COME, FOLLOW ME

WORDS
OF THE
WEEK

COME, FOLLOW ME

WORDS
OF THE
WEEK

WEEK-BY-WEEK INSIGHTS
ON SIGNIFICANT WORDS IN
THE NEW TESTAMENT

ERIC D. RICHARDS

CFI

An imprint of Cedar Fort, Inc.
Springville, Utah

ISBN 13: 978-1-4621-4428-0

Published by CFI, an imprint of Cedar Fort, Inc.
2373 W. 700 S., Suite 100, Springville, UT 84663
Distributed by Cedar Fort, Inc., www.cedarfort.com

Library of Congress Control Number: 2022946340

Cover design by Courtney Proby
Cover design © 2023 Cedar Fort, Inc.
Edited by Valene Wood

Printed in Colombia

10 9 8 7 6 5 4 3 2 1

Printed on acid-free paper

Other works by this author

BOOKS

Preparing for the Second Coming

AUDIO PUBLICATIONS

*Great Mess to Greatness: 10 Scriptures That Will
Change Your View of the Atonement*

Are You a Bushel or a Candlestick?

Bad Day, Great Life

Recipe for Revelation

Don't Look Back (You're Not Going That Way!)

Change Your Words, Change Your World

Contents

CONTENTS

Introduction

OUR WORDS ARE POWERFUL. BY CHANGING a single word, we can completely change the way that we are understood. Author Mark Twain wrote, "The difference between the right word and the almost right word is the difference between *lightning* and a *lightning bug*."[1] This is especially true in writing, where a stray punctuation mark can change the tone of a message entirely.

God knew the power of words when He inspired the authors and translators of ancient writings to select certain words as they wrote or translated His divine messages. Indeed, if we carefully study why certain words were used in scripture and gain a better understanding of the breadth, depth, and meaning behind these words, we will find a deep ocean of interpretation and personal application.

"*Language is divine*," Elder Charles Ditier of the Seventy wrote:

> One word—just a single, simple word—can bring a variety of thoughts and influences. Words can get things done, fulfill commitments or accomplish miracles. We may, because of words, be moved to tears or to laughter, feel great or miserable, be exalted or condemned. *Language is divine*.[2]

There are many tasks that we use writing for in our everyday lives. With all the anxiety that composing an important email brings, imagine how much larger the challenge was for these great men of God in choosing the best word for each translation or composition of holy scripture. With

---

1. "Topic: Words," *Everyone's Mark Twain*, Compiled by Caroline Thomas Harnsberger (South Brunswick and New York: A. S. Barnes and Company, 1972) 669.
2. "Language: A Divine Way of Communicating," *Ensign*, Nov. 1979.

literally tens of thousands of beautiful word options glistening in their brilliant minds, many sought for the Holy Ghost to pinpoint which one to use to best portray the Divine message.

The Bible: A Brief History

Writing hasn't always been as accessible as it is today. For centuries, the abilities to read and write were reserved for a privileged few. Then, in the mid-15th century, Johannes Gutenberg, a German craftsman, revolutionized the ability to share written words. His invention, movable type, streamlined the printing process and made books and pamphlets easily and widely accessible. This created a thirst for knowledge and literacy throughout Europe for decades to come. With the written word becoming more accessible, it was time for the Bible to become more accessible, too.

Martin Luther used this new invention to spread his questions about Bible translations. This led to his writing of "The Ninety-Five Theses" in 1517, beginning the Protestant Reformation.

William Tyndale (1494–6 October 1536) was another prominent figure in the Protestant Reformation and an amazing man of faith. He is most renowned for his translation of the Bible into English. Fluent in eight languages, he felt that a direct translation from Greek and Hebrew into English would be superior to John Wycliffe's translation from Latin. He believed in making the Bible accessible to everyone at a time when this belief faced great opposition, and he famously once said, "If God spare my life, ere many years I will cause a boy that driveth the plough shall know more of the scripture than thou dost."[3] These were bold words spoken to a scholar. William Tyndale was eventually murdered for his scriptural efforts, but his translations have been used for subsequent English translations, including the King James Version that is widely used today.[4]

The King James Version (KJV) was a seven-year project commissioned by King James I in England that began three centuries after Tyndale's execution. It resulted in a word-for-word translation of the Bible, published in A.D. 1611, that was meant to be understood by common readers.

---

3. As quoted in John Foxe, "The Actes and Monuments of these Latter and Perilous Days, touching Matters of the Church," *Foxe's Book of Martyrs*.
4. See D. Todd Christopherson, "Preparations for the Restoration and the Second Coming: 'My Hand Shall Be over Thee,'" *Ensign*, Nov. 2005, 90.

This translation of the Bible was no small feat. Nearly 50 translators were involved in the project.[5] Divided into six panels (two at Oxford, two Cambridge, and two at Westminster), two panels oversaw the translation of the New Testament, three oversaw the translation of the Old Testament, and one oversaw the translation of the Apocrypha.[6] Using the Bishop's Bible of 1568 as the basis for this revision, The Old Testament was translated entirely from Hebrew (with a few passages written in Aramaic, a language close to Hebrew) and the New Testament was translated from Greek. The groups worked independently from each other and once their work was complete, it was sent to the other panels for comment and revision. The chief members of the six panels then met to make final decisions on all suggested revisions.[7] In other words, the process, although influenced by political and ecclesiastical pressures, was careful and precise. Under this system, no one translator could "go rogue" and insert his own ideas or interpretations without being subjected to peer review, evaluation, and approval.

The King James Bible was well received. Madeleine and J. Lane Miller wrote in praise about the KJV translation of the Old Testament and New Testament, saying:

> Its Old Testament far surpassed any English translation in its faithfulness to the Hebrew text and the simplicity of its style. Its New Testament is so expressive in language and form that it is said to rival the original Greek as literature. Its majestic, direct, forceful prose has never been surpassed in English literature.[8]

It's wonderful to imagine the beauty and the care that these strangers in the past put into the King James Bible so that we could have it to study today. This is worth celebrating, regardless of any theological bias the translation team may have been affected by.

The Church of Jesus Christ of Latter-day Saints prefers to use the King James Version for its English-speaking members. This may cause us to ask, is it safe to use other and more modern English translations? Absolutely yes. Other translations often explain passages that are difficult to understand.

---

5. By June 30, 1604, James had approved a list of 54 revisers, although records show that approximately 47 scholars actually participated in the process.
6. See Ken Curtis, "Story Behind King James Bible?" *Christianity.com*, 28 Apr. 2010.
7. See Ron Rhodes, "The Story Behind the King James Version," *CBN*, www1.cbn.com/churchandministry/the-story-behind-the-king-james-version.
8. Madeleine Sweeny Miller and John Lane Miller, *Harper's Bible Dictionary*, 8th ed. (New York: Harper & Row, 1973) 165.

Comparing verses with other translations opens a whole new world of application and growth towards Jesus Christ.

The Beauty of Translation

Scriptures are inspired by God. That is, God personally oversaw the word choices within scripture, guiding the prophet-authors and subsequent translators. This is taught in the scripture from Timothy, "All scripture is given by inspiration of God, and is profitable for doctrine, for reproof, for correction, for instruction in righteousness" (2 Timothy 3:16). Just as the English word *apostle*, which came from the Greek a*postolos*, literally means "messenger" or "one who is sent forth," our scriptures have literally been "sent forth" by The Messenger Himself, our Lord.

Anciently, the scriptures were painstakingly copied by scribes, including Jewish councils, groups, and secretaries such as the Sopherim, the Zugoth, the Tannaim, and the Masoretes. These scribes had a deep admiration and reverence for the ancient texts they were copying and translating, and they worked with great care. Consideration was taken about the type of parchment to use, the size and width of the columns, the type of ink, and the spacing of words. Most translations were done by committee to help guard against individual prejudice or theology.

Despite the general carefulness and precautions of these scribes and translators, the Book of Mormon teaches that "many plain and precious things [were] taken away" during the many copies and translations of Biblical text that ensued (see 1 Nephi 13:28). For example, there are few references within the Old Testament to the first principles and ordinances of the gospel, and it's hard to find the words faith, repentance, baptism, and the Holy Ghost.

When translating from one language to another, and especially from an ancient language to modern, difficult choices must be made along the way by translators and linguists. The translators of the Bible certainly wrestled with questions such as, Should the translated word be the exact original word, even if the meaning of that word is unclear to the modern reader? Should a word be used that portrays the general idea and not the exact word? Or should we create a new word that conveys the original meaning?

Joseph Smith must have encountered a few of these questions as he began his translation of the King James Bible in June 1830.[9] The Joseph

---

9. Based on the 1828 Webster Dictionary, available to Joseph Smith while he was

Smith translation assists in restoring some of the plain and precious things that have been lost from the Bible (see 1 Nephi 13–14). It offers many interesting insights and can aid us in our biblical interpretation and understanding. This translation is yet another witness that Prophet Joseph Smith was a prophet of God, as it is the translation that agrees most closely with the language and doctrine contained within latter-day scripture.

Each translation shows us something a little different, which is one reason why we have so many different translations and interpretations of the Bible (see Joseph Smith—History 1:12). Thankfully, modern revelation and modern translation tools help correct and restore any truths lost in the Bible translation (see 1 Nephi 13:39–40).

Despite the challenges of translation, we can know that the words used in the scriptures are exactly what the Lord wanted us to have. Peter taught, "For the prophecy came not in old time by the will of man: but holy men of God spake as they were moved by the Holy Ghost" (2 Peter 1:21).

Etymology

To help us accomplish our goal of better understanding the breadth, depth, and meaning of the words used in scripture, we will study the etymology of these words.[10]

What is etymology, exactly?

Etymology is like a map of the wheel-ruts left behind by the early pioneers of languages. Etymologists are researchers who carefully study how a word has evolved over time and authoritatively tell us about the cultures and history from which a word emerged, and then help us understand the original meaning and definition of words.

To put it simply, etymology is the history of words.

A word's etymology is not its definition; it's an explanation of what a word meant long ago.[11]

---

translating the Bible and Book of Mormon, the word *translate* did not just mean "to replace one word from one language into another"; it meant to transfer, convey, interpret, or explain. Hence, many use the term "Joseph Smith's Inspired Version of the Bible" when speaking of his work, giving room for his work not being an exact translation and for him to use his work as a teaching resource more than an exact translation.

10. Unless otherwise noted, the Online Etymology dictionary was exclusively used for each word's background in this book (see www.etymonline.com). The founders of this online resource use a variety of sources to determine word roots (see https://www.etymonline.com/columns/post/sources).

11. *Epistemology* is a close cousin to etymology; it is the investigation of what distinguishes justified belief from opinion.

Exegesis

Here's another word you may or may not be familiar with: *exegesis*. It means analyzing a text to discern what the author intended to communicate. *Exegesis* comes from the Greek and literally means *"to explain"* or *"to narrate"* or *"to show the way."*[12] It's the process of carefully studying scripture passages to produce correct (and useful) interpretations.[13]

Simply stated, *exegesis* means doing a bit more work with the text to discover the author's intent.

Think of exegesis this way. A young adult girl who is deeply in love with her handsome fiancé gets a long text message from him. It's longer than usual. She reads it carefully. Why? She wants to understand what her fiancé is trying to communicate. Why? She doesn't want to *misunderstand* what he wrote.

Just like a young couple hoping to build a solid foundation for their relationship based on clear communication, we, too, in our relationship with the word of God should examine the cultural setting of the text and word origins to be sure we don't misunderstand the Lord's intent. *Exegesis* guards against taking verses or passages out of context, which can lead to misunderstanding and misapplication.

The opposite of *exegesis* is *eisegesis*, which means applying meaning into a text that isn't actually there. We don't want to twist scripture into saying something that it doesn't actually say. *Exegesis* is not about discovering what *we* think a text means (or what we *hope* it means) but trying to discover what the scriptural author meant—and what he or she intended the readers to understand.

Don't feel overwhelmed. Our goal in doing *exegesis* isn't to become world experts in biblical literature. Rather, our goal is to have a deeper experience with God through a deeper study of His word. Learning the broader story of the words in scripture will bring a broader relationship with the Author.

Ancient Languages

As part of the rich history of these words we'll study, we'll also look at their translations in Greek, Hebrew, and/or Latin. And if you don't speak these languages? Don't worry one bit!

---

12. See "exegesis," *Online Etymology Dictionary*, www.etymonline.com.
13. David Noel Freedman, "Exegesis," *Anchor Yale Bible Dictionary*, vol. 2 (New Haven, CT: Yale University Press, 1992).

Thanks to modern-day technology, there are many websites that can show you each word in the New Testament, in context with their surrounding words and verses, and will provide translations for you. Biblical technology is a huge blessing! It is a rich experience to study the word of God from the Bible while learning what each word originally was and what it meant. Not only does it provide an avenue of learning, it provides a route for revelation and personal, relevant application.

Consider using sites like www.blueletterbible.org or www.biblehub.com. (There are dozens of highly reputable online parallel Bibles that will show you the Greek, Hebrew, and Latin meanings of each word, presented in a verse-by-verse manner).

Yes, it does take a few extra minutes to read in this manner, but the journey is absolutely remarkable!

Notes from the Author

As we explore the history, meaning, and definitions of various words in the New Testament, please know that I believe that each word in canonized scripture is divinely inspired. I believe that the Lord spoke to the hearts and minds of those ancient copiers and translators and linguists and that each was inspired to use certain words to give deeper understanding of Heavenly Father's plan for our lives.

I believe the Lord touched the minds of prophets and translators to choose some of the best words and phrases to translate the record into English (and other languages). I believe that we can gain great insights about the gospel and our relationship with Jesus Christ by studying those words deeply.

I firmly believe that our modern scholars and Church translation team carefully and meticulously seeks God's will as they translate books, talks, and documents in our day. I believe that we can learn more deeply by studying the word use of General Authorities carefully and meticulously. Indeed, a close look at the original definitions of words used by inspired authors unlocks a trove of personal application to become more Christ-like.

This book can help you improve your scriptural understanding and interpretation, but it must be used with caution. This book (and most all commentaries) will never be a substitute for the scriptures, just as a good cookbook is not a good substitute for food.[14]

---

14. See Dallin H. Oaks, "Scripture Reading and Revelation," *Ensign*, Jan. 1995.

Elder Oaks taught that we should be cautious of relying on commentaries, as they often focus on a single meaning, blinding us to other possibilities:

> Sometimes those other, less obvious meanings can be the ones most valuable and useful to us as we seek to understand our own dispensation and to obtain answers to our own questions. This is why the teaching of the Holy Ghost is a better guide to scriptural interpretation than even the best commentary.[15]

On that same point, Elder Oaks concluded, "If we depend only upon our own reasoning or the scholarship or commentaries of others, we will never obtain the understanding that can come only by revelation."[16]

To correctly understand the words of the scriptures, we must pray for and receive revelation. This Spirit-to-spirit communication is what will lead us to God. The Spirit of the Lord is essential to understand the Word of the Lord. The Lord revealed, "he that receiveth the word by the Spirit of truth receiveth it as it is preached by the Spirit of truth" (D&C 50:21). When we discover application in scripture through study and revelation, we come to know the true Author and He who assisted in each translation, our Father in Heaven.

---

15. Dallin H. Oaks, "How Rare a Possession—the Scriptures!" *Ensign*, Sept. 1976, 4.
16. Dallin H. Oaks, "Scripture Reading and Revelation," *Ensign*, Jan. 1995.

Chapter 1

We Are Responsible for Our Own Learning

WHAT A JOY IT IS TO be responsible for our own learning! This introductory lesson for our New Testament study reminds us how important the scriptures are as the foundation for our teaching and learning.

Let's consider the word "canon." This word has been used for centuries to describe the scriptures. "Canon" is a word of Greek origin. It originally meant "a rod for testing straightness" (think of its root word, cane).[1] *Canon* is now used to denote the authoritative collection of the sacred books used by the true believers in Christ (see Bible Dictionary, "Canon").[2]

President Harold B Lee taught that the canon of scriptures "are the standards by which we measure all doctrine and if anything is taught which is contrary to that which is in the scriptures, it is false. It is just that simple."[3] Clearly this principle of measurement coincides with the etymology of the word "canon."

---

1. Norman Doe, *Canon Law in the Anglican Communion: A Worldwide Perspective* (Clarendon Press, 1998).
2. The term originally pertained to a measuring rod, but eventually referred to the standards which regulated various trades in the ancient world.
3. See Harold B. Lee, "Viewpoint of a Giant," Address to religious educators, 18 July 1968. While we believe that our canon of scripture contains the fullness of the gospel, it does not contain all things necessary for running the Church. Hence, we, as Latter-day Saints, believe that God continues to make known His will through the First Presidency and the Quorum of the Twelve Apostles, who are prophets, seers, and revelators inspired by the Holy Ghost (see D&C 107:27).

Compare this etymology of *canon* to the metaphor of the iron rod. Elder David A. Bednar taught that holding to the iron rod requires a reliance on the holy scriptures:

> Holding fast to the iron rod entails, in large measure, the prayerful, consistent, and earnest use of the holy scriptures as a sure source of revealed truth and as a reliable guide for the journey along the strait and narrow path to the tree of life—even to the Lord Jesus Christ.[4]

We can measure our discipleship based on what the Lord has revealed in His sacred canon, the scriptures.

For those of us who are parents, it is our duty to help our children grow strong in the gospel and become responsible for their own learning. The Church's seminary program helps high-school-aged youth around the world build roots in the gospel canon by meeting regularly to study the Bible, the Book of Mormon, the Doctrine and Covenants, and the Pearl of Great Price. All youth ages 14 to 18, whether members of the Church or not, are invited to participate in this wonderful program.

Our *Come, Follow Me* curriculum mirrors what is taught in seminary each year. Seminary is a supporting element to home-centered gospel learning.

Discussing the shift to align the seminary curriculum with *Come, Follow Me*, Elder Jeffrey R. Holland of the Quorum of the Twelve Apostles said, "We think it is a wonderful alignment . . . with what the rest of the Church is doing. And we believe that it's going to be wonderfully symbiotic with the . . . Church-supported—and now we add seminary-supported—home-centered gospel study."[5]

Elder Kim B. Clark, Commissioner of the Church Educational System, added, "We want to . . . give the students an opportunity to really dive deep, and really understand the doctrines of the gospel. . . . We also want them to be able to see the power that comes from weaving different books of scripture together."[6]

Fittingly, the Latin word for *seminary* is *seminarium* which means "a plant nursery" or "seed plot." The literal definition comes from, "a plot where plants are raised from seeds." Attendance and active participation helps youth plant gospel seeds in their hearts as they learn and feel the

4. David A. Bednar, "Lehi's Dream: Holding Fast to the Rod," *Ensign*, Oct. 2011.
5. See Aubrey Eyre, "Seminaries to Align with Come, Follow Me Curriculum and Schedule in 2020," *Church News*, 22 Mar. 2019.
6. Ibid.

truthfulness of the gospel. Ultimately, the purpose of seminary is to help students understand and rely upon the teachings and Atonement of Jesus Christ, qualify for the blessings of the temple, and prepare themselves, their families, and others for eternal life with their Father in Heaven.[7]

Seeing our children as seeds planted in the gospel can be a helpful metaphor as we help them to grow strong. Spending time with them in the scriptures and helping them understand the gospel now can help further understanding and prevent future pain.

President Gordon B. Hinckley extended this metaphor in a story he told about a tree that he planted outside his home. As the years went by, he paid little attention to it. Then one winter day, he noticed that it was misshapen and out of balance. He went out and braced himself against it, trying to push it upright, but the trunk was nearly a foot in diameter and his strength was nothing against it. Ultimately, he took out a saw and cut off the great heavy branch that was pulling it down in an effort to restore its balance, leaving an ugly scar.

President Hinckley concluded, "How serious was the trauma of its youth and how brutal the treatment I used to straighten it. When it was first planted, a piece of string would have held it in place against the forces of the wind. I could have and should have supplied that string with ever so little effort. But I did not, and it bent to the forces that came against it."[8]

The efforts that we put in today to become responsible for our own learning and help our children become responsible for theirs will help us stand strong and tall in the future. Let's take the time to hold tight to the iron rod and nurture our seedlings today.

---

7. see *Gospel Teaching and Learning: A Handbook for Teachers and Leaders in Seminaries and Institutes of Religion* (The Church of Jesus Christ of Latter-day Saints, 2012), x.
8. Gordon B. Hinckley, "Bring Up a Child in the Way He Should Go," *Ensign*, Nov. 1993.

Six Tips for How to Study Scripture

1. "Develop a *systematic plan* for study."[9]
2. *"Establish a regular time* to study the scriptures."[10]
3. "Set a *consistent time and place* to study when you can be alone and undisturbed."[11]
4. "Couple *prayer* with scripture study. It will give increased success in your daily activities. It will bring increased alertness to your minds."[12]
5. *"Read slowly* and more carefully and with more *questions* in mind. . . . Ponder and examine every word, every scriptural gem. . . . Such an examination may unearth a treasure hidden in a field."[13]
6. *"Memorize scriptures* that touch your heart and fill your soul with understanding. . . . They have . . . power that is not communicated when paraphrased."[14]

9. Howard W. Hunter, "Reading the Scriptures," *Ensign*, Nov. 1979, 64.
10. Henry B. Eyring, "A Discussion on Scripture Study," *Ensign*, July 2005, 24.
11. M. Russell Ballard, "Be Strong in the Lord, and in the Power of His Might, Brigham Young University fireside, 3 Mar. 2002, speeches.byu.edu.
12. Ibid.
13. Jeffrey R. Holland, "Students Need Teachers to Guide Them," CES satellite broadcast, 20 June 1992, 4.
14. Richard G. Scott, "He Lives," *Ensign*, Nov. 1999, 87.

Chapter 2

Matthew 1; Luke 1

Don't miss these Words of the Week

"Genealogy" (Matthew 1:1)
"Espoused" (Matthew 1:18)

**"The book of the generation [genealogy]
of Jesus Christ, the son of
David, the son of Abraham."
(Matthew 1:1)**

WHEN MATTHEW BEGAN TO WRITE HIS gospel account, he had no shortage of captivating experiences to pull from. He could have begun with the time the Savior walked on water, or when He multiplied the loaves and the fishes. After all, what reader could resist such stories? But instead, Matthew started with a long list of the Savior's family history.

At first glance, this may not seem quite as exciting or inspiring as the other stories, but the Apostle knew what he was doing.

Matthew was teaching us very empowering principles right from the beginning. Most of us just need a little help recognizing those principles in between all of the "so-and-so begat so-and-so's."

In this verse, the Greek word *geneseōs* is used for genealogy.[1] It means *birth, lineage, descent*. The English word *genealogy* comes from the Latin

---

1. *Strong's*, 1078.

word *genealogia* or "tracing of a family"[2] and from the Greek word *genealo-gia* "the making of a pedigree."[3]

When both Matthew and Luke recorded Christ's genealogy, they did something interesting—they didn't include everyone. Instead, they seem to have handpicked a select few of Jesus's ancestors, including people who have what we might call a colorful past: David with his infidelity, Solomon and his multiple marriages, and Rahab and her promiscuity.

So how is this list supposed to inspire us? Simple: If Jesus rose and became great despite an imperfect line of ancestry, so can we. Despite hiccups in our family history, we can rise and become all that God knows we are capable of.

Family therapist Carlfred Broderick said that God can help us break the chains of destruction without families:

> God actively intervenes in some destructive lineages, assigning a valiant spirit to break the chain of destructiveness in such families. Although these children may suffer innocently as victims of violence, neglect, and exploitation, through the grace of God some find the strength to "metabolize" the poison within themselves, refusing to pass it on to future generations. Before them were generations of destructive pain; after them the line flows clear and pure. Their children and children's children will call them blessed.[4]

We can follow the Savior's example and break cycles. We, too, can choose the path our lives will follow.

But that isn't all we can learn from Matthew's choice to begin his account with genealogy. The prefix "gene" refers to family, which becomes interesting in the context of the word "generous." To be generous means we treat people with the level of love and kindness that should be found in families. And learning to do so might be more useful than you even think.

Jack Welch, the highly successful CEO of General Electric, called being generous "one unique characteristic that all great leaders have."[5]

---

2. See "genealogy," *Online Etymology Dictionary,* www.etymonline.com.
3. Matthew (and Luke) present Jesus's genealogy showing His pedigree and tracing His family back to ancient prophets. Matthew's genealogy shows Jesus's royal lineage, establishing His rights to the throne of David, while the genealogical account given by Luke is a personal pedigree, demonstrating descent from David without rights to the throne through family tracing.
4. Carlfred Broderick, "I Have a Question," *Ensign,* Aug. 1986, 38–39.
5. David Carlin, "Do you have the Generosity Gene?" *Forbes Magazine,* 15 Jan. 2020.

Social science researchers agree with Welch and have provided reasons why this is true[6]:

- Teams led by generous managers are happier, more effective, and more productive than other teams.
- When a manager is more generous, employees work harder and provide significantly better customer service.
- Companies that offered opportunities for employees to give back to their communities saw improvements in job satisfaction and performance.
- Generous employees are promoted more quickly than their more self-focused peers.
- People who are generous are physically healthier on average; they have lower levels of the stress hormone cortisol, which has been linked to a variety of diseases.
- Being generous makes people happier.

We are also encouraged to be generous within the gospel. Elder Jeffrey R. Holland shared a moving example of what generosity looked like in the life of President Thomas S. Monson:

> I have been blessed by an association with this man for 47 years now, and the image of him I will cherish until I die is of him flying home from then-economically devastated East Germany in his house slippers because he had given away not only his second suit and his extra shirts but the very shoes from off his feet. More than any man I know, President Monson has "done all he could" for the widow and the fatherless, the poor and the oppressed.[7]

As you read the names found in Jesus's genealogy, let it remind you to be *generous*, to treat the people around you as loving family members. As we do so, we will find a deeper sense of belonging and happiness, and a clearer path we can all walk together—as brothers and sisters with a common *genealogy*—back to our heavenly home.

6. Adam Grant, *Give and Take* (United States: Penguin Publishing Group, 2014).
7. Jeffery R. Holland, "Are We Not All Beggars?" *Ensign*, Nov. 2014.

"Now the birth of Jesus Christ was on this wise: When as his mother Mary was espoused to Joseph, before they came together, she was found with child of the Holy Ghost." (Matthew 1:18)[8]

MARRIAGE IS A SACRED COVENANT; AND while most youth and young adults today shudder at the idea of their parents choosing a spouse for them, in biblical Jewish culture, parents were responsible for choosing appropriate spouses for their children (and children were expected to accept their parents' arrangements).

The Greek word used for *espoused* here in Matthew 1 is *mnēsteutheisēs*. It means *to ask in marriage.*[9] The Latin root reflects the same meaning; the Latin *sponsalia* means "betrothal" or "wedding."[10] Betrothal in that day and age was similar to engagement as we now know it, but it was much more binding. Once a couple was betrothed, they were considered legally married, even though the marriage was not yet consummated. Thus Mathew and Luke refer to Mary as Joseph's *"espoused."*[11] No wonder that Joseph had to wrestle with what to do when Mary became pregnant (see Matthew 1:18–20).

In a devotional address in 1978, President Gordon B. Hinckley agreed with Syndey Harris, a columnist, who wrote of the truth about a person's commitment and investment into a marriage relationship:

> One of the grand errors we tend to make when we are young is supposing that a person is a bundle of qualities, and we add up the individual's good and bad qualities, like a bookkeeper working on debits and credits. If the balance is favorable, we may decide to take the jump [into marriage]. . . .
>
> The world is full of unhappy men and women who married their mates because . . . it seemed to be a good investment.
>
> Love, however, is not an investment; it is an adventure. And when the marriage turns out to be as dull and comfortable as a

---

8. Information taken from "Historical and Cultural Background," *Savior of the World Production*, www.churchofjesuschrist.org.

9. *Strong's,* 3423.

10. "Espousal," *Online Etymology Dictionary,* www.etymonline.com.

11. When "proposing" marriage, the groom made a ritual statement, such as the one found in Hosea 2:19–20, formally consecrating himself to his bride. The use of five virtues in this particular statement—"in righteous, in judgment, and in loving kindness, and in mercies, . . . in faithfulness"—symbolizes God and invites Him into the covenant being made.

sound investment, the disgruntled party soon turns elsewhere for adventure, . . .

Ignorant people are always saying, "I wonder what he sees in her," not realizing that what he sees in her (and what no one else can see in her) is the secret essence of love.[12]

Though marriage often begins with feelings of great excitement and romance, inevitably the day-to-day responsibilities of life can wear upon a couple. None of us are perfect and in no relationship do the imperfections of another human being become more evident than when we commit to share our hearts and our lives with one another. When challenges arise, we must remember that a successful marriage requires consistent effort. We can view our endeavors to maintain and improve our marriage as burdensome work or as a worthwhile labor of love. Granted, in some situations, it is wise to seek counsel about divorce, but in many cases, remembering that a truly good marriage is often laden with episodes of monotony, melancholy—and even unanticipated drama and chaos—will help us stay committed to covenants, even as Joseph chose to stay committed to his betrothed Mary.

FOR FURTHER STUDY

- Consider looking up the meanings of each name in the genealogy of Jesus (Matt. 1:1–16) within the scriptures; use the footnotes in this section to help.

- Research laws surrounding engagement in Jesus's day. For example, www.gotquestions.org has a great entry under "Marriage Customs."

- Look up what the title "Emmanuel" means using www.blueletterbible.com.

- Study the meaning of the word angel and the doctrines surrounding their ministry using www.blueletterbible.com or www.biblehub.com.

What other unique or insightful words did you find in your study this week?

12. Sydney Harris, "Love and Marriage," *Deseret News,* 18 Oct. 1977; as quoted in Gordon B. Hinckley, "'And the Greatest of These Is Love,'" Brigham Young University devotional address, 14 Feb. 1978, speeches.byu.edu.

_____

_____

_____

_____

_____

Please share with us!
Visit www.ComeFollowMeWOW.com and
share your word discoveries and insights!

Chapter 3

Luke 2; Matthew 2

Don't miss these Words of the Week

"Bethlehem" and **"Jerusalem"** (Matthew 2:1)
"Swaddling Clothes" and **"Manger"** (Luke 2:7)

**"Now when Jesus was born in Bethlehem
of Judæa in the days of Herod the king,
behold, there came wise men from
the east to Jerusalem."
(Matthew 2:1)**

WE ALL STRIVE FOR THOSE MOMENTS of precious peace when our heavy thoughts and feelings are replaced by God's soothing sense of calm. *Jerusalem*—a city we learn so much about but perhaps is far from our thoughts—might be able to help us, as it stands as a symbol for peace.

The name *Jerusalem* was the Greek form of the Hebrew name *Hierosolyma.1 Jerusalem's* root *Salem actually* means *peace.*[2] Long ago, around 2000 BC, this city was the home of King Melchizedek, one of the greatest leaders in the world's history.[3] He led his people to "obtain heaven" (JST, Gen. 14:34) and they did just that: they were translated because of their immense faith.

---

1. *Strong's,* 2414.
2. See Bible Dictionary, "Salem."
3. See Genesis 14:18; Hebrews 7:1–2; Alma 13:17–18.

Wouldn't it be amazing to be swept up into your mansion on high to chat with great men and women of faith in the heavens? But God has a different plan for us right now.

After Melchizedek's people were translated, the Jebusites moved into the area around what we know as Jerusalem and put their own spin on things. *"Jebus,"* meaning "City of the Jebusites" (very clever), was added. Over time, the city became known as *Jeru-Salem* or simply *Jerusalem:* the city of peace.

Why is this important? Think about Jerusalem and its thousands of years of history. Both temporally and spiritually, it has known magnificence and tragedy, years of prosperity and poverty. The Prince of Peace, Christ Himself, walked the streets and brought "healing in his wings" (see Malachi 4:2). Your life, with all its miracles and misfortune, mirrors that of Jerusalem's, the city of peace.

Let's travel a little bit south from Jerusalem to an obscure little village. *Bethlehem* in Hebrew, *bet lehem,* means "house of bread." Bread has been the staple food for millennia, as it may be a staple in your own home (even if you wish it wasn't!).

The scriptures are *full* of references to our favorite carb. Adam and Eve, after partaking of the forbidden fruit, were told that Adam would work and earn his bread "by the sweat of his brow" (see Genesis 3, 18–19). Bread is found in the Lord's Prayer: "Give us this day our daily bread" (see Luke 11:2–4). Moses fed his people in the desert with a type of bread which fell from heaven (see Exodus 16). Bread was used during the last supper (see Luke 22:7–38). Jesus used bread to feed crowds of thousands (see Matthew 14:13–21).

How significant of all places on planet Earth that Jesus, the "Bread of Life" would come from *Bethlehem*, the "house of bread"! (see John 6:48).[4]

Christ's birthplace in Bethlehem shows us that background, popularity, and wealth have little significance in God's eyes. In fact, the scriptures show time and again that humble circumstances lead to the most powerful spiritual growth. So, take heart! If you haven't come from the most illustrious places on the earth, you are in wonderful company—and you, too, can do great things!

---

4. Micah, an Old Testament prophet, emphasized Bethlehem's lack of significance to the world in a prophesy about Christ's birth: "But thou, Bethlehem . . . though thou be little among the thousands of Judah, yet out of thee shall he come forth . . . to be ruler in Israel: whose goings forth have been from of old, from everlasting" (Micah 5:2).

"She brought forth her firstborn son, and wrapped him in swaddling clothes, and laid him in a manger; because there was no room for them in the inn." (Luke 2:7)

MANY COUPLES SPEND WEEKS, MONTHS, EVEN years planning out the perfect spot in their homes for their newborns to sleep. When we think of Mary and Joseph, who brought the literal Son of God into the world, we can imagine the pressure they must have felt—on top of the pressure that all parents feel—to give their son the best that they could.

If they could have, we can imagine that Mary and Joseph might have sprung for one of the $2,000 bassinets sold today, with all the bells and whistles to protect the most important child who has ever been born, but the newborn Jesus's bed was neither a crib nor a cradle, but a manger—a trough where horses, donkeys, and cattle ate (see Luke 13:15).[5]

Luke is the only writer to use the word *manger* in the scriptures. In Greek, the word for *manger* is *phatnē*, which means *a feeding-trough*.[6] In Latin, *manger* refers to *chewing* or *eating*. Essentially, a *manger* was a trough where horses, donkeys, and cattle ate (see Luke 13:15).[7]

Newborn Jesus's bed was a food bowl for slobbering animals! As Jesus said: "Foxes have holes, and birds of the air have nests, but the Son of Man has nowhere to lay his head" (Luke 9:57–58).

It hurts to imagine the desperation that Mary and Joseph must have felt, having no better place to lay their newborn, but think of the richness of this moment! Bethlehem (the Hebrew word for "house of bread") is where Jesus ("the Bread of Life," according to John 6:35) was laid into a trough used for *feeding*. No wonder that He would later teach, "He that cometh to me shall never hunger" and "He that eateth of this bread shall live forever" (John 6:35, 58). Later, at the Last Supper, Jesus took the bread and said, "This is my body, which is given for you." (See Luke 22:19.) As Christ's manger nourished the animals, Christ also nourishes us.

This week, think of what you can do to follow Christ and feed His sheep as He would.

---

5. "Manger," *Online Etymology Dictionary*, www.etymonline.com.
6. *Strong's*, 5336; from *pateomai*; a crib.
7. "Manger," *Online Etymology Dictionary*.

FOR FURTHER STUDY

- Consider a study of the biography of Caesar Augustus and how he came to power.[8] You can just type in "History of Caesar Augustus" or "Caesar Augustus Biographical Facts" to find fascinating tidbits about his life.

- Look up fun facts on the internet by typing in "The Christmas Star" or "The Star of Bethlehem" into a web browser.[9]

- There have been a few discussions about the advantage of giving birth in a stable over a public inn.[10] Use the internet to look up to see what scholars have suggested.

- There's much more about the group of shepherds who were visited by the angel and what their role was in providing sacrificial animals for temple worship. Do a search for "migdal eder" using www.blueletter-bible.com or www.biblehub.com and see what you find.

- Look up the significance of the names "Anna" and "Simeon" using an online dictionary such as *Hitchcock's Bible Names Dictionary* (https://www.ccel.org/ccel/hitchcock/bible_names.toc.html) and see how their name meanings relate to the Christmas story.

What other unique or insightful words did you find in your study this week?

_____

_____

_____

_____

Please share with us!
Visit www.ComeFollowMeWOW.com and
share your word discoveries and insights!

---

8. See Michael Grant, "Augustus: Roman Emperor," *Britannica,* www.britannica.com.
9. For example, see: Colin R. Nicholl, "9 things you didn't know about the Star of Bethlehem," *The Washington Post,* 22 Dec.2015, www.washingtonpost.com.
10. For example, see: Mario Seiglie and Tom Robinson, "Was There Really 'No Room in the Inn'?" *United Church of God: an International Association,* 8 Nov. 2012, www.ucg.org.

Chapter 4

John 1

Don't miss these Words of the Week

"Word" (John 1:1)
"Created/Made" (John 1:3)
"Light" (John 1:4–5)
"Bethabara" (John 1:28)
"Guile" (John 1:47)

**"In the beginning was the Word, and the Word
was with God, and the Word was God."
(John 1:1)**

It's AMAZING THE POWER THAT A single word can have. Think about your name, for instance. It's a single word that draws to mind so much more than just the sounds of the word itself, like the color of your hair, the shape of your face, your likes and dislikes. You hear it and you think, "Oh, that's me."

When Christ created the world, His name, or title, was *the Word*. President Russell M. Nelson wrote:

Under the direction of the Father, Jesus bore the responsibility of Creator. His title was "the Word," spelled with a capital W (see JST, John 1:16, Bible appendix). In the Greek language of the New Testament, that Word was Logos, or "expression."[1] That terminology may seem strange, but it is appropriate. We use words to

---

1. See *Strong's*, 3056.

express our ideas to others. So Jesus was the Word, or expression, of His Father to the world.[2]

Our words can express thoughts and influence feelings, help communicate messages, and get things done. Words often bring miracles to pass. So, too, it is with the Word of God, Jesus Christ. Through our Savior, our Heavenly Father communicated a message of His love; through the Word, He created the world and performed other miracles. Our self-esteem and feelings of self-worth can be elevated as we truly understand the Word of God, Jesus Christ.

This week, remember the power of your words. The words that we choose have a huge impact. Think about how a single compliment can improve your day, or how a single rude remark can worsen it. Your words can create closeness or separation; they can calm or excite. Your job is to motivate others to step forward and begin a new life. So practice being more aware of the words that come from your thoughts and the actions that will follow your words.

"All things were made by him; and without him was not any thing made that was made." (John 1:3)

THE CREATION OF THE EARTH CAN teach us so much about our divine nature. As people, we can't help but create, whether it's delicious food, magnificent buildings, or a perfectly timed joke. When we use our sacred skills to make something new, we are drawing closer to our Heavenly Father, the divine creator.

Under the direction of Heavenly Father, Jesus Christ created the heavens and the earth. In the work of the Creation, the Lord organized elements that had already existed (see Abraham 3:24). He did not form the world "out of nothing," as some believe. His work can be divided into divisions and additions:

Divisions	Additions
Day 1 Divide light from dark.	*Day 4* Add sun, moon, stars.
Day 2 Divide water above from water beneath.	*Day 5* Add fish & fowl.

---

2. Russell M. Nelson, "Jesus the Christ: Our Master and More," *Ensign*, April 2000.

Day 3 Divide dry land from water.	*Day 6* Earth brings forth life. Man is organized, given dominion.

The Greek form of *made* is *egeneto* meaning *to cause to be*.[3] The Old English word (*macian*) meant "*bring into existence; construct, do, be the author of, produce; prepare, arrange, transform*," and each of these meanings fit so well with what John taught in John 1.

Often, we think about making or creating in the terms of a grand skill, like a stunning musical composition or art piece. But creation comes in many forms; you just need to look at all the things that cause you to "move, progress, advance or become."

The word *made* appears in several scriptural passages (including John 1:3) and is taught beautifully by modern-day prophets. President Thomas S. Monson has said that while the creation of the earth was completed several millennia ago, there are endless things God left for us to create:

> God left the world unfinished for man to work his skill upon. He left the electricity in the cloud, the oil in the earth. He left the rivers unbridged and the forests uncut, and the cities unbuilt. God gives to man the challenge of raw materials, not the ease and comfort of finished things. He leaves the pictures unpainted and the music unsung and the problems unsolved, that man might know the joys and glories of creation.[4]

You may have an idea that's just waiting to be formed, or a relationship that's waiting to be strengthened, or possibly even a family that's waiting to be created. Take notice of the many things you create today; you'll be surprised at all you can do!

"In him was life; and the life was the light of men. And the light shineth in darkness; and the darkness comprehended it not." (John 1:4–5)

FROM THE VERY BEGINNING OF THE Old Testament (see Genesis 1:2) to the opening words in the New Testament stated above, *light* is the first of the Creator's attributes, manifesting Himself in a world that is darkness and chaos without Him.

---

3. *Strong's,* 1096.
4. Thomas S. Monson, "In Search of the Abundant Life," *Ensign*, Aug. 1998.

The Greek word used for *light* in John 1 literally means "source of light"[5] (see also Doctrine and Covenants 88:7–12) while the Old English means "to illuminate, fill with brightness."[6] We see a powerful contrast between light and darkness throughout the Old and New Testaments, teaching us that Christ, our source of light, will always have the power to overcome the darkness that inevitably comes when we drift away from Him and His teachings.

President Henry B. Eyring said: "Each time you choose to try to live more like the Savior, you will have your testimony strengthened. You will come in time to know for yourself that He is the Light of the World. . . . You will reflect to others the Light of Christ in your life."[7]

This week, think about what you can do to better reflect the Light of Christ in your life.

"These things were done in Bethabara beyond Jordan, where John was baptizing." (John 1:28)

THE RIVER JORDAN WAS THE SITE Jesus chose for John to baptize Him (see Matthew 3:15) and, according to John, the place where this ordinance was performed was in "Bethabara" (John 1:28). This location is virtually the lowest body of fresh water on earth.[8] This symbolism is so rich! This location may have been chosen to symbolize Christ's humility and to teach us that He literally descended beneath all things to rise above all things.[9]

Interestingly, the word "Jordan" is a Hebrew word that means "to go down." The exact location, Bethabara, means "the crossing" or "house of the crossing." President Russell M. Nelson taught that this location could symbolize a spiritual crossing into the kingdom of God:

> Could it be that Christ chose this location for His baptism in the River Jordan as a silent commemoration of the crossing of the faithful Israelites under Joshua's direction so many years before (see Josh. 3), as well as a symbol that baptism is a spiritual crossing into the kingdom of God?[10]

---

5. *Strong's*, 5457.
6. "Light," *Online Etymology Dictionary*.
7. Henry B. Eyring, "A Living Testimony," *Ensign*, May 2011, 128.
8. See David K. Lynch, "Land Below Sea Level," *Geology.com*, geology.com/below-sea-level.
9. See Russell M. Nelson, "Why Palestine?" Missionary Training Center, 11 Oct. 1994.
10. Russell M. Nelson, "In This Holy Land," *Ensign*, Feb. 1991.

Baptism today can be viewed as our "crossing place." As this ordinance is administered, it points our minds toward a new beginning. This covenant allows us to take the name of Jesus Christ, keep His commandments, and serve Him to the end (see Mosiah 18:8–10; D&C 20:37). Baptism begins a crossing into a new life—one dedicated to following Jesus Christ—as sins are forgiven through the receipt of the gift of the Holy Ghost. The Lord will help, comfort, and guide us as we cross onto the path that leads to eternal life, just as Jesus and the Children of Israel began a new life as they entered the waters of the Jordan at Bethabara.

As you navigate your life, always remember that Jesus has been to Bethabara. He's been lower than any of us can ever go. If you feel like you are "below water" and drowning with life, reach to Him. He's below you—and can help you rise.

"Jesus saw Nathanael coming to him, and saith of him, Behold an Israelite indeed, in whom is no guile!" (John 1:47)[11]

GUILE IS A WORD THAT WE don't hear very often, so the meaning might be lost on us. In Greek the word for guile is *dolos*, meaning *deceit, treachery or a trick*.[12] When Jesus saw Nathanael coming toward Him, He exclaimed of Nathanael, "Behold an Israelite indeed, in whom is no *guile*!" (John 1:47). Elder Joseph B. Wirthlin taught that being without guile means being honest, true, and righteous:

> To be without guile is to be free of deceit, cunning, hypocrisy, and dishonesty in thought or action. . . . A person without guile is a person of innocence, honest intent, and pure motives, whose life reflects the simple practice of conforming his daily actions to principles of integrity. . . . If we are without guile, we are honest, true, and righteous. . . . Those who are honest are fair and truthful in their speech, straightforward in their dealings, free of deceit, and above stealing, misrepresentation, or any other fraudulent action.[13]

---

11. The psalmist wrote, "Blessed is the man . . . in whose spirit there is no guile" (Ps. 32:2), and then admonished, "Keep thy tongue from evil, and thy lips from speaking guile" (Ps. 34:13).
12. *Strong's*, 1388.
13. Joseph B. Wirthlin, "Without Guile," *Ensign*, May 1988.

To restate that in simple terms: we should strive to be genuine. This is what being without *guile* is all about. Our honest desire to be righteous in word and deed will draw us nearer to Christ.

FOR FURTHER STUDY

- Read about the premortal and mortal ministry of John the Baptist (see the Bible Dictionary, John; or Robert J. Matthews, "There is not a greater Prophet," *Ensign*, Jan. 1991.)
- Spend some time studying the creation and what the scriptures teach about "The Beginning" (John 1:1) in Genesis 1–2, Moses 1–3, and Abraham 3–5.
- Look up the meaning of "grace" and "truth" (John 1:14) in the Bible Dictionary, www.biblehub.com, and www.blueletterbible.org.

What other unique or insightful words did you find in your study this week?

_____

_____

_____

_____

_____

Please share with us!
Visit www.ComeFollowMeWOW.com and
share your word discoveries and insights!

Chapter 5

Matthew 3; Mark 1; Luke 3

Don't miss these Words of the Week

"Repent" (Matthew 3:1)
"Dove" (Matthew 3:16)
"Confess" (Mark 1:5)

**"In those days came John the Baptist, preaching
in the wilderness of Judæa, and saying, Repent
ye: for the kingdom of heaven is at hand."
(Matthew 3:1)**

ELDER THEODORE M. BURTON OF THE Seventy once said, "Because of the
Savior's Atonement, repentance is a beautiful word!"[14] Now, what makes
repentance such a beautiful word?

After the death of Jesus and his apostles, many of the truths found in
the doctrine of repentance were lost. The Old Testament (originally written
in Hebrew), used the word *shube* for repentance, which means "the turn
from" or "to turn to." Throughout the Old Testament, a fundamental theme
was forsaking or turning from evil and doing good, which captured the idea
of repentance very well.

---

14. See Theodore M. Burton, "The Meaning of Repentance," *Ensign*, Aug. 1988.

The New Testament (originally written in Greek) used the word *meta-neoeo* for repentance, which means "a change of mind or thinking."[15] The first part of *metaneoeo*, "meta," simply means "change" (think of *metabolism* and *metamorphosis*). The suffix *neoeo* means "air, mind, thought, or spirit," depending on how it is used.[16] Thus, in the context where *meta* and *neoeo* are used in the New Testament, the word *metaneoeo* means a change of mind or thought or thinking so powerful and so strong that it leads to change.

When the New Testament was translated from Greek into Latin, the Greek word *metaneoeo* was translated into a Latin word with painful meanings. Elder Theodore H. Burton taught that the Latin word used for repentance caused fear and dread:

> The beautiful meaning of Hebrew and Greek was changed in Latin to an ugly meaning involving hurting, punishing, whipping, cutting, mutilating, disfiguring, starving, or even torturing. Small wonder then that most people have come to fear and dread the word repentance. . . . People must somehow be made to realize that the true meaning of repentance is that we do not require people to be punished or to punish themselves, but to change their lives so they can escape eternal punishment. If they have this understanding, it will relieve their anxiety and fears and become a welcome and treasured word in our religious vocabulary.[17]

The Guide to the Scriptures teaches that repentance is, "A change of mind and heart that brings a fresh attitude toward God, oneself, and life in general. . . . True repentance comes from a love for God and a sincere desire to obey His commandments."[18] With a true knowledge of what repentance means, repentance is indeed a beautiful word.

---

15. *Strong's,* 3340.
16. *Neoeo* is sometimes transliterated as *pn*, as in the French word *pneu*, meaning "air-filled"; we also find *pneu* in pneumatic (pneumatic hammer or a pneumatic drill: air-driven tools) and pneumonia, an air sickness of the lungs.
17. Theodore M. Burton, "The Meaning of Repentance," Brigham Young University devotional, 26 Mar. 1985, speeches.byu.edu.
18. Guide to the Scriptures, "Repent, Repentance," scriptures.ChurchofJesusChrist.org.

"And Jesus, when he was baptized, went up straightway out of the water: and, lo, the heavens were opened unto him, and he saw the Spirit of God descending like a dove, and lighting upon him." (Matthew 3:16)

IN GREEK, THE WORD *PERISTERAN* IS used here to describe a pigeon or dove.[19] Much debate has been given about the actual or symbolic appearance of a dove following Jesus's emergence from the waters of baptism. Matthew wrote that, "The Spirit of God descended like a dove" (see Matthew 3:16). Nephi penned, "After Jesus was baptized, the Holy Ghost came down in the form of a dove" (1 Nephi 11:27). And John added, "I, John, bear record, and lo, the heavens were opened, and the Holy Ghost descended upon him in the form of a dove" (see D&C 93:15). We know that God's "every word shall be established"[20] in the mouth of two or three witnesses, and here we've got Matthew, Nephi, and John's pure testimony.

The Bible Dictionary teaches that the Sign of the Dove was "a prearranged sign by which John the Baptist would recognize the Messiah" and that, "The sign of the dove was instituted before the creation of the world as a witness for the Holy Ghost."[21] The Prophet Joseph Smith taught that the "sign of the dove" was given as a witness that Jesus's baptism had divine approval.[22]

The idea that the Holy Ghost can appear as a bird (dove) is a misconception. Facsimile in the Book of Abraham No. 2, Figure 7 shows that the Sign of the Dove appears to represent that the Holy Ghost Himself was present at Jesus's baptism. Similar signs seem to have been given to Abraham, and likely to other prophets since Adam.

Regardless of whether or not an actual feathered bird flew down from the sky when Jesus arose from the Jordan river, or whether the personage of the Holy Ghost gave a sign to John or other witnesses, one application emerges: We should identify and embrace things that bring the Holy Ghost into our lives, as well as identify and eliminate the things that repel Him.

---

19. *Strong's*, 4058.
20. Matthew 18:16.
21. Bible Dictionary, "Dove, sign of."
22. Joseph Smith, *History of the Church*, 5:261.

"[They] were baptized of him in Jordan, confessing their sins." (Mark 1:5)

WHEN WE HEAR THE WORD *CONFESS*, many of us imagine a criminal in an interrogation room or a nervous partitioner sitting outside of a booth speaking with a religious leader. The word confess comes from Latin *confessare*, which comes from *com* (together) and *fateri* (to admit, or speak).[23] The Greek version is *exomologoumenoi* meaning "to acknowledge or agree fully."[24]

Confession is a common Christian practice as it has roots back to John receiving confessions of sin at the time of Christ's baptism (see Mark 1:5) and also in James 5:14–16.

Elder C. Scott Grow shared a story that illustrates the blessings and beauty of people humbly seeking out a priesthood leader to confess sin:[25]

> One evening a few years ago, I was interviewing adults for renewal of their temple recommends. A middle-aged woman came in for her interview. She had been married in the temple and was active in the Church all her life.
>
> I sensed a deep sadness in her soul. As the interview progressed, I received a spiritual impression. I said to her, "Sister, I have the impression that you made a serious mistake when you were a teenager that you haven't confessed to a priesthood leader. Would you be willing to tell me about it?"
>
> She immediately began to cry. She told me that was true, but she had always felt too embarrassed to confess it to a bishop. As she confessed what she had done, she shared sufficient detail for me to make a determination of her worthiness.
>
> The confession of her sin to a priesthood leader marked the end of her repentance process rather than the beginning. She had unnecessarily carried the burden and sorrow of that sin for more than 30 years. . . .
>
> I want you to know that I do not remember her name. The Lord can remove such memories from bishops. What I do remember is that through confession to her priesthood leader, a middle-aged woman was relieved of feelings of guilt that she had carried far too many years.

23. "Confess," *Online Etymology Dictionary*.
24. *Strong's*, 1843.
25. C. Scott Grow, "Why and What Do I Need to Confess to My Bishop?" *New Era*, Oct. 2013.

If you are in the same arena as this sweet sister in Elder Grow's story, consider the blessings that come through confessing major transgressions to an ecclesiastical leader. It only takes a few seconds to type a text to ask for the process to begin. In fact, a simple, "Bishop, I need some help" message is enough to start that process.

FOR FURTHER STUDY

- Research the symbolism of camel's hair and John's unique diet to find modern-day relevance; to do this, use a web browser and type in phrases like, "Spiritual Symbolism of John's the Baptist clothing,"[26] or "Locusts and Wild Honey as Object Lessons."[27]

- Understand the role that confession has in the repentance and baptism processes (see Matthew 3:6). Consider studying the word "confession" and other scripture that speak to this process in the Bible Dictionary, www.biblehub.com, and www.blueletterbible.org.

- Study the role of the Holy Ghost and the process and purpose of confirmation following baptism, based on Matthew 3:11. As you study, be sure to look up the word "confirmation" in the Bible Dictionary, BibleHub.com, and www.blueletterbible.org. Consider modern-day application and meaning.

- Read what the Book of Mormon teaches about how Jesus fulfilled all righteousness (see 2 Nephi 31).

---

26. See Philip Kosloski, "The spiritual symbolism of John the Baptist's unusual clothing," *Aleteia*, 29 Aug. 2019, aleteia.org.
27. See Andrew Wilson, "Locust and Wild Honey: An Object Lesson?" *Think*, 13 Apr. 2015, thinktheology.co.uk.

What other unique or insightful words did you find in your study this week?

_____

_____

_____

_____

_____

_____

_____

Please share with us!
Visit www.ComeFollowMeWOW.com and
share your word discoveries and insights!

Chapter 6

Matthew 4; Luke 4

Don't miss these Words of the Week

"**Tempted**" and "**Devil**" (Matthew 4:1)
"**Fasting**" and "**Forty**" (Matthew 4:2)

"Then was Jesus led up of the Spirit into the wilderness to be tempted of the devil." (Matthew 4:1)

TEMPTATION IS A TEST OF A person's ability to choose good instead of evil. Temptation comes from Greek *peirasthēnai* meaning "to try or tempt,"[1] while Latin *temptare* means "to feel, attempt to influence, or test." One of the Latin variants for this word is *tentare*, which introduces an even more hands-on experience.[2] *Tentare* means "*to handle*" or "*to touch*." Think of that: when we are tempted, it points us to the imagery of Satan hoping to handle or touch us.

When the devil came to Jesus, it indeed was a one-on-one confrontation, an enticement for Jesus to sin and follow Satan instead of His Heavenly Father.

Since the Fall of Adam and Eve, people have been inclined to follow earthly desires and to succumb to appetites and passions. In our latter days, it's been prophesied that "perilous times" (2 Timothy 3:1) would come. The

---

1. *Strong's,* 3985.
2. "Tempt," *Online Etymology Dictionary.*

influence of the adversary is widespread and seductive. Satan tries to deceive and to make sin seem appealing. But each individual can defeat Satan and overcome temptation (see Alma 13:28).

The Latin and Greek root for *devil* means *slanderer*, which means "oral or spoken defamation." The word for devil used in Matthew 4:1 is *diabolos* and means *tracucer*: to expose to shame or blame by means of falsehood and misrepresentation.[3]

Slander is a legal term for the act of harming a person's reputation by saying something that is untrue and damaging about that person to one or more people. With so many avenues for people to slander each other, including social media, blogs, and podcasts, we see many headlines, comments, and articles that are designed to get clicks by the very act of slandering another person, institution, or group of people.

Slander is something that grieves the Spirit of God and it is something that is simply not an acceptable behavior for a Christian.

The Lord taught that sacred things "must be spoken with care" (D&C 63:64). Sister Jean B. Bingham, First Counselor in the Primary General Presidency, taught: "Words have surprising power, both to build up and to tear down. . . . Choosing to say only that which is positive about—and to—others lifts and strengthens those around us."[4] As we choose our words carefully, both in person and online, we are refusing to allow the devil to influence our message as we choose to reject the temptation to slander our brothers and sisters. Always think twice before you speak or post online; do not fall for the devil's deceit of *slander*.

"And when he had fasted forty days and forty nights, he was afterward an hungred." (Matthew 4:2)

THE GREEK NUMBER FOR 40 IS *tesserakonta,5* while the English *quarantine* looks very similar to the Latin *quadraginta* and the Italian *quaranta*, both meaning "40 days." The number 40 typically refers to a time of waiting and testing, and Jesus faced such a time of testing when he fasted for forty days.[6]

Anciently, when a ship arriving in port was suspected of being infected, it had to forego contact with the shore for a period of about 40 days.

---

3. *Strong's*, 228.
4. Jean B. Bingham, "I Will Bring the Light of the Gospel into My Home," *Ensign*, Nov. 2016, 7.
5. *Strong's*, 5062.
6. "Forty," *Online Etymology Dictionary*.

Scripturally, there are several examples of the number 40 referring to periods of testing and quarantining:

- 40 days and 40 nights of rain when God flooded the Earth as Noah and his family quarantined in the ark (see Genesis 7:4).
- After Jacob (Israel) died, he was embalmed for 40 days (see Genesis 50:3).
- 40 years of wandering in the wilderness for Israel (see Numbers 32:13)
- 40 days of Moses on the mount receiving the 10 Commandments; while there, "he neither ate bread nor drank water" (see Exodus 34:28; Deuteronomy 9:11).
- Elijah sojourned in the wilderness for 40 days until he reached Horeb, the mountain of God (1 Kings 19:8).
- Every morning for 40 days, Goliath approached the army of Israel (1 Samuel 17:16).
- 40 days given to Nineveh to repent or be destroyed.
- 40 days of Jesus being tempted by Satan while alone in the wilderness (Matt. 4:2).
- 40 years of rule for many of Israel's Judges (kings Saul, David, and Solomon each reigned for 40 years).
- Nephi writes that after they had separated from the Lamanites, in the space of 40 years they had contention (2 Nephi 5:34).
- Ammon wandered in the wilderness 40 days before finding King Limhi and his people (Mosiah 7:4–5).

By way of application, we are being tested here on Earth through our trials and troubles of mortality. While we do not know the length of time our struggles will last (just as those in the scriptures did not know how long their eventual 40-day or -year periods of testing were going to last), we do know if our periods of testing and spiritual quarantining are leading to great outcomes while we are in the middle of them. And just as many great men and women in the scriptures gained strength during their 40-day or -year quarantine and trying experiences, we can also find spiritual progression and improvement by clinging to our covenants during our time of testing, just as Jesus did while being tempted by the devil.

FOR FURTHER STUDY

- Study how the temptations that the devil presented to Christ mirror the temptation to Adam and Eve in the Garden of Eden (see Genesis 3 and Moses 4).

- Look up information about the prison and prison conditions that John was in (Matthew 4:12).

- Study the history of fasting within the Church.[7] (See "I have a Question," *Ensign*, Mar. 1998 or Howard W. Hunter, "Fast Day," *Ensign*, Nov. 1985.)

- Set some goals to improve your next fast.

What other unique or insightful words did you find in your study this week?

_____

_____

_____

_____

_____

Please share with us!
Visit www.ComeFollowMeWOW.com and
share your word discoveries and insights!

!

---

7. KSL News has a wonderful article summarizing the updates of fasting: Carter Williams, "Looking back at the history of fasting in religion and within the Church of Jesus Christ," *KSL.com*, 8 Apr. 2020, www.ksl.com.

Chapter 7

John 2-4

Don't miss these Words of the Week

"Miracle" (John 2:11)
"Born Again" (John 3:3)
"Love" (John 3:16)
"Living Water" (John 4:11)
"Messiah" (John 4:25)

**"This beginning of miracles did Jesus in Cana
of Galilee, and manifested forth his glory;
and his disciples believed on him."
(John 2:11)**

FOR HIS FIRST OF MANY MIRACLES, Jesus chose to take filthy, bacteria-laden water used for cleansing as part of a wedding celebration and turn the water into the best wine of the night (see John 2:10). John mentions in John 2:11 that this was the first miracle of Jesus.

When the miracle of turning water to wine happened at Cana, it appears that only those disciples that were closest in proximity to Jesus witnessed this first miracle (the wedding guests most likely had no idea that a miracle had taken place). Likewise, those that are closest to Christ in our day will be those that clearly see miracles occurring in their lives and in the world.

The Greek word used here is *sēmeiōn,* referring to *supernatural signs1,* while the Latin word for *miracle* is *miraculum* which means "object of wonder" or "a marvelous event caused by God."[2] The root and origin of this word is *smeiros,* which means "to smile or to laugh." Think of that implication: miracles are founded in smiling and heavenly happiness. Indeed, miracles bring us joy and smiles, and we wonder if the same sentiments are found in the Orchestrator of these divided events as well.

Think of it: miracles are etymologically tied to smiling and blissful laughter. Indeed, those who have seen the hand of the Lord in their lives are left smiling—and sometimes even chuckling or laughing with delight over the tender mercy they have received. As Job declared, "He [shall] fill thy mouth with laughing, and thy lips with rejoicing" (Job 8:21).

Jesus can take the dirtiest things in our lives and make them absolutely clean and sweet. He can transform the most natural, fallen person into a Celestial Saint. It's no wonder that changing filthy water to sweet wine was His first miracle; He wanted us to know early on that He has the power to change anything and anybody—to transform not just a liquid called water, but the life of anyone that comes to Him. And that *miracle* should indeed make us smile.

"Jesus answered and said unto him, Verily, verily, I say unto thee, Except a man be born again, he cannot see the kingdom of God." (John 3:3)

NICODEMUS WAS A VERY EDUCATED AND important ruler who seems to have been impressed with what Jesus had been teaching. When Jesus said to him, "Unless a man is born again, he cannot see the kingdom of God" Nicodemus responded with a quizzical expression (there's been debate about his reply; was he being sarcastic, or was he being sincere?).

Here's one reason why Nicodemus may have been confused. The use of the word *again* in *born again* may have been a play on words. *Again* is from the Greek word *anothen,* which means *above* (from the root *ano* meaning *upward* or *above*).[3] Being "born again" might have been understood as being "born from above," but it appears that Nicodemus could only see the

---

1. *Strong's,* 4592.
2. "Miracle," *Online Etymology Dictionary.*
3. *Strong's,* 509.

physical absurdity of a person re-entering his or her mother's womb and being born a second time.

Regardless of Nicodemus's questions or confusion, being born again is a fundamental doctrine of Jesus Christ. Further, there are several elements of physical birth that relate to spiritual rebirth:

Physical Birth	Spiritual Rebirth
Conception begins with two people.	Being born again begins with two people: the Lord and one of his children.
It typically takes one cell 40 weeks to grow into a fetus with tissues, bones, heart, nails, ears, etc.	Being born again takes time; a person needs sufficient time to grow into a new creature in Christ.
The fetus is anchored in by an umbilical cord.	Before being born again, most people are spiritually connected to leaders or friends who have been previously converted.
The umbilical cord helps to cleanse, feed, and protect the fetus.	The "spiritual umbilical cord" helps a person to repent and grow spiritually self-sufficient.
Before being born, the baby sheds lanugo (hairs) and vernix caseosa (waxy coating).	Before being born again, a person sheds sins and improper habits.
The fetus initiates the birthing process—the baby's hypothalamus sends a message to the pituitary gland to the adrenal glands to release cortisol through the umbilical cord to the placenta.	It's usually up to the individual that wants to be reborn to initiate the process. In exceptional cases (Alma the Younger, Saul, etc) the Lord will intervene and initiate repentance.
Occasionally, labor must be induced and when that happens, it's a bit harder on mom and on the baby.	It is much easier to choose to be reborn than to be forced into change.
Following the pain and pressure of birth, the baby is now in a new environment.	After repentance, those that are born again find themselves in a new spiritual environment.
Newborn babies are covered in blood and water.	Those who are spiritually reborn have the emblems of Christ's Atonement operative in their lives.
At the time of birth, the heart changes form and function.	A change of heart accompanies being born again.

The baby is named and will ultimately receive an inheritance from his or her parents.	Those who are born again receive the name of Christ and are qualified to inherit all the Father has.

Jesus's teaching about a physical and a spiritual baptism to Nicodemus helps us understand that both our own actions (faith, repentance, baptism, and the receipt of the Holy Ghost) and assistance from God and His power and through Christ's Atonement are needed for a lasting transformation. Being born again is a change from a natural man or woman to a saint (see Mosiah 3:19).

"For God so loved the world, that he gave his only begotten Son, that whosoever believeth in him should not perish, but have everlasting life." (John 3:16)

WE FREQUENTLY FIND WORDS TRANSLATED FROM Greek or Hebrew that don't have a meaning quite as powerful in English as they do in their original language. *Love* in this scripture is one of them. The Greek word translated for *love* in John 3:16 is ēgapēsen and it means "to take pleasure in" or "long for"[4] while the Proto-Germani liubi connotes love as joy. [5]

Another word for love found throughout the New Testament is *agapao*. It's used over 200 times in the New Testament. *Vine's Expository Dictionary* explains *agapao* as a deep and constant love:

> In respect of *agapao* as used of God, it expresses the deep and constant love and interest of a perfect Being towards entirely unworthy objects, producing and fostering a reverential love in them towards the Giver, and a practical love towards those who are partakers of the same, and a desire to help others to seek the Giver.[6]

We could all agree it would be a beautiful thing if we had an increase in "reverential love" for our Maker and Giver and for those who follow Him.

This attitude of *agapao* is poorly expressed in the English language by both *love* and *charity*. There doesn't seem to be another suitable word in our language that appropriately expresses this attitude of doing good to another

---

4. *Strong's*, 25.
5. "Love," *Online Etymology Dictionary*.
6. W. E. Vine, *Vine's Complete Expository Dictionary of Old and New Testament Words* (New York: Thomas Nelson Publishers, 1985), 381–82.

without a hope of reward from the feelings they may have about the person to whom the good deed is being extended.

It is this "agapo attitude" that we must possess to fulfill our duty to "Love [our] enemies, bless those who curse [us], do good to those who hate [us], and pray for those who spitefully use [us] and persecute [us]" (see Matthew 5:43–44). The "agapo attitude" implores us to do good to people even if they curse us, hate us, spitefully use us, and persecute us. We simply try to love them with the same love God demonstrated when He sent His only begotten Son.

Search for this pure love as you interact with others today and your understanding of our Heavenly Father's sacrifice will grow.

"From whence then hast thou that living water?" (John 4:11)

MOST OF US IN THE WESTERN world are blessed with clean running water. In Biblical times, water sources were limited to two: running water (found naturally in streams and rivers or in rainstorms) or man-made wells or cisterns which were made to collect water. As Jesus conversed with the Samaritan woman at Jacob's well, He presented a concept to her of *living water*. The phrase *living water* in Greek describes water that had a source and which generally would be available all year long, generally a spring or a river.[7] This *living water* was not stagnant water, but flowing water, which would make life much easier due to the reduction in transportation to access it.

Water is a frequently found symbol of Jesus Christ and His gospel. As water is essential to sustain physical life, the Savior and His teachings (living water) are essential for eternal life. Describing our day, the prophet Jeremiah wrote, "My people . . . have forsaken me the fountain of living waters, and hewed them out . . . broken cisterns, that can hold no water" (Jeremiah 2:13). Elder Robert L. Simpson added,

> Throughout history men have always been looking for the easy way. [Some] have devoted their lives to finding the "fountain of youth," a miracle water which would bring everlasting life. Today [many] are still seeking . . . some magic "fountain" that [will] bring forth success, fulfillment, and happiness. But most of this searching is in vain. . . . It is only this "living water," the gospel of Jesus Christ, that

---

7. *Strong's,* 2198.

can and will bring a happy, a successful, and an everlasting life to the children of men.[8]

What's the difference between dead and living water? Two words: The Source. The Lord provides the living water to eliminate droughts of truth; the world's water sources are stagnant. Thanks to Him, we need not spend time carving out broken cisterns of worldly gain that won't last. His living water satisfies our natural thirst for truth. His beautiful gospel quenches spiritual thirst. Just as Jacob's well was a unique source of living (spring) water, Jesus is the only source of living truth and saving ordinances available to us today. Turn to Him and apply His living truths to find living waters for your life.

"The woman saith unto him, I know that Messiah cometh, which is called Christ: when he is come, he will tell us all things." (John 4:25)

IN THE OLD TESTAMENT, THE JEWISH people longed for the day when God would send a King, an "anointed (or chosen) one." This is where our English word *Christ* originated.

The word *Christ* is from the Latin *Christus*, in turn from the Greek *Christos*, which meant "the Anointed,"[9] the perfect title for Jesus.[10] He was chosen by the Father to be the savior of the world, the savior of each of us, while in the pre-earth life. By calling Jesus the *Christ* or the *Messiah* (an Aramaic word), the woman at the well in John 4 is suggesting that she knew He was the anointed one.

But where do we get the meaning of the word anointed? The idea and imagery of anointing stems from the Old Testament. Kings and high priests ceremonially had oil placed on their heads as part of their rituals. Olive oil was used to anoint the tabernacle of the congregation, the ark of the testimony, as well as to anoint Aaron and his sons (see Exodus 30:22–31). Being the purest of oils, it was perfect for anointings and also provided sustenance, healing, and light—each of which are perfect symbols for Christ, the anointed, or chosen, Son of God.

---

8. Robert L. Simpson, In Conference Report, Oct. 1968, 96.
9. *Strong's*, 5547.
10. See "Christ," *Online Etymology Dictionary*.

FOR FURTHER STUDY

- Research Jewish wedding ceremony customs and traditions and look for symbolism that points you to Christ; www.gotquestions.org has a wonderful entry under "Marriage Customs;" www.myjewishlearning.com has a great article titled "Ancient Jewish Marriage."

- Look up Jewish purification rituals and look for connections to modern-day gospel ordinances; for example, earlychurchhistory.org has information under its page titled "Medicine and Jewish Cleanliness" and www.encyclopedia.com has a wonderful article titled "Jewish Purification."

- In John 2, we learn of Jesus cleansing the temple. Many have wondered about the show of emotion at this moment. Take some time and look up Church magazine articles about emotions and how they affect discipleship.

- Study the mission of the Holy Ghost described in John 3.

- Read about where the Samaritans came from and why this conversation would have been controversial to appreciate the significance of Jesus's conversation with the Samaritan woman by looking up the history of the Jews and Samaritans.[11]

- Review the history of Jacob's Well using the internet.[12]

- Review John 4:39's witness of the power of everyday missionary work. Consider making goals to improve sharing the gospel with your neighbors and friends.

11. See Don Stewart, "Who Were the Samaritans?" *Blue Letter Bible,* www.blueletterbible.org/faq/don_stewart/don_stewart_1319.cfm; "Samaritan: Judaism," *Britannica,* www.britannica.com.
12. See Randall Niles, "Jacob's Well in Samaria," *Drive Thru History, 24 June 2061,* drivethruhistory.com; "Jacob's Well," *Wikipedia,* wikipedia.org, accessed 16 Aug. 2022.

What other unique or insightful words did you find in your study this week?

_____

_____

_____

_____

_____

_____

Please share with us!
Visit www.ComeFollowMeWOW.com and
share your word discoveries and insights!

!

Chapter 8

Matthew 5; Luke 6

Don't miss these Words of the Week

"Blessed" (Matthew 5:3)
"Salt" (Matthew 5:13)
"Lust" (Matthew 5:28)
"Perfect" (Matthew 5:48)

**"Blessed are the poor in spirit: for
theirs is the kingdom of heaven."
(Matthew 5:3)**

WE OFTEN REFER TO THE NINE virtues and characteristics taught by Christ in Matthew 5–7 as the beatitudes. The word "blessed" (*makarios* in Greek*)* comes before each passage wherein Christ teaches a characteristic of the beatitudes. *Makarios* literally means "fortunate," "blessed," or "happy."[1] We get "beatitude" from the Latin word *beatus,* which means "happy."[2] So, we could read each of these passages as, "[Happy, or Fortunate] are the":

Beatitude	Blessing	Principle/Ordinance
Poor in Spirit (who come unto me)	Kingdom of Heaven	Faith
Mourn	Comfort	Repentance

---

1. *Strong's,* 3107.
2. "Blessed," *Online Etymology Dictionary.*

Beatitude	Blessing	Principle/Ordinance
Meek	Inherit the Earth	Baptism
Hunger and Thirst	Filled w/ Holy Ghost	Gift of the Holy Ghost
Merciful	Obtain Forgiveness	Melchizedek Priesthood and Temple Blessings (see Doctrine and Covenants 107:18–19)
Pure in Heart	See God	
Peacemakers	Kingdom of Heaven	
Persecuted	Rewarded in Heaven	

But happy are the *poor?* Happy are those who *mourn?* Happy are the *meek?* Fortunate are those who *hunger* and *thirst?* Happy are those who are *persecuted?* None of those pairs seem to go very well together. Yet each virtue is an invitation to come to Christ and use His Atonement to be refined through our trials. As King Benjamin taught:

> And moreover, I would desire that ye should consider on the blessed and happy state of those that keep the commandments of God. For behold, they are blessed in all things, both temporal and spiritual; and if they hold out faithful to the end they are received into heaven, that thereby they may dwell with God in a state of never-ending happiness. O remember, remember that these things are true; for the Lord God hath spoken it. (Mosiah 2:41)

Happiness is found in obedience to God and coming unto Christ by making and keeping sacred covenants through ordinances. The Beatitudes give us a pattern for coming unto Christ—and those that come unto Christ will ultimately be blessed with happiness despite the challenges that face them during life on earth.

"Ye are the salt of the earth: but if the salt have lost his savour, wherewith shall it be salted? it is thenceforth good for nothing, but to be cast out, and to be trodden under foot of men." (Matthew 5:13)

IN JUST ABOUT EVERY CULTURE ON the planet, we use food to connect with others. Can you think of a single celebration that doesn't involve food? From birthdays to Christmas, we love to break bread with one another. And one of the most vital ingredients to most of these dishes is salt.

Salt has been associated with the gospel since the beginning of time. Under the law of Moses, priests put salt on offerings (see Leviticus 2:13; Ezekiel 43:23–24).[3] Salt was even sprinkled on the ramp leading to the altar to prevent the priests from slipping. Salt was also used to describe our covenants with God; at least twice in scripture, the phrase "covenant of salt" is used to describe the everlasting covenants between God and man (see Numbers 18:19; 2 Chronicles 13:5).

In Biblical times, salt was considered a form of wealth. Soldiers in the Roman army were paid a sum of money to buy salt for themselves. The Greek word for "salt" was *halas*,[4] while the Latin word was *sal*. The money given to the Roman soldiers was called *salarium*, which later became the English word "salary."[5]

Besides its use as currency, salt brings flavor (think of a meal or popcorn without salt). It can also inhibit the growth of harmful mold and bacteria and preserve and cure food.[6] Salt also keeps our electrolytes in balance and helps regulate insulin and blood pressure. Popcorn aside, we need salt to live.

In application, as salt prevents decay, we can be personally sanctified through covenants, and we can help halt the spread of moral decay by living righteously. Because salt is a preservative and because God refers to His "everlasting covenant," those who make and keep covenants can extend eternal blessings to others. And as salt enhances flavor, we can enhance our spiritual capabilities through seeking for the Holy Ghost.

Interestingly, the only way that salt can lose its savor is through outside contamination. When protected against outside influences, salt will remain at its full strength for years and years. Why, then, would the Savior say, "If the salt has lost his savour, wherewith shall it be salted? it is thenceforth good for nothing, but to be cast out, and to be trodden under foot of men" (Matthew 5:13). When salt is mixed with other substances, it becomes corrupted and cannot be used to preserve or flavor food.[7] In application,

---

3. Herod's temple included a salt chamber to store salt for sacrifices and other rituals.
4. *Strong's*, 217.
5. See "Salt-cellar," *Online Etymology Dictionary*.
6. When salt comes in contact with the surface of food, the salt molecules try to achieve a balance between the number of salt molecules inside and outside the food. It does this by drawing water molecules out of the food and inserting salt molecules into the food through osmosis across semipermeable cell membranes. As a result, the number of free water molecules is reduced to a point where most bacteria cannot survive and most enzymes cannot operate because, basically, they get dehydrated (see "The Salt of the Earth," New Era, June 2013).
7. Some dishonest merchants would add fillers to the salt; this would increase the volume of the salt, increasing their earnings.

we must strive to keep ourselves unstained by the things of our world in order to serve our purpose. The Lord declared, "When men are called unto mine everlasting gospel, and covenant with an everlasting covenant, they are accounted as the salt of the earth and the savor of men" (D&C 101:39). To perform our duties as disciples and as the salt of the earth, we must be different from those around us.

Our presence on this earth can make a big difference! Those who strive to keep covenants can make the world a better place. This is the greatest *salary* that the *salt of the earth* would ever desire.

"I say unto you, That whosoever looketh on a woman to lust after her hath committed adultery with her already in his heart." (Matthew 5:28)

LUST ISN'T SOMETHING WE TALK ABOUT in our society today. However, understanding what lust really is can lead to an ability to combat its temptation.

The word "lust" speaks to appetites or pleasures. Its Latin root *lascivus* means "a wanton or playful desire."[8] The notion that lust means "sinful sexual desire" most likely developed in late Old English from Bible translations such as "lusts of the flesh" (see I John 2:16). Lust's Greek descendant is *laste* which means "harlot."[9]

In His sermon on the Mount, the Lord emphasized the importance of not letting lust interfere with our discipleship. Based on earlier definitions of the word "lust," it's easy to surmise that His message to avoid lustfulness may have extended beyond sexual purity. A few millennia previously, the children of Israel "fell a lusting" for food beyond that which God had already given them:

> And the children of Israel also wept again, and said, Who shall give us flesh to eat? We remember the fish, which we did eat in Egypt freely; the cucumbers, and the melons, and the leeks, and the onions, and the garlick: But now our soul is dried away: there is nothing at all, beside this manna, before our eyes. (Numbers 11:4–8)

And the consequence for lusting after more than manna?

---

8. See "Lust," *Online Etymology Dictionary*.
9. See "Lascivious," *Online Etymology Dictionary*.

And there went forth a wind from the Lord, and brought quails from the sea, and let them fall by the camp . . . And the people stood up all that day, and all that night, and all the next day, and they gathered the quails . . . And while the flesh was yet between their teeth, ere it was chewed, the wrath of the Lord was kindled against the people, and the Lord smote the people with a very great plague; . . . there they buried the people that *lusted*. (Numbers 11:31–34)

Elder Jeffrey R. Holland provided five tips for keeping the Lord's command to avoid the temptation of lust[10]:

1. Separate yourself from "people, materials, and circumstances that will harm you."
2. Seek help from your Father in Heaven, priesthood leaders, and Church resources.
3. Exercise self-control, even in small moments like deciding what movie to watch or who to develop a relationship with.
4. Watch your thoughts and replace lewd thoughts with uplifting ones.
5. Be where the Spirit is and seek to cultivate the Spirit in your home.

As we try to protect ourselves and our families against the temptation to lust, we will feel closer to God and experience happiness through our purity.

"Be ye therefore perfect, even as your Father which is in heaven is perfect." (Matthew 5:48)

SCRIPTURES HAVE DESCRIBED NOAH, SETH, AND Job as *perfect* men (See Gen. 6:9; D&C 107:43; Job 1:1). The use of the word "perfect" within the lives of these great men of God does not necessarily mean that they never made mistakes. The etymology behind the word "perfect" sheds light on its true meaning. The Greek word *teleios*, which is the English version of *perfect*, means, "completed; a person who has become fully initiated in the rituals of a religion."[11] The Latin word history carries the same meaning: "being complete or finished."[12] This definition from the Greek brings inspired light upon the Lord's doctrine of being *perfect*.

---

10. Jeffrey R. Holland, "Place No More For the Enemy of my Soul," *Ensign*, May 2010.
11. *Strong's*, 5046.
12. See "Perfect," *Online Etymology Dictionary*.

Matthew 5:48 ("Be ye therefore perfect, even as your father in heaven in perfect")[13] has often been misunderstood to mean that God requires us to live a sinless, perfect life, leaving us feeling defeated since we know we can't be sinless. Many have questioned why Jesus would ask us to be perfect when He knows it's not possible for us. Elder Jeffrey R. Holland noted, "Such celestial goals seem beyond our reach. Yet surely the Lord would never give us a commandment He knew we could not keep."[14]

As we lay aside most dictionaries' definition of perfect ("being entirely without fault or defect") and then turn to the original meaning, we find hope for our imperfections. Indeed, participation in the rituals of our religion, such as baptism, confirmation, and temple ordinances help us to become more like Jesus Christ.[15]

Professor Hugh Nibley taught that *teleios* means fulfilling all requirements of the covenants we make:

> [*Teleios* means] living up to an agreement or covenant without fault: as the Father keeps the covenants he makes with us . . . the completely initiated who has both qualified for initiation and completed it is *teleios*, literally, "gone all the way," fulfilling all requirements, every last provision of God's command.[16]

President Russell M. Nelson taught that the Savior understands that we cannot yet achieve perfection in this life:

---

13. Interestingly, Greek philosophers also used the word *teleios* in regards to something that is in its intended function—in its intended place—which has great implications for our need to be found at church each week and at the temple as often as time permits (see J. Ayodeji Adewuya, *Holiness in the Letters of Paul* [Cascade Books, 2016]). The word *telios* is also used by Paul in Hebrews 5:14–6:1 to distinguish between the initial teachings and the full instruction (see John W. Welch, "New Testament Word Studies," *Ensign*, Apr. 1993). In Matthew 5:48, *teleios* is rendered as, "to put someone in the position in which he can come or stand before God" (Gerhard Kittel, ed., *Theological Dictionary of the New Testament* (Grand Rapids, Michigan: Eerdmans, 1967), 8:82; citing Heb. 7:19; Heb. 10:1).

14. Jeffrey R. Holland, "Be Ye Therefore Perfect—Eventually," *Ensign*, Nov. 2017.

15. See Walter Bauer, *Greek-English Lexicon of the New Testament* (Chicago: University of Chicago Press, 1957), 817; see also Demosthenes, *De Corona* 259, in C. A. Vince, tr., *Demosthenes* (Cambridge: Harvard University Press, 1971), 190–91. *Telousei* is also translated as "initiations" (Kittel, *Theological Dictionary*, 8:69; 10).

16. As quoted in John W. Welch, "New Testament Word Studies," *Ensign*, Apr. 1993; see Hugh Nibley, unpublished notes from his Sunday School class on the New Testament, commentary on Matt. 5:48, in the Hugh Nibley Archive, Foundation for Ancient Research and Mormon Studies, Provo, Utah.

The perfection that the Savior envisions for us is much more than errorless performance. . . . Perfection is pending. It can come in full only after the Resurrection and only through the Lord. It awaits all who love him and keep his commandments.[17]

Elder Holland further said that to be perfect means to be finished and complete:

May we refuse to let our own mortal follies, and the inevitable short-comings of even the best men and women around us, make us cynical about the truths of the gospel, the truthfulness of the Church, our hope for our future, or the possibility of godliness. If we persevere, then somewhere in eternity our refinement will be finished and complete—which is the New Testament meaning of *perfection*.[18]

In Matthew 5:48, Jesus invites us to become more and more like Him within our current state. What He seems to be asking and looking for is maturity, not sinlessness. What Jesus asks of us in Matthew 5:48 is not an impossible task. As the Old Testament prophet Samuel wrote, "God is my strength and power: and he maketh my way *perfect*" (2 Samuel 22:33).

---

17. Russell M. Nelson, "Perfection Pending," *Ensign*, Nov. 1995.
18. Jeffrey R. Holland, "Be Ye Therefore Perfect—Eventually," *Ensign*, Nov. 2017.

FOR FURTHER STUDY

- Re-read the virtues presented in the Beatitudes and look for a pattern.

- Research what the word "Raca" means in Matthew 5:22 using www. biblehub.com or www.blueletterbible.org. What principle may have the Savior tried to teach with its use?

- What does it mean to "agree with thine adversary quickly" in Matthew 5:25? Look at other New Testament translations using www.biblehub.com or www.blueletterbible.org to see alternate translations of this phrase.

- Research to see when divorce is permissible in the latter days; Jesus addresses adultery in Matthew 5:27–32. (See Gospel Topics, "Divorce," topics.churchofjesuschrist.org).What does it mean to let your communications be "yea yea" and "nay nay" in Matthew 5:37? Look at other New Testament translations using www.biblehub.com or www.blueletterbible.org to see alternate translations of this phrase.

- Consider the question, when should we "go the extra mile" and "turn our cheek" and "give our cloaks"—and when should we take a stand or defend ourselves?

What other unique or insightful words did you find in your study this week?

_____

_____

_____

_____

_____

Please share with us!
Visit www.ComeFollowMeWOW.com and
share your word discoveries and insights!

Chapter 9

Matthew 6-7

Don't miss these Words of the Week

"Vain" (Matthew 6:7)
"Judge Not" (Matthew 7:1-2)
"Rain" (Matthew 7:24-25)

"But when ye pray, use not vain repetitions."
(Matthew 6:7)

THE COMMANDMENT TO NOT TAKE THE name of the Lord in *vain* is a rare commandment as it finds itself repeated in each of the standard works:

- "Thou shalt not take the name of the Lord thy God in vain." (Exodus 20:7)
- "Thou shalt not take the name of the Lord thy God in vain; for the Lord will not hold him guiltless that taketh his name in vain." (Mosiah 13:15)
- "Keep yourselves from evil to take the name of the Lord in vain, for I am the Lord your God, even the God of your fathers, the God of Abraham and of Isaac and of Jacob." (Doctrine and Covenants 136:21)

We are probably most familiar with the first declaration to not take the Lord's name in vain when He revealed it to Moses on Mount Sinai in Exodus 20; other translations of that passage containing the word "vain" read as follows:

- "You must not *make wrong use* of the name of the Lord your God." (Revised English Bible)
- "You shall not *misuse* the name of the Lord your God." (New International Version)

In latter-day revelation, the Lord cautioned that the Lord's name is sacred and should be used with care and authority:

Wherefore, let all men beware how they take my name in their lips— For behold, verily I say, that many there be who are under this condemnation, who use the name of the Lord, and use it in vain, having not authority. . . . Remember that that which cometh from above is sacred, and must be spoken with care, and by constraint of the Spirit; and in this there is no condemnation (D&C 63:61–62, 64).

The word "vain" comes from the Latin and means "void, empty or fruitless."[1] In Greek, the word is *mátaios* connoting "to no purpose."[2]

As one biblical scholar has observed, vain implies "emptiness—a wandering in shadows without substance, a life without the possibility of satisfaction."[3] As we speak of God or act in His name, we should do so with meaning, thoughtfulness, and feeling as we actively speak His holy name.[4]

How, then, may we become guilty of taking the name of God in vain? Certainly through profanity and vulgarity.[5] We also may be guilty of offense when we use His name without serious thought, without appropriate reflection—in other words, in vain (empty, void, and fruitless).

---

1. See "Vain," *Online Etymology Dictionary.*
2. *Strong's,* 3155.
3. Lawrence O. Richards, *Expository Dictionary of Bible Words* (Grand Rapids, Mich.: Zondervan Publishers, 1985), 608.
4. Think, too, of how we use the name and symbols of Christ and His body and blood each week with the administration of the sacrament; participation in this ordinance certainly should not be done in vain (void, empty, or fruitlessly).
5. President Spencer W. Kimball underwent surgery many years ago. While he was wheeled from the operating room to the intensive care room, the attendant who pushed his gurney stumbled and let out an expression using the name of the Lord. President Kimball, who was barely conscious, said weakly, "Please! Please! That is my Lord whose names you revile." There was a deathly silence; then the young man whispered with a subdued voice, "I am sorry." He later went on to counsel: "It is not enough to refrain from profanity or blasphemy. We need to make important in our lives the name of the Lord. While we do not use the Lord's name lightly, we should not leave our friends or our neighbors or our children in any doubt as to where we stand. Let there be no doubt about our being followers of Jesus Christ" (*The Teachings of Spencer W. Kimball,* ed. Edward L. Kimball [1982], 198).

Being flippant, sacrilegious, and irreverent with His name is simply out of bounds of covenant keeping Christians. Obedience to this commandment and to Jesus's teaching during His sermon on the Mount has much to do with living and speaking with purpose and meaning, especially when we act in the name or speak of the Lord.[6]

"Judge not, that ye be not judged. For with what judgment ye judge, ye shall be judged." (Matthew 7:1-2)

MANY PEOPLE TODAY TALK ABOUT FRIENDS and neighbors and criticize their choices or their idiosyncrasies. It's nearly impossible to go a single day in our world without hearing or reading about someone judging another person. Jesus Christ, realizing our tendency to make unrighteous judgment, was very clear about the importance of not making eternal judgments on those around us (see Matthew 7:1–2). In essence, unless we are without fault, we are not qualified to judge. It's really that simple.

In Greek, the word *krinete* is used for "judgment" and it means "to distinguish, to try or condemn."[7] And too many people don't understand that judgment in terms of condemnation is up to the Lord.

President Dallin H. Oaks taught that there are two kinds of judging: final judgments (which we are forbidden to make and which God is authorized to make), and intermediate judgments (which we are directed to make, using righteous principles, such as judging a movie to watch or activity to consider—or even when a bishop acts as a judge in Israel).[8] So when do we know when it is acceptable to judge? President Oaks gave these guidelines:

First, a righteous judgment must, by definition, be intermediate. It will refrain from declaring that a person has been assured of exaltation or from dismissing a person as being irrevocably bound for hellfire.

Second, a righteous judgment will be guided by the Spirit of the Lord, not by anger, revenge, jealousy, or self-interest.

Third, to be righteous, an intermediate judgment must be within our stewardship. We should not presume to exercise and act upon judgments that are outside our personal responsibilities.

---

6. See Robert L. Millet, "Honoring His Holy Name," Ensign, Mar. 1994.

7. *Strong's*, 2919.

8. Dallin H. Oaks, "Judge Not and Judging," Brigham Young University fireside, 1 March 1988, speeches.byu.edu.

Fourth, we should, if possible, refrain from judging until we have adequate knowledge of all the facts.

Elder Dieter F. Uchtdorf of the Quorum of the Twelve Apostles added more clarity on when judging others is within bounds:

> When it comes to hating, gossiping, ignoring, ridiculing, holding grudges, or wanting to cause harm, please apply the following: Stop it! It's that simple. We simply have to stop judging others and replace judgmental thoughts and feelings with a heart full of love for God and His children.[9]

As Sister Bingham learned from a dear friend, "The greatest form of charity may be to withhold judgment."[10]

Be sure to leave all eternal and weighty judgments on the Lord's perfect judgment. And when it comes to imperfections we see in other people or opportunities, be sure to use wisdom as you judge which things come from God and which ones do not (see Moroni 7:16).

"The rain descended, and the floods came, and the winds blew, and beat upon that house; and it fell not." (Matthew 7:24-25)

JESUS CHRIST EXPLAINED HOW TO BUILD on a foundation of truth with a story. You may have heard the popular Primary song about the wise man and the foolish man strum in your mind as you read Matthew 7:24–25.

Most of the symbols in this parable are well known. The wise man and the foolish man represent us, and the houses symbolize the lives we build—either on the rock of our Redeemer or on the sandy foundations of worldly pursuits.

Many overlook the symbol of the *rain*. First, know that the word "rain" simply refers to precipitation—water that falls from the atmosphere. The Greek word for rain used here is *brochē* meaning a "heavy rain"[11] while the Latin word, *rigare*, seems to suggest a less prominent rain as the word means "to wetten" or "to moisten" (same root as *irrigate*).[12]

---

9. Dieter F. Uchtdorf, "The Merciful Obtain Mercy," *Ensign*, May 2012, 75.
10. Sandra Rogers, in Jean B. Bingham, "I Will Bring the Light of the Gospel into My Home," *Ensign*, Nov. 2016, 6.
11. *Strong's*, 1028.
12. See "Rain," *Online Etymology Dictionary*.

While the rain in the Savior's parable may be a symbol for trials and struggles, one scriptural interpretation for what the rain represents is found in the Old Testament. In Deuteronomy 32:2, the Lord teaches, "My *doctrine* shall drop as the *rain*." What a truth! Both the wise and foolish will have doctrine drop rain into their lives. Those that have built their faith and testimony on Christ will endure it well, while those who have based their faith in other people or the programs or sociality of the gospel are candidates for having their homes destroyed. It's no wonder that the Book of Mormon prophet Nephi taught that our foundations impact the way that we receive God's truth:

> And in fine, wo unto all those who tremble, and are angry because of the truth of God! For behold, he that is built upon the rock receiveth it with gladness; and he that is built upon a sandy foundation trembleth lest he shall fall. (2 Nephi 28:28)

As you seek to build your life on Jesus Christ and His gospel, you will be able to more fully embrace truths and doctrines from scriptures and modern prophets.

FOR FURTHER STUDY

- Study almsgiving and the history of tithing and fast offering within our faith (see "Almsgiving" under the Topical section on www.bible-hub.com, the article "Tithing" on churchofjesuschrist.org, and the article "Fast offerings" on thechurchnews.com.[13]

- Based on Matthew 6:5–15, consider making goals to improve your personal prayers.

- What does the word "fast" mean (Matthew 6:16–18)? (See www.biblehub.com and www.blueletterbible.org.)

- What does the word "mammon" mean in Matthew 6:24? (See www.biblehub.com and www.blueletterbible.org.)

- In Matthew 6:34, the Savior taught, "Sufficient unto the day is the evil thereof." Look at other translations of this phrase using www.biblehub.com or www.blueletterbible.org to better understand its meaning.

What other unique or insightful words did you find in your study this week?

_____

_____

_____

_____

_____

_____

Please share with us!
Visit www.ComeFollowMeWOW.com and
share your word discoveries and insights!

---

13. "Fast Offerings," *Church News*, 14 June 1997, www.thechurchnews.com/archives/1997-06-14/fast-offerings-130382.

Chapter 10

Matthew 8-9; Mark 2-5

Don't miss these Words of the Week

"Healed" (Matthew 8:16)
"Storm" (Mark 4:37)
"Astonish" (Mark 5:32)

"He healed all that were sick."
(Matthew 8:16)

THE MOMENT THAT HIS SERMON ON the Mount was over, the Savior came down from the mountain and began healing, first starting with a leper, then the centurion's servant, then Peter's mother-in-law, and many that were possessed with devils. Matthew recorded that He "healed all that were sick" (Matt. 8:16). He then returned to His hometown (Matt. 9:1), where He healed a man confined to bed with palsy, healed a woman with a 12-year issue of blood, raised Jairus's daughter from the dead, restored the sight of two blind men, and then cast out a devil that took the ability to speak from a man.

In the New Testament, at least two Greek words are used when documenting the Savior's healing: *iaomail* and *therapeuo.*[2] Most of the time when we read of the physical healings that Jesus performed, we think of the definition of *therapeuo*: to heal, cure, restore to health (think of our

---

1. *Strong's,* 2390.
2. *Strong's,* 2323.

English word *therapy*). Yet oftentimes, the Greek word *iaomai* is found within the text. *Iaomai* means "to make free from errors and sins, to bring about [one's] salvation."

Using a Greek lexicon, we can search for each instance of *iaomai* and each instance of *therapeuo*. Here are a few people that received forgiveness of sin in addition to their physical healing, based on the author's use of the word *iaomai*:

- Matthew 8:13—Healing the Centurions' servant
- Mark 5:29—Healing the woman with the issue of blood
- Luke 8:47—Offering forgiveness to the woman taken in adultery
- Luke 22:51—Healing the Roman soldier's ear when Jesus was being arrested

Often, when the word "healing" appears in the New Testament, it's accompanied by the word "teaching." It seems there is a connection between good teaching and physical and spiritual healing and wholeness. President Dallin H. Oaks reminded that gospel teachers should not only teach but also assist in the Lord's work:

> A gospel teacher is concerned with the results of his or her teaching, and such a teacher will measure the success of teaching and testifying by its impact on the lives of the learners. A gospel teacher will never be satisfied with just delivering a message or preaching a sermon. A superior gospel teacher wants to assist in the Lord's work to bring eternal life to His children.[3]

Adding to this principle, Elder Jeffrey R. Holland taught that gospel teachers should try to fortify their students to be free from evil:

> Let me be a little more specific. [As you teach,] rather than just giving a lesson, please try a little harder to help that spiritually blind basketball star really see, or that spiritually deaf homecoming queen really hear, or the spiritually lame student body president really walk. Could we try a little harder to fortify others to be truly free from evil? . . . Can you try a little harder to teach so powerfully and so spiritually that you can take that student—that boy or girl who walks alone to school and from school, who sits alone in the lunchroom, who has never had a date, who is the brunt of every joke, who weeps in the dark of the night—can you unleash the

---

3. Dallin H. Oaks, "Gospel Teaching," *Ensign*, Nov. 1999, 80.

power in the scriptures and the power in the gospel and "cleanse" that leper, a leper not of his or her making, a leper made by those on our right and on our left and sometimes by us?[4]

The next time you have the opportunity to teach (or sing or perform a musical number), do so with the intent of healing those that are listening.

"There arose a great storm of wind." (Mark 4:37)

HAVE YOU EVER SEEN A STORM raging outside your window and felt so safe to be inside, out of the unforgiving winds and freezing rain? Maybe you've been caught in such a storm and sought desperately for shelter. The Greek word *lailaps,* which is used here for "storm," is used to paint the picture of much more than just a downpour. A lilap is a "whirlwind with tempestuous winds and squalls."[5] While the Italian word *stormo* shows equal intensity as it means "a fight."[6] It's not an isolated single gust nor a steady wind, but a storm breaking forth with thunderclouds and furiously violent and damaging gusts with floods of rain. Storms like this are mentioned at least twice during the ministry of Jesus Christ, first here in Mark 4:37 and then again in Luke 8:23.

During our lives, we may face physical lilap-type storms, and we may also face lilap-type trials. When faced with these storms, as feelings of despair or fear settle in as we wonder when we'll find relief, remember where to go for refuge: our Heavenly Father and the gift of the Atonement through Jesus Christ. As the Savior said to the Prophet Joseph Smith in Liberty Jail:

My son, peace be unto thy soul; thine adversity and thine afflictions shall be but a small moment; And then, if thou endure it well, God shall exalt thee on high. (Doctrine and Covenants 121:7–8)

Heavenly Father can make our trials a small moment in our lives, if we will trust in Him and His son.

---

4. Jeffrey R. Holland, Address to religious educators at a symposium on the New Testament, Brigham Young University, 8 Aug. 2000; as quoted in Jeffrey R. Holland, "Therefore, What?" *Teaching Seminary: Preservice Readings,* Church Educational System (The Church of Jesus Christ of Latter-day Saints, 2004).

5. *Strong's,* 2978.

6. "Storm," *Online Etymology Dictionary.*

"And straightway the damsel arose, and walked; for she was of the age of twelve years. And they were astonished with a great astonishment." (Mark 5:42)

THE WORD "ASTONISHED" DENOTES SURPRISE. THE phrase "exceedingly astonished" and "astonished beyond measure" greets us a few times in holy writ. When reading, we readers feel a sense of surprise, or total surprise, that something completely unexpected has happened. The Greek word *ekstasei* used here means "bewilderment."[7]

As Jesus was teaching and preaching and healing, people were struck with great astonishment on at least 18 occasions in the New Testament, beginning with the healing of the damsel in Mark 5:42.

In English, the word "astonish" is taken from the Latin root word *"tonare"*—meaning "thunder." Literally "to leave someone thunderstruck."[8] This root certainly sheds light on the responses of those who witnessed the miracles of Jesus or heard powerful testimony from Him and His disciples.

Elder Jeffrey R. Holland reminded all teachers that we should think about, pray for, and hope for truly astonishing teaching:

> We need to *astonish* those students and do it with the "power and authority of God" that is given to a teacher—professional or volunteer—who teaches the gospel of Jesus Christ boldly and honestly. . . . As teachers of the gospel, we are to be spiritual arsonists. Our lessons are to be incendiary devices.[9]

He goes on to counsel all teachers to teach by the Spirit:

> I am not talking about raising the decibels of your voice, about being theatrical in a presentation; I'm especially not talking about false emotion. I am talking about something that is essentially, simply a matter of spirit, a spirit that will manifest in many different ways as different as you are. . . . If the Spirit is the key to astonishing teaching—and it is—there is great risk in speaking from old notes. . . . Remember, a student is not a container to be filled. A student is a fire to be ignited. . . . Please, go out there, you angels of glory all over this globe . . . please go and astonish your students.[10]

---

7. *Strong's*, 1611.
8. See "Thunder," *Online Etymology Dictionary*.
9. Jeffrey R. Holland, "Angels and Astonishment," Church Educational System Training Broadcast, 12 June 2019.
10. Ibid.

The next time you have a chance to teach, prepare to *astonish* your students, as Jesus did.

FOR FURTHER STUDY

- There is wonderful symbolism behind the cleansing process of leprosy. Look up the process and see how it points to Christ (Matthew 8:1–4). Leviticus 13 and 14 in the Old Testament give "The Law of the Leper's Cleansing."

- The history of the centurion soldiers and their rule over the Jews is intense; certainly the disciples must have felt some emotions when the centurion soldier asked Jesus to heal his servant (Matthew 8:5–13). Spend a few minutes researching the history between the Romans and Jews. See the "The Roman Period" section of the Judaism article on *Encyclopedia Britannica*.[11]

- Look up the origins of the word "infirmities" in www.biblehub.com and www.blueletterbible.org as you study Matthew 8:17.

- Look up other translations of Matthew 8:22 using www.biblehub.com and www.blueletterbible.org

- In Matthew 8:28–34, what is the symbolism of the devils being cast into the herd of swine?

- We first encounter the apostle Matthew in Matthew 9:9. Look up some facts about him and his profession. See the article "Saint Matthew" on *Encyclopedia Britannica*.[12]

- In Matthew 9:22, the Savior uses the title "daughter." Research what this term means using www.biblehub.com and www.blueletterbible.org.

---

11. Link: www.britannica.com/topic/Judaism/The-Roman-period-63-bce-135-ce.
12. Link: www.britannica.com/biography/Saint-Matthew.

What other unique or insightful words did you find in your study this week?

_____

_____

_____

_____

_____

_____

Please share with us!
Visit www.ComeFollowMeWOW.com and
share your word discoveries and insights!

Chapter 11

Matthew 10-12;
Mark 2; Luke 7; 11

Don't miss these Words of the Week

"Disciple" (Matthew 10:1)
"Yoke" (Matthew 11:29-30)
"Meek" (Matthew 11:30)
"Sabbath" (Matthew 12:10)

**"When he had called unto him his twelve
disciples, he gave them power."
(Matthew 10:1)**

THE WORD FOR "DISCIPLE" AND THE word for "discipline" both come from the same Latin root *discipulus*, which means "pupil."[1] In Greek, the word is *mathētas*, also meaning "a pupil or learner."[2] President James E. Faust wrote that disciples of Christ must be disciplined:

> Self-discipline and self-control are consistent and permanent characteristics of the followers of Jesus, as exemplified by Peter, James, and John, who indeed "forsook all, and followed him." . . . The disciples of Christ receive a call to not only forsake the pursuit

---

1. "Disciple," *Online Etymology Dictionary.*
2. *Strong's,* 3101.

of worldly things but to carry the cross daily. [Discipleship] also means self-mastery.[3]

John Tanner, President of BYU-Hawaii, taught that disciples are rigorously instructed and trained. He said:

Disciples submit themselves to be instructed and trained by the person or in the area of study they wish to follow. This strict training was called *disciplina*. . . . Discipleship involves learning discipline—meaning instruction, rigorous training, or mastery of a body of knowledge and skill. Because such discipline was often administered with a firm hand, the term came to be synonymous with correction or punishment, but its root meaning is instruction or training. The verb "to discipline" did not originate from the idea of punishing but in the idea of teaching someone to follow rules with exactness in order to master a skill, or body of knowledge, or code of conduct. The original meaning of discipline is still evident in the term "self-discipline." When we think of self-discipline we do not think of people who punish themselves by engaging in self-flagellation. Rather we think of someone who has self-control, willpower, grit.[4]

Disciples of Jesus Christ, whether the 12 chosen 2,000 years ago or modern-day followers of Christ, are asked to submit their will to His and to develop by divine discipline. In Matthew 10, Jesus clearly forewarned His followers and us about the cost of journeying with Him. His discipleship requires self-renunciation, firm commitment, and an identity tied to Jesus. There is no easy road to discipleship. However, the rewards are absolutely amazing if we will discipline ourselves and try our best to be His disciples.

"I am meek." (Matthew 11:29)

OUR WORLD PUSHES US TO BE faster and louder. Do more! Work harder! It's hard to find a moment of reflection or a listening ear. In ancient times, the virtue of **meekness** was held in high esteem.

So what is "meekness"? In Greek, the word *praus* meaning "gentle" is used in place of meek.[5] Most modern translations of the Bible replace

---

3. James E. Faust, "Discipleship," *Ensign*, Nov. 2006.
4. John Tanner, "Disciplined Disciples," Brigham Young University—Hawaii devotional, 18 Sept. 2018, speeches.byuh.edu.
5. *Strong's*, 4239.

"meekness" with "gentleness" or "humility."[6] One definition of meekness is being "Godfearing, righteous, humble, teachable, and patient under suffering."[7] Meekness allows us to create those moments of reflection and be the listening ear that we crave.

The world might tell us that being Godfearing, humble, and patient is weakness, but it takes strength to place our strength in subjection to God.

President Spencer W. Kimball taught that to be meek is to be bold, brave, and courageous:

> [Meekness is] boldly denouncing evil, bravely advancing righteous works, courageously meeting every problem, becoming the master of himself . . . and being near oblivious to personal credit. . . . It is not weak, vacillating, nor servile.[8]

Adding a second witness, Elder David A. Bednar of the Quorum of the Twelve Apostles described being meek as being strong, active, courageous, retrained, modest, and gracious:

> Meekness is strong, not weak; active, not passive; courageous, not timid; restrained, not excessive; modest, not self-aggrandizing; and gracious, not brash. A meek person is not easily provoked, pretentious, or overbearing and readily acknowledges the accomplishments of others.[9]

What is the only word that Jesus used to describe Himself? The answer is simple: meek.[10]

Elder Neal A. Maxwell said meekness is "the subtraction of self."[11] As this quote describes, the Savior's meekness shone in His submission of His will to the will of the Father.

Think about the flow of a river. The water rises slowly and patiently when it meets an obstacle, and ultimately it runs over the obstruction and wears it away. As we achieve meekness through submitting our wills to the will of God, we will gain new strength and power to rise above the obstacles of mortality.[12]

---

6. See NIV Ephesians 4:2–3; Titus 3:1–2; Galatians 6:1.
7. Guide to the Scriptures, "Meek," scriptures.ChurchofJesusChrist.org.
8. Spencer W. Kimball, "Humility," Brigham Young University devotional, 16 Jan. 1963, speeches.byu.edu.
9. David A. Bednar, "Meek and Lowly of Heart," *Ensign*, May 2018.
10. See Matt. 11:29; 21:5; 2 Cor. 10:1.
11. Neal A. Maxwell, "Meekness—A Dimension of True Discipleship," *Ensign*, Mar. 1983.
12. See Leland H. Monson, *Look to the Mount: A study of the Sermon on the Mount* (Salt Lake City: Deseret Book, 1968), 14.

Consider studying more about meekness this week. It is one of the most wonderful and empowering virtues to seek for in mortality.

"My yoke is easy, and my burden is light." (Matthew 11:30)

OXEN OR CATTLE ARE OFTEN YOKED (tethered or bound together) to accomplish difficult tasks and to produce power that far exceeds what they could do alone. The yoke enables the farmer to link two animals of unequal strength together in such a way that neither animal is pulling more weight than it can bear. The ideal relationship is to yoke two "equally yoked" animals (two beasts of equal size and strength), yet this is often impossible due to so many variations in animals.

This unequal yoking is the case with us and the Savior: He, of course, has ultimate power and strength, while we are weak and inexperienced. Yet by yoking (linking) ourselves with Christ, He is able to carry more of the workload that might otherwise overwhelm us. The Greek word for yoke is *zygos* and is defined as "a coupling of servitude or a beam of balance." This definition invokes images of how, without the Savior's eternal service to us and our willing servitude to Him, our life becomes unbalanced and off centered.

Notice that Matthew 11 uses the term "my yoke." If we take *His yoke*, we will find rest and strength. His yoke might include temple trips and church attendance and ministering to neighbors. Notice that He's not guaranteeing us peace and strength by asking Him to take "our yokes" (our employment, our busy schedules, etc). But if we take His yoke, putting Him first, we will find strength to accomplish His work—and consequently will find extra time and strength to also accomplish our work as well.

Why face life's burdens alone? Standing side-by-side with a God that will provide strength, stamina, balance, and perspective to help us accomplish our tasks here in mortality is the offer He extends to us, if we take His yoke upon us.

"For the Son of man is Lord even of the sabbath day." (Matthew 12:8)

FOR MANY FAMILIES, SUNDAYS FEEL CHAOTIC. We know that we're supposed to keep the Sabbath day holy, but what does that mean when our kids are going crazy, dinner needs to be started, and church starts in ten minutes?

A command to honor the Sabbath day was first given in Old Testament times (see Exodus 20:8–11). The Lord established that people were to work six days a week (Exodus 20:9) and rest on the seventh day (Exodus 20:10). The Lord followed this pattern when He created the world, and we, too, should rest once a week (Exodus 20:11).

The Savior reaffirmed this ancient command in Matthew 12 when He taught about keeping the Sabbath day holy.

"Sabbath" comes from Greek *sabbatou*[13] and the Latin *Shabbath* which meant "a day of rest."[14] The Pharisees in Jesus's day had become very stringent about not working on the Lord's Day but they lost sight of the why. They tried to condemn Jesus for healing someone on the Sabbath (Mark 6:1–3). When His disciples even plucked a head of grain (Mark 2:23), the Pharisees claimed they were working on the Sabbath. Essentially, the Pharisees took the commandments of the Old Testament and created fence laws, or their versions of the commandments, that were enacted to help people not get close to breaking actual commandments.

Like the Pharisees, it is easy for us to fall into a black-and-white list of things to do and not do on the Sabbath. But if we follow President Russell M. Nelson's advice to think about our activities and attitudes on the Sabbath as a sign between us and our Heavenly Father, the path will be made clear. President Nelson taught:

> How do we *hallow* the Sabbath day? In my much younger years, I studied the work of others who had compiled lists of things to do and things *not* to do on the Sabbath. It wasn't until later that I learned from the scriptures that my conduct and my attitude on the Sabbath constituted a *sign* between me and my Heavenly Father (see Exodus 31:13). With that understanding, I no longer needed lists of dos and don'ts. When I had to make a decision whether or not an activity was appropriate for the Sabbath, I simply asked myself, "What *sign* do I want to give to God?" That question made my choices about the Sabbath day crystal clear.[15]

We can keep the Sabbath day holy, even when our Sundays aren't serenely perfect.

This week, consider what you can do this coming Sabbath to make Sunday a delight. Think of people to serve and activities to do that will bring you and others closer to the Lord of the Sabbath.

---

13. *Strong's*, 4521.
14. See "Sabbath," *Online Etymology Dictionary*.
15. Russell M. Nelson, "The Sabbath is a Delight," *Ensign*, May 2015.

FOR FURTHER STUDY

- Look up what each of the 12 disciples' names mean in Matthew 10 using *Hitchcock's Bible Names Dictionary*[16]; consider studying how each died.[17]

- Because Matthew 10 addresses the calling of apostles, think of a few ways that you can sustain and support our modern-day apostles.

- Read the Joseph Smith Translation of the phrase, "be ye therefore wise as serpents, and harmless as doves" from Matthew 10:16.

- Matthew 11:6 addresses a principle of offense. Study the word "offend" using www.blueletterbible.org and www.biblehub.com and see what applications there are with its origin.

- Matthew 12:25 speaks about unity in our associations. Study the word "unity" using www.blueletterbible.org and www.biblehub.com and see what applications can help your home or circle of friends be more united.

- The word "blasphemy" has a fascinating origin. Look it up using www.etymonline.com.

- Matthew 12:31–32 talks about blasphemy against the Holy Ghost. There is a difference between unforgivable sin and unpardonable sin. Consider studying the differences. (See "Unpardonable Sin" within the Guide to the Scriptures on scriptures.ChurchofJesusChrist. org and the article "Forgiveness and Pardon" from Internet Bible College.[18])

---

16. Link: https://www.biblestudytools.com/dictionaries/hitchcocks-bible-names.
17. See David Snell, "How Did Each of the Original Twelve Apostles Die?" *ThirdHour*, 28 Apr. 2018, thirdhour.org.
18. "Forgiveness and Pardon," *The Work Internet Bible College*, 15 Feb. 2006, www.internetbiblecollege.net.

What other unique or insightful words did you find in your study this week?

_____

_____

_____

_____

_____

_____

_____

Please share with us!
Visit www.ComeFollowMeWOW.com and
share your word discoveries and insights!

Chapter 12

Matthew 13; Luke 8; 13

Don't miss these Words of the Week

"Parable" (Matthew 13:3)
"Good" (Matthew 13:8)
"Seed" (Matthew 13:31)

"He spake many things unto them in parables."
(Matthew 13:3)

JESUS CHRIST TOLD BEAUTIFUL PARABLES THAT helped His followers, both in His day and the present, to better understand gospel principles. President Thomas S. Monson counseled that we should study the parables as if they were spoken to us today:

> Learn the background and setting of the Master's parables and the prophets' admonitions. Study them as though they were speaking to you, for such is the truth. . . . I promise you . . . that if you will study the scriptures diligently, your power to avoid temptation and to receive direction of the Holy Ghost in all you do will be increased.[1]

In Matthew 13, the Savior taught about the restoration of the gospel using several parables. The word "parable" is Greek in origin and means "a setting side by side" or "a comparison."[2] Christ presents pure truth and doctrine in

---

1. Thomas S. Monson, "Be Your Best Self," *Ensign*, May 2009.
2. See "parable," *Online Etymology Dictionary*.

the New Testament through analogies or stories that allow us to see ourselves in the stories; perhaps we are the prodigal son, or the shepherd going after lost sheep. Study the parables with the word "comparison" in mind and ponder how Christ would have you compare His teachings to your life.

	Reference	Symbol
The Wheat and Tares	Matthew 13:24–26	If the righteous and wicked are separated too soon, "you will destroy the wheat, or the Church, with the tares; therefore it is better to let them grow together until the harvest, or the end of the world" (*Teachings of the Prophet Joseph Smith*, 98).
The Mustard Seed	Matthew 13:31–32	"Let us take the Book of Mormon, which a man took and hid in his field, securing it by his faith, to spring up in the last days. . . . It is truth, and it has sprouted and come forth out of the earth, and righteousness begins to look down from heaven, and God is sending down His powers . . . to lodge in the branches thereof" (*Teachings*, 98).
The Leaven	Matthew 13:33	"It may be understood that the Church . . . has taken its rise from a little leaven that was put into three witnesses. Behold, how much this is like the parable! It is fast leavening the lump, and will soon leaven the whole" (*Teachings*, 100).
Hidden Treasure	Matthew 13:44	"See the Church . . ., selling all that they have, and gathering themselves together unto a place that they may purchase for an inheritance, that they may be together and bear each other's afflictions in the day of calamity" (*Teachings*, 101).
Pearl of Great Price	Matthew 13:45–46	"See [the Saints] traveling to find places for Zion . . ., who, when they find the place for Zion, or the pearl of great price, straightway sell that they have, and buy it" (*Teachings*, 102).
The Fish Net	Matthew 13:47–50	"Behold the seed of Joseph, spreading forth the Gospel net upon the face of the earth, gathering of every kind, that the good may be saved in vessels . . ., and the angels will take care of the bad. So shall it be at the end of the world" (*Teachings*, 102).
New and Old Treasures	Matthew 13:52	"For the works of this example, see the Book of Mormon . . ., also the translation of the Bible [the Joseph Smith Translation]—thus bringing forth out of the heart things new and old" (*Teachings*, 102).

3

---

3. Table modified from "Matthew 13: Parables on the Gathering," *New Testament Teacher*

"But another fell into good ground, and brought forth fruit." (Matthew 13:8)

THERE ARE SO MANY USES OF the word "good" within the scriptures and our lives. We say that our day was good, a dog is good, and the scriptures talk about good works and, here, good ground. Each of these examples has a slightly different meaning. So, what does it mean to be *good*?

The parable of the soils describes what becomes of seed that is sown in four different types of soil. The first type of soil is hard. This seed does not penetrate the soil at all and is quickly snatched up by birds. The second type of soil is rocky and shallow. This seed quickly germinates, but it is hindered by a lack of depth and moisture. The third soil is thorny, and the germinated seed is eventually crowded out by the thorns. The fourth soil is good, and the seed produces a bountiful crop.

The seed that the Master sows is a *good* seed (see Alma 32:28–34), and it thrives in *good* soil.

The word *good* has a fascinating root. The Hebrew word for "good" is *tov*, which is best translated as "functional" (the Hebrew word *ra* is its opposite and means "dysfunctional"). In the book of Genesis, after each period of creation, God comments that His creations are *good*, meaning *functional*; this may be akin to being like a well-oiled machine—everything worked. God also uses *good* to name The Tree of Knowledge of Good and Evil, or the tree of *tov* and *ra*, meaning the tree of function and dysfunction; the Greek word used here for good is *kalēn* and means "beautiful."[4]

One purpose of life is to simply become functional to God—or simply, *good* (see Romans 3:10–12, 23; Matthew 7:16; Romans 12:2; Galatians 6:9). That is, that we function under the order of God's commandments. President Gordon B. Hinckley said that we must do good, rather than just be good:

> You are good. But it is not enough just to be good. You must be good for something. You must contribute good to the world. The world must be a better place for your presence.[5]

As we seek to be functioning and good members of society and of the Church, the Lord will bless our efforts. God is good—and we should be as well.

Resource Manual, Church Educational System (The Church of Jesus Christ of Latter-day Saints, 1999), 39.

4. *Strong's,* 2570.

5. Gordon B. Hinckley, "Stand Up for Truth," Brigham Young University devotional, 17 Sept. 1996, speeches.byu.edu.

"The kingdom of heaven is like to a grain of mustard seed." (Matthew 13:31)

HAVE YOU EVER TRIED TO GROW a plant from a seed? It's hard work! With the amount of steps it takes to get from a seed to a fully grown plant, it's a wonder that anything ever grows at all.

The Greek word *kokkō* and the Latin word *granum* both mean "seed."[6] The definition of what seeds are is very simple: "grains of plants used for sowing." If we take a deeper look into some of the steps that seeds take to grow, we will find several symbols and good gospel applications.

- SOIL and GERMINATION. The term "germination" means "to expand into a greater being from a small existence; to begin to grow after a period of dormancy." When a seed is exposed to the proper conditions, it will germinate. Likewise, gospel seeds need the right conditions to germinate. The scriptures and prophets teach us that we are all born with the light of Christ (see D&C 84:46). These "seeds" of light are dormant within us until the conditions are proper for germination.

- DORMANT: "Dormant" means "lying asleep; inactive; capable of being activated." Dormant seeds are ripe seeds that do not germinate because of less-than-ideal environmental conditions. Likewise, when the children of God expose themselves to less-than-ideal conditions in mortality, "gospel seeds" are challenged to germinate properly.

- WATER: The uptake of water by seeds is called imbibition. This leads to the swelling and the breaking of the seed's coat. Likewise, Christ invites us to come unto Him with a "broken heart" (see 3 Nephi 9:19–20). Once our hard hearts are softened and broken (much like the process of imbibition), there is space for the Spirit to operate. Jesus Christ called Himself "Living Water." As we take up His living water, our hearts soften and change.

- OXYGEN: If a seed is buried too deeply within the soil, the seed can be oxygen starved. This can happen to our "gospel seeds" when we try to forcefully shove the gospel into people's lives. We need to give them space to breathe.

---

6. *Strong's*, 2848.

- LIGHT and DARKNESS: Many seeds will not germinate until they have enough light and warmth to grow. So, too, our testimonies will remain dormant until we bring gospel light into our lives by studying the scriptures and words of the prophets. We must also shun the dark things of this word as we seek to let "gospel seeds" germinate in their lives.[7]

- HOMEGROWN vs STORE-BOUGHT: Several studies show that homegrown food has more nutrients and flavor than store-bought food. Likewise, our testimonies are usually richer when they are grown at home.

FOR FURTHER STUDY

- Jesus used several parables as He taught. Consider spending some time studying each of them. The Institute's "Parables of Jesus" (Religion 390R) student manual may be a great resource to supplement your study.

- A fascinating study is looking at soil fertilizers and what they do to help lawns and gardens—and relate each nutrient to gospel principles. (See the article "How does a fertiliser work?" from LovetheGarden.com[8])

- Do a study of the words "wheat" and "tare" using www.biblehub.com and www.blueletterbible.org and see what gospel principles are found.

- In Luke 13:11–17, the Savior delivers from bondage. Look up the meaning of the word "bondage" using www.biblehub.com and www.blueletterbible.org and see what applications are found in its definition.

What other unique or insightful words did you find in your study this week?

---

7. Elder David A. Bednar of the Quorum of the Twelve Apostles reminded us of the importance of being clean when it comes to preparing to receive revelation when he taught, "If something we think, see, hear, or do distances us from the Holy Ghost, then we should stop thinking, seeing, hearing, or doing that thing. If that which is intended to entertain, for example, alienates us from the Holy Spirit, then certainly that type of entertainment is not for us. Because the Spirit cannot abide that which is vulgar, crude, or immodest, then clearly such things are not for us." (David A. Bednar, "That We May Always Have His Spirit to Be with Us," *Ensign*, May 2006).

8. Link: www.lovethegarden.com/uk-en/article/how-does-fertiliser-work.

_____

_____

_____

_____

_____

_____

_____

Please share with us!
Visit www.ComeFollowMeWOW.com and
share your word discoveries and insights!

Chapter 13

Matthew 14–15; Mark 6–7; John 5–6

Don't miss these Words of the Week

"Fourth Watch" (Matthew 14:25)
"Bethesda" (John 5:2)
"Whole" (John 5:14)

"And in the fourth watch of the night Jesus went unto them."
(Matthew 14:25)

In Jesus's time, the night was divided into four watches: the first watch was from six in the evening until nine at night, the second watch from nine until midnight, the third watch from midnight until three in the morning, and the fourth watch from three in the morning until six. The Greek term *tetartē phylakē* means "fourth guarding of a time, place or condition."[1]

In Matthew's gospel, he wrote that, "The ship was . . . tossed with waves" (Matthew 14:24), and then we read that Jesus came to them during the fourth watch of the night. We don't fully know the reason that Jesus chose this time of day to come to the aid of the disciples, but it must have been important, since Matthew included this detail.

---

1. *Strong's,* 5067 and 5438.

An application of this timed appearance may be this: we worship a "fourth-watch" God. Most of us appreciate help early and often—a "first-watch" hope for help. But there are many passages of scripture that help us understand that He truly is a fourth-watch God.[2] The Lord seems content to let us grow and stretch and feel some degree of pain before He comes to fully rescue us.

Author S. Michael Wilcox wrote that waiting can cause us to doubt, but Heavenly Father and Jesus Christ will always come to help us:

> When we advance into the second watch and he doesn't come, a certain cold fear often begins to spread through us as the wind's velocity does not diminish. As we move into the third watch we may be tempted to make some assumptions that are very dangerous and foolish to make. "God is not listening to me." "He doesn't care." Or, more dangerous yet, "He is not there." At times the universe can seem so very empty—all that dark space filled with cold stars. Or, very common to Latter-day Saints, we assume, "I'm not worthy." "He's not listening." "He doesn't care." "No one is there to respond." Because if He were there and if He were listening or if I were worthy, He would certainly come.
>
> When you feel somewhat desperate, when it seems like your prayers aren't answered and the winds still blow, take comfort in the knowledge that He is on the hillside watching. Remember, you might not know that He's watching as you struggle in the boat, but He is on the hillside watching, and He will come. But He generally comes in the fourth watch—after we have done all we can do.[3]

It may take until the fourth watch, but Heavenly Father is always there for us, aware of us, and asking us to trust Him.

---

2. Joseph Smith was visited "at the very moment when I was ready to sink into despair and abandon myself to destruction . . . just at this moment of great alarm, I saw a pillar of light exactly over my head" (JS—H 1:16).
3. S. Michael Wilcox, *When Your Prayers Seem Unanswered* (Salt Lake City: Deseret Book, 2013).

"Now there is at Jerusalem by the sheep market a pool, which is called in the Hebrew tongue Bethesda." (John 5:2)

IN THE FIFTH CHAPTER OF JOHN, the Savior visits the pool of Bethesda. Tradition had it that when the waters of the pool moved, they were troubled by an angel (see John 5:2), and the first person to make it to the water would be healed of their malady. The Greek word *Bēthzatha*, marks this name of Chaldee origin and defines it as a "house of kindness,"[4] while the Latin name *Bethesda* means "house of mercy" or "house of grace."[5]

The Bible Dictionary shares that there was possibly an intermittent spring flowing into the pool, which produced a bubbling at the surface. But imagine the fierce longing of those who hoped to be first in the water, and the intense despair of those who could never make it in time to be healed by what they thought was water blessed by an angel.

In John 5, the Savior went to a man who had been waiting for 38 years to be healed of his invalidity. This healing of the invalid has a wonderful application, explained by Sister Ann E. Taylor in the following:

> There are many in the Church today who wait, metaphorically speaking, by the pool of Bethesda hoping to be carried into the healing waters. War veterans might suffer from horrific memories and broken bodies. Other Saints might suffer from the isolation of depression or addiction. Widows live alone or face failing health; families feel devastated by a child's illness or an unexpected accident; and caregivers work long, lonely hours taking care of a family member. Who will carry these infirm to the pool?[6]

Consider looking for those in your circles who need your help—your gifts and talents and attributes—and seek ways to help them become whole through your mercy and grace.

"Behold, thou art made whole." (John 5:14)

AFTER JESUS FORGAVE AND CLEANSED SOMEONE from sin, He often proclaimed that they were made *whole*. The word "whole" is used often in the

---

4. *Strong's*, 964.
5. See "Bethsesda," *Online Etymology Dictionary*.
6. Ann E. Tanner, "Carry Others to the Pool of Bethesda," *Ensign*, Jan. 2011.

New Testament and translations of the King James version of the Bible and describe "whole" as "sound," "normal," or simply "well."

The Greek word used here is *hygies* or "made well" with similes of "health, pure and wholesome"[7] (same root as "hygiene"). The Old English rendered "whole" as "safe; healthy, sound."[8]

In John 5:14, Jesus encounters the man who had been healed at the pool of Bethesda walking around at the temple and Jesus says that he has been "made whole" (John 5:14). Something to keep in mind is the fact that Christ had already physically healed this man, but he was not pronounced whole until he went to the temple. What a beautiful message for our lives about where to find wholeness, or wellness.

For those of who have disabilities or suffer from mental illness or physical ailments—or just the stresses of everyday life—the promise is certain: one day, we will be made *whole*. Free. Normal, Sound. Well. What a thrilling moment that will be! And that journey might just start as you find yourself in the temple.

"Our fathers did eat manna in the desert." (John 6:31)

How wonderful would it be to simply gather up prepared food when it was time to eat? We would never again have to worry about forgetting to take the chicken out of the freezer! In the Old Testament, we learn that the Lord provided manna—small pieces of food that tasted like honey (see Exodus 16:14–31)—one day at a time to feed the children of Israel during their forty years in the wilderness (see Exodus 16).

Manna (or *man-hu* in Hebrew) literally translates as, "What is it?", presumably because the Israelites didn't know what it was (see Exodus 16:15). [9] The Greek word *manna* means "edible gum."[10]

In John 6, manna is used as a symbol for Christ. Christ taught, "I am the bread of life: he that cometh to me shall never hunger; and he that believeth on me shall never thirst" (John 6:35). The Bread of Life (see John 6:31–35). Manna can stand as a testament of Christ because it teaches us the importance of daily sustenance. We know how important it is to be physically fed, we don't want to go a day without food! But equally as important is our spiritual nourishment through consistent gospel living.

---

7. *Strong's*, 5199.
8. See "Whole," *Online Etymology Dictionary*.
9. It was also called "angels' food" and "bread from heaven" (Ps. 78:24–25; John 6:31).
10. *Strong's*, 3131.

Elder D. Todd Christofferson of the Quorum of the Twelve Apostles poignantly taught that we can learn to trust Christ as we turn to Him for daily sustenance:

> By providing a daily sustenance, one day at a time, Jehovah was trying to teach faith to a nation that over a period of some 400 years had lost much of the faith of their fathers. He was teaching them to trust Him, to "look unto [Him] in every thought; doubt not, fear not" (D&C 6:36). He was providing enough for one day at a time. Except for the sixth day, they could not store manna for use in any succeeding day or days. In essence, the children of Israel had to walk with Him today and trust that He would grant a sufficient amount of food for the next day *on* the next day, and so on. In that way He could never be too far from their minds and hearts.[11]

Just as manna provided a daily reminder of the Lord for the children of Israel, we can use prayer and scripture study as daily reminders of Christ in our own lives.

---

11. D. Todd Christofferson, "Give Us This Day Our Daily Bread," Brigham Young University fireside, 9 Jan. 2011, speeches.byu.edu.

FOR FURTHER STUDY

- What principles are taught by the Lord's silence following the woman's request for help in Matthew 15:21–28? What thoughts may have come to her mind when Jesus didn't answer her?

- In Matthew 14–15, Jesus feeds 5,000 and 4,000. Study the meaning of those numbers. [12]

- In John 5 as the man at the pool of Bethesda is healed, Jesus asks him to take his bed with him. Why? What message is there in taking his bed with him? (See the article "What does John 5:8 mean?" on www.bibleref.com[13])

- Read Mark's version of the account of the storm and Jesus walking on the water. What detail did he leave out of his account, and why do you think he didn't include that detail? (See Mark 6:45–52).

- What principle is taught by the accelerated arrival to the shore in John 6:21?

What other unique or insightful words did you find in your study this week?

_____

_____

_____

_____

_____

Please share with us!
Visit www.ComeFollowMeWOW.com and
share your word discoveries and insights!

---

12. See: Shawn Brasseaux, "Feeding the 4,000 and Feeding the 5,000—Same of Different?" *For What Saith the Scriptures?* 28 Mar. 2020, forwhatsaiththescriptures.org.
13. Link: www.bibleref.com/John/5/John-5-8.html#commentary.

Chapter 14

Matthew 16-17; Mark 9; Luke 9

Don't miss these Words of the Week

"Reveal/Revelation" (Matthew 16:17)
"Transfigured" (Matthew 17:1-2)
"Perverse" (Matthew 17:17)

**"Flesh and blood hath not revealed it unto
thee, but my Father which is in heaven."
(Matthew 16:17)**

WE TALK ABOUT REVELATION A LOT as Latter-day Saints, but it can be difficult to describe because it *is* so personal. We can look at it as guidance or inspiration from God, but the Greek word may provide a deeper meaning for us. The English word "revelation" is translated from the Greek word *apocalypse*, which means "to make known" or "uncover." It literally means "to unveil."[1]

Revelation comes from God through the Holy Ghost or by other means, such as visions, dreams, or visitations.[2] We may hear the Holy Ghost as a literal voice, have a persistent thought, or feel one of the "fruits of the spirit."[3]

---

1. See "Reveal," *Online Etymology Dictionary.*
2. See Bible Dictionary, "Revelation."
3. Galatians 5:22

"The Holy Ghost is a revelator," said Joseph Smith, and "no man can receive the Holy Ghost without receiving revelations."[4]

When we are seeking revelation, we are in essence asking God to allow us to see "behind the veil." When revelation does come, it will likely come "in the less spectacular way—that of deep impressions, without spectacle or glamour or dramatic events. Expecting the spectacular, one may not be fully alerted to the constant flow of revealed communication."[5]

When we are blessed to have a "removal of the veil" (revelation), we will understand things in our mind and feel things in the heart by the Holy Ghost (see D&C 8:2–3; 11:13). This is one principle that Jesus was teaching His disciples when He said to Peter, "Blessed art thou, Simon Bar-jona: for flesh and blood hath not *revealed* it unto thee, but my Father which is in heaven. And I say also unto thee, That thou art Peter, and upon this rock I will build my church; and the gates of hell shall not prevail against it" (Matthew 16:17–19).

With full confidence, you can seek His will by asking Him to let you experience a "look behind the veil" as you seek revelation in your life.

"Jesus . . . bringeth them up into an high mountain apart and was transfigured before them." (Matthew 17:1–2)

IN ELEMENTARY SCHOOL, CHILDREN OFTEN LEARN about the fantastical process of metamorphosis. Teachers bring caterpillar eggs or tadpoles into class, and over the next few months the class watches the eggs and tadpoles transform into butterflies and frogs. Can you remember ever doing a similar activity?

The Greek word for "transfigured," *metemorphōthē*, is closely related to our English word "metamorphosis." Both words mean "to transform."[6] The Latin root means "to change the shape or form of."[7]

In the scriptures, we get examples of both transfiguration and translation, but what is the difference between the two?

"Transfigure" comes from the prefix *trans* (change, carry) and *figure* (form, image). In the scriptures, transfigured people are temporarily changed in appearance and nature (lifted to a higher spiritual level) so that they can

---

4. *Teachings of the Presidents of the Church: Joseph Smith* (The Church of Jesus Christ of Latter-day Saints, 2007), 132.

5. Spencer W. Kimball, "To His Servants the Prophets," *Instructor*, Aug. 1960, 257.

6. *Strong's*, 3339.

7. See "Transfigure," *Online Etymology Dictionary*.

endure the presence and glory of heavenly beings.[8] Peter, James, and John saw the Lord glorified and transfigured before them (see Matthew 17:1–9). At this event, the Savior, Moses, and Elias (Elijah) gave keys of the priesthood to Peter, James, and John.

"Translated," in contrast, means "to change one's form." "Translate" comes from *trans* (to change, carry) and *late* (over, slow, dead/death). Translated people have been changed so that they do not experience pain or death until their resurrection to immortality.[9] All translated beings will eventually experience physical death and resurrection to further the work of the Lord.[10]

Whether or not we are ever *transfigured* or *translated* in the technical sense, Heavenly Father and His Only Begotten Son change us all. Just as a baby frog or butterfly is unrecognizable in its adult form, the Atonement can change us fundamentally and make us brand new if we let it. This week, ponder how you can better allow the Atonement to transform you.

"O faithless and perverse generation." (Matthew 17:17)

SOMETIMES WE KNOW THE RIGHT DIRECTION to go, the right decision to make, but we don't take it. For various reasons, we ignore our better judgment and betray ourselves to make a different choice.

Jesus often called those living in His day and ours a "faithless and perverse generation" (see Matthew 17:17; Helaman 13:29; Matthew 16:4; Philippians 2:14–16; Doctrine and Covenants 33:2; 34:6). There are a dozen passages in the Book of Mormon that contain the word "pervert," which originates from the word "perverse."

Rather than its current sexual derivative, the original Latin word *pervertere* meant "to turn the wrong way" or "one who has forsaken a true doctrine" or "apostate."[11] Similarly, the Greek word *diestrammenē* means "oppose, distort or misinterpret."[12] Apply these definitions to each passage containing the word "perverse" or "pervert:"[13]

---

8. See Guide to the Scriptures, "Transfigured," scriptures.ChurchofJesusChrist.org.
9. See Guide to the Scriptures, "Translated Beings," scriptures.ChurchofJesusChrist.org.
10. See Bruce R. McConkie, "Translated Beings," *Mormon Doctrine* (Bookcraft, 1958), 807–8.
11. See "Pervert," *Online Etymology Dictionary*.
12. *Strong's*, 1294.
13. See the Index to the Triple Combination, "Pervert, Perverse, Perversion," www.churchofjesuschrist.org.

- The abominable church *perverts* right ways of the Lord (1 Nephi 13:27)
- All who *pervert the right* way of the Lord shall be thrust down to hell (2 Nephi 28:15)
- Sherem claims that Jacob leads away people that they *pervert* right way of God (Jacob 7:7)
- Priests of Noah have *perverted* ways of the Lord (Mosiah 12:26)
- Unrighteous king *perverts* ways of righteousness (Mosiah 29:23)
- Lawyers lay plans to *pervert* ways of righteous (Alma 10:18)
- Korihor *perverts* the ways of the Lord (Alma 30:22, 60)
- Zoramites *pervert* ways of the Lord (Alma 31:1, 11)
- They who say little children need baptism *pervert* the ways of the Lord (Moroni 8:15–16)
- Nephites have become strong in *perversion* (Moroni 9:19)

What is the solution for one who perverts the ways of God, or turns from or forsakes true doctrine? One answer is found in Alma 30:11, when Alma and his brethren chose to preach the word to those who had fallen away:

> Yea, in fine, they did pervert the ways of the Lord in very many instances; therefore, for this cause, Alma and his brethren went into the land to preach the word unto them.

The word of God can correct any perverse person, can correct any perverse practice, and can clarify any doctrine that has been perverted. President Boyd K. Packer, President of the Quorum of the Twelve Apostles, frequently taught that understanding true doctrine changes behavior. He said:

> True doctrine, understood, changes attitudes and behavior. The study of the doctrines of the gospel will improve behavior quicker than a study of behavior will improve behavior.[14]

When true doctrine is taught by the Holy Ghost, it can bring about a mighty change of heart (see 1 Corinthians 2:4; 1 Thessalonians 1:5; Mosiah 5:2; Alma 5:7; D&C 68:4). When we teach and receive His word and His doctrine by His Spirit, the Holy Ghost cleanses, clarifies, and redirects (see John 6:63; 2 Nephi 33:1; D&C 84:45). To avoid *perversion* and *perverse* behaviors (those "wrong ways" that betray true doctrine), following the Spirit is key, as it will enlighten our minds and change our hearts.

---

14. Boyd K. Packer, "Little Children," *Ensign*, Nov. 1986, 17.

FOR FURTHER STUDY

- Consider studying what the word "rock" means in Matthew 16:16–19 using www.blueletterbible.org and www.biblehub.com.

- There are a few interesting facts about the history of the location of the Mount of Transfiguration (Matthew 17). Do a deep dive into that mountain's history (see the Wikipedia article "Mount of Transfiguration," to start[15]).

- In Matthew 17:15, Matthew records the miracle of Jesus healing a lunatic. The word lunatic has a fascinating origin. Consider researching it using www.blueletterbible.org and www.biblehub.com.

What other unique or insightful words did you find in your study this week?

_____

_____

_____

_____

_____

_____

_____

Please share with us!
Visit www.ComeFollowMeWOW.com and
share your word discoveries and insights!

---

15. Link: en.wikipedia.org/wiki/Mount_of_Transfiguration.

Chapter 15

Easter

Ironies of the Life of Jesus Christ

"IRONY" SIMPLY MEANS, "A DIFFERENCE BETWEEN the actual result and the expected result."[1] Some irony is bitter. Some ironies are painful. Some are humorous. Irony has the ability to punctuate any incident and give a deeper meaning to any story. With Christ's power as the only Begotten Son of God, we may have expected Him to live a less troubled life than what He really experienced. However, we can learn so much from the challenges and betrayals He faced.

Christian author Max Lucado wrote that betrayal is more than rejection:

Rejection opens a wound; betrayal pours the salt. It's more than loneliness. Loneliness leaves you in the cold; betrayal closes the door. It's more than mockery. Mockery plunges the knife; betrayal twists it. It's more than an insult. An insult attacks your pride; betrayal breaks your heart.[2]

Christ was betrayed not only by His own people, but by a friend and apostle as well. Though we will not experience betrayal on Christ's scale, we can consider some of the ironies and betrayals of His life to gain greater compassion and understanding for our savior.

The life of Christ is riddled with ironies. For this week's study, consider some of the following:

---

1. *Merriam-Webster Dictionary*, "irony."
2. Max Lucado, *And the Angels Were Silent: The Final Week of Jesus* (Walker and Company, 1993).

Jesus was sold for the price of a _____, yet He came to serve
　　us all (Matthew 27:9; Exodus 21:32)
IRONY: Jesus was sold for 30 pieces of silver, the price of a slave according to
　　Exodus 21:32, yet He came to serve us.

Jesus (The Way, the Truth, the Life) had _____ told about Him.
IRONY: Jesus, whose life was completely founded on truth, endured cruel
　　stings of lies being told about Him, His role, and the purpose of His
　　ministry.

Jesus was _____, yet he bore every sin ever committed.
IRONY: Jesus, who committed no sin, had to endure the pains of every sin
　　ever committed.

Judas betrayed Jesus. Judas is the Greek version of the Hebrew name
　　who betrayed Joseph in the Old Testament. (see Genesis 37:26)
IRONY: Israel's son Judah proposed the sale of Joseph in the Old Testament
　　(See Genesis 37:26). In the New Testament, Judas (the Greek version
　　of the Hebrew Judah) was the one that sold Jesus to the Romans.

The God of love was betrayed by Judas with a_____ .
　　(Matt. 26:48)
IRONY: Kisses are a modern sign of love and intimacy, and Jesus, the
　　embodiment of love, was betrayed by this intimate act.

The_____ of the World was taken in darkness.
IRONY: Jesus is the Light of the World (see John 8:12) and yet was arrested
　　and falsely tried in the dark of the night.

Jesus was the Son of God, yet was arrested for_____.
IRONY: The only person that could ever say He was the son of God was
　　arrested for saying He was the son of God!

The Prince of_____was violently arrested by a mob carry-
　　ing swords and clubs.
IRONY: Jesus was the Prince of Peace, yet was treated violently by the
　　Roman soldiers and others.

Jesus, the judge of all men was_____by men.

IRONY: It's rare to find a judge on trial, yet Jesus, the perfect judge of all men, was put on trial by imperfect men.

Pilate released_____rather that Jesus, the Son of the Father.
IRONY: Bararaba's name means "son of the father" (Matthew 27:16–17— Bar/Ben = Son of; Abba = The Father) and he was chosen to be released rather than The Son of The Father, Jesus.

The man released before Jesus was killed was in jail for _____, yet Jesus was on earth to give life (Mark 15:7)
IRONY: Barabbas was serving time in prison for taking life, yet Jesus was condemned for offering eternal life.

Jesus was forced to wear the crown of thorns which is a symbol of _____.
IRONY: The one who overcame the effects of the fall of Adam and Eve was forced to wear one of the many symbols of the fall, a crown of thorns.

Pilate said he was innocent of shedding Jesus's blood (and washed his hands of the crime), but the only way he (and we) can be innocent is to be washed by_____.
IRONY: As Elder Neal A. Maxwell said, "Pilate sought to refuse responsibility for deciding about Christ, but Pilate's hands were never dirtier than just after he had washed them."[3]

Jesus hung naked on the cross, yet he provided our covering. Ironically, the word_____means "a covering."
IRONY: Jesus provided an atonement for all mankind; the word atonement means "a covering." Some historical records indicate that Jesus hung naked and free from covering on the cruel cross of Calvary (see (John 19:23–24).

Jesus died on Nisan 14 which corresponds with_____ in our calendars.
IRONY: Jesus may have died on His birthday, April 6 (see Doctrine and Covenants 20:1).

---

3. Neal A. Maxwell, "Why Not Now?", *Ensign*, Nov. 1974, 12.

What other unique or insightful words did you find in your study of Easter this week?

_____

_____

_____

_____

_____

_____

Please share with us!
Visit www.ComeFollowMeWOW.com and
share your word discoveries and insights!

Chapter 16

Matthew 18; Luke 10

Don't miss these Words of the Week

"**Forgive**" (Matthew 18:21)
"**Samaritan**" (Luke 10:33)
"**Neighbor**" (Luke 10:29)
"**Careful**," "**Chosen**," "**Troubled**" (Luke 10:41–42)

"Lord, how oft shall my brother sin against me, and I forgive him?" (Matthew 18:21)

FROM OVERCOMING FEELINGS SURROUNDING DIVORCE, TO coping with living in a broken home, to conquering feelings of rejection or enduring abuse or mistreatment, many have asked, "How can I tell when I have completely forgiven another person?" One answer to this question is found in Matthew 18 where the Savior commands His followers to forgive "seven times seventy times" (Matthew 18:22). While this mathematical response most likely refers to forgiving completely and without limit, true, lasting, and genuine forgiveness is a blessing that can be elusive to achieve.

The word "forgive" simply means "to remit a debt" or "to pardon an offense." Interestingly, the etymology of the word "forgive" points to a complete giving up. The Old English word was *forgiefan; for* which here means "completely," and *giefan* "to give." In other words, "to give completely."[1] The Greek word for "forgive," *aphesis,* is defined as "a dismissal or release, a

---

1. See "Forgive," *Online Etymology Dictionary.*

letting go."[2] To forgive means to completely release a person from a debt, a wrong, or an obligation. Forgiveness does not mean approving or excusing behavior and it does not mean reconciliation. Furthermore, the decision to forgive is not associated with a feeling; rather, forgiveness is a choice.

There are at least two types of forgiveness. Unilateral forgiveness is forgiving someone who has not asked for forgiveness; it is forgiveness that goes in "one direction." A second type of forgiveness is transactional forgiveness. This is forgiving a person after that person has made an effort to right their wrong. Here, a transaction has occurred on behalf of the offender: the offending person has requested forgiveness and demonstrated their sorrow and remorse and has tried to make things better.

It does not matter when the wrong occurred, how long we have been withholding forgiveness, or how long we have been working and waiting to feel peace after extending forgiveness. There is no offense that cannot be overcome through the Atonement of Jesus Christ. It is never too late to take the "first steps," whether it is the first or fourth time. President Gordon B. Hinckley shared, "Somehow forgiveness, with love and tolerance, accomplishes miracles that can happen in no other way."[3]

As you read Matthew 18 this week, think of a few people that you might consider forgiving; seek the Lord's help to take the first steps of forgiving them and to start enjoying the peace that comes from complete forgiveness.

"A certain Samaritan, as he journeyed, came where he was." (Luke 10:33)

THE GREEK AND LATIN WORDS FOR "Samaritan" (*Samaritēs* and *Samarītānus* respectively) both simply connote an inhabitant from the land of Samaria.[4] With a deeper look, the details of the Good Samaritan story appear to contain several symbols of the Plan of Salvation.

---

2. *Strong's*, 859.
3. Gordon B. Hinckley, "Forgiveness," *Ensign*, Nov. 2005, 84.
4. *Strong's*, 4541.

Good Samaritan Story	Possible Plan of Salvation Symbolism
He came down from Jerusalem.	Our journey from the pre-earth life.
He fell among thieves that stripped him of his raiment.	We fall into temptation and sin that rob us of our true nature.
He was left wounded; half dead.	We encounter two deaths in mortality: physical death and spiritual death.
A Levite and a Priest pass by.	Leaders of other faiths who have partial authority.
The Samaritan poured in wine and oil.	Symbols of the sacrament and Atonement of Jesus Christ.
The Samaritan places him on his beast and takes him to an inn.	The inn is a temporary station; this may symbolize Church attendance and its power to prepare people for temple ordinances.
The Samaritan offers the host a two pence payment and more as needed.	The Savior's payment through His Atonement.
The Samaritan promises to return.	The Second Coming of Jesus Christ.

Remember to be *good* in each role you play; the "Good Samaritan" was just a regular man who chose to do good—and he's now famously known as "The Good Samaritan" because of his kindness. You, too, can become "The Good Husband" or "The Good Fast-Food Worker" or "The Good Student" or "The Good Grandfather" by finding ways to serve those in need.

"And who is my neighbour?" (Luke 10:29)

IN LUKE 10:29 A LAWYER ASKED Jesus, "And who is my neighbour?" (Luke 10:29). Jesus replied with the parable of the Good Samaritan. In the parable, a man is robbed and beaten, but he is ultimately rescued by the kindness of a Samaritan (since Jewish society had established that Jews and Samaritans didn't interact, it was a surprise that he was the one to stop and help).

Jesus then told the lawyer that the one who showed the man mercy was the true neighbor:

Which now of these three, thinkest thou, was neighbour unto him that fell among the thieves? And he said, He that shewed mercy on him. Then said Jesus unto him, Go, and do thou likewise. (Luke 10:36–37).

The Greek word for neighbor is *plēsion* meaning simply "one who lives near another" (notice how the prefix of the English neighbor is closely related to "nigh," meaning "near"), while the Latin is *vicinus* closely linked to our word "vicinity" which also means "near."[5]

So who is OUR neighbor? Far from the dictionary definition of what a neighbor is, the Lord's definition of neighbor is likely an individual that society says we should ignore. The Savior taught that our neighbor is the person that has broken the law. Our neighbor might include a spouse who was unfaithful or the parent who was absent or the boss who was a tyrant. "Our neighbor" might be an annoying co-worker or the man that that stole your wallet or a gay community member who fights angrily for gay marriage.

The Lord beckons us to love our enemies and to love them as much as we love ourselves (see Matthew 5:43–48).

So who is your neighbor? Your neighbor is probably the person you can't quite forgive or the person you have no compassion for.

It's that person who came to mind as you read this.

"Martha, Martha, thou art careful and troubled about many things." (Luke 10:41)

As Martha worried over providing sustenance during the Savior's visit, Luke records that the Savior noticed that she was "careful and troubled" (see Luke 10:41). We read "careful" today and feel that Martha was simply trying to provide a thoughtful meal. And while she undoubtedly was serving with care, the original Greek word for "careful" sheds a different light.

The Greek word for "careful," *Merimnaó,* is used in Luke 10:41 and it translates to the English word "anxious."[6] While Greek for "troubled" is *thorubeo,* and it translates to English as "disturbed, panicked, or agitated."[7] Simply, Martha was feeling anxious, and the Savior was trying to help her be aware of her emotions.

Most every one of God's mortal children will be anxious at some point in their lives. We find examples of this in the scriptures. The great Book of Mormon missionaries Ammon and his brethren were depressed at one point (See Alma 26:27; 56:16). Esther 4:4 relates that queen Esther and her

---

5. *Strong's,* 4139.
6. *Strong's,* 3309.
7. *Strong's,* 2350.

maidens were "exceedingly grieved." And on more than one occasion, the disciples were "terrified" or "frightened" (see Matthew 17:6, for example).

The English word "anxious" is from Latin *angere* and means "to choke, squeeze, constrict, cause tightness."[8] Literally, it means that a person is having great difficulty breathing. Elder Jeffrey R. Holland bore witness that one day, each of our feelings of anxiousness would melt away:

> I bear witness of that day when loved ones whom we knew to have disabilities in mortality will stand before us glorified and grand, breathtakingly perfect in body and mind. What a thrilling moment that will be! I do not know whether we will be happier for ourselves that we have witnessed such a miracle or happier for them that they are fully perfect and finally "free at last."[9]

What a blessing that we will literally be able to "breathe again" once we are resurrected and made perfect in Christ. Meanwhile, remember that anxiety is a very common feeling. When you feel anxiousness and are feeling choked by your life's situations, take heart knowing that Christ is the master Healer. Remember His admonition to not let yourself be "careful or troubled about [too] many things."

"Mary hath chosen that good part." (Luke 10:42)

MAKING DECISIONS IS PROBABLY THE MOST important thing we ever do. And the story of Mary and Martha and their individual decisions is a perfect example of how we can choose the better things in life.

The Greek word here, *exelexato*, means "to pick out for myself, to choose or select."[10] The English word *decision* comes from the Latin *decisionem* which means, "To cut off" (from *de* "off" + *caedere* "to cut").[11] By way of etymological application, making a decision is really just choosing to "cut off" different parts of our lives or schedule.

---

8. See "Anxious," *Online Etymology Dictionary*.
9. Jeffrey R. Holland, "Like a Broken Vessel," *Ensign*, Nov. 2013, 42.
10. *Strong's,* 1586.
11. The Valley of Decision is a biblical name given to the Valley of Jehoshaphat by the prophet Joel (see Joel 3:14). Joel teaches that all the armies of the world will come into this Valley where the Lord will pronounce judgment on all of them. This divine judgment will cause mass death; it will take seven months for the Israelis to bury all of the dead (see Ezekiel 39:12–16).

It's important to remember that *choosing* and *deciding* do not mean "cutting *you* off"; in fact, making a decision frees people from the shackles of endless choices so that they can get to where they want to go.

Indecision is where the Adversary loves to function. As people decide what to keep in their life and what to cut off from their lives, progress happens. From deciding to declutter a home to deciding to distance oneself from a toxic relationship to deciding to say no to extracurricular responsibilities, each of these choices to "cut out" the clutter from life actually frees us and gives us more opportunities. Author James Clear wrote that we should be careful about what and who we say "yes" to:

> When you say no, you are only saying no to *one* option. When you say yes, you are saying no to *every other* option. . . . No is a decision. Yes is a responsibility.[12]

President Thomas S. Monson taught that we should take a look at our responsibilities to make sure that we're focusing on the things that truly matter to us:

> We become so caught up in the busyness of our lives. Were we to step back, however, and take a good look at what we're doing, we may find that we have immersed ourselves in the "thick of thin things." In other words, too often we spend most of our time taking care of the things which do not really matter much at all in the grand scheme of things, neglecting those more important causes.[13]

You see, productivity isn't about deciding to get *more* done, it's about deciding to get the *right things* done. And that comes through deciding what to keep in one's life and what to cut off, as illustrated in the story of Mary and Martha.

FOR FURTHER STUDY

- Study the difference between "childish" and "childlike" (see Matthew 18:1–6) using www.biblehub.com and www.blueletterbible.org.

---

12. James Clear, "The Ultimate Productivity Hack is Saying No," *James Clear*, 26 Mar. 2019, jamesclear.com/saying-no.
13. Thomas S. Monson, "What Have I Done for Someone Today?" *Ensign*, Nov. 2009.

- Look up the meaning of the word "offense" (see Matthew 18:7–14) using www.biblehub.com and www.blueletterbible.org
- Look up the meaning of the word "talent" using www.biblehub.com and www.blueletterbible.org and calculate the total owed in Matthew 18:21–35.
- In Luke 10, the Lord commissions the Seventy to be witnesses. Scripturally, the terms "special witness" (D&C 107:23) and "especial witness" (D&C 107:25) are used. Study the difference between those two words on www.biblehub.com and www.blueletterbible.org.
- Look up the roles and responsibilities of the men called into the Quorum of Seventy (see Luke 10:1–16).
- Study the history of the Jews and Samaritans to shed more light on Luke 10:25–42 (see Encyclopedia Britannica's article "Samaritan" to get started[14]).

What other unique or insightful words did you find in your study this week?

_____

_____

_____

_____

_____

Please share with us!
Visit www.ComeFollowMeWOW.com and
share your word discoveries and insights!

---

14. Link: www.britannica.com/topic/Samaritan.

Chapter 17

John 7-10

Don't miss these Words of the Week

"**Truth**" (John 8:32)
"**Adultery**" (John 8:3)
"**Sin no more**" (John 8:11)
"**Sheep**" (John 10:11)

**"Ye shall know the truth, and the truth
shall make you free." (John 8:32)**

LIVING IN SUCH A DIGITAL AGE, where anyone can post anything and pretend that it's true, it is becoming harder and harder to find and know the truth. If you've ever Googled a question before, you know how many vastly different answers there are for something as simple as how to feed your baby. So what is *truth* and how can we know it?

The hymn "O Say, What Is Truth?," written over 100 years ago, attempts to answer this vital question. In its first verse, the song describes truth as the brightest prize and noblest desire that we can aspire to:

Yes, say, what is truth? 'Tis the brightest prize
To which mortals or Gods can aspire.
Go search in the depths where it glittering lies,
Or ascend in pursuit to the loftiest skies:
'Tis an aim for the noblest desire.

The third verse of the song describes truth as a pillar in our lives that will endure forever and withstand every attack:

The sceptre may fall from the despot's grasp
When with winds of stern justice he copes.
But the pillar of truth will endure to the last,
And its firm-rooted bulwarks outstand the rude blast
And the wreck of the fell tyrant's hopes.[1]

Truth can be defined in a few ways:

- The Greek word *alētheian* and the Latin *veritas* are both defined as truth.[2]
- Truth is "knowledge of things as they are, and as they were, and as they are to come" (see D&C 93:24).
- Truth is light or revelation from heaven.
- *"Faith"* and *"covenants"* are two synonyms for truth (Online Etymology Dictionary).
- Sir Francis Bacon said the three parts of truth are inquiry, knowledge, and belief, or the wooing of it, the presence of it, and the enjoyment of it.[3]

Satan seeks our captivity and bondage by trying to "turn hearts away from the truth" (D&C 78:10). The Lord's way is a way of freedom.

Jesus taught that truth brings freedom (and ignorance brings bondage and captivity) in His discourse about truth and light. Lehi taught that eternal life brings liberty:

Wherefore, men are free according to the flesh; and all things are given them which are expedient unto man. And they are free to choose liberty and eternal life, through the great Mediator of all men, or to choose captivity and death, according to the captivity and power of the devil; for he seeketh that all men might be miserable like unto himself. (2 Nephi 2:27)

We can find truth in the gospel. We are free to choose happiness through a pursuit and application of this eternal truth—or we can choose a path of misery through a life of gospel ignorance and spiritual shortsightedness. We are free to choose truth and freedom or remain in darkness and limitations.

---

1. "O Say, What Is Truth?" *Hymns*, no. 272.
2. *Strong's*, 225.
3. See "Of Truth," in *Essays* [n.d.], 18.

Seek truth—and strive to be changed by the Savior's truths! He truly is the Way, the Truth, and the Light!

"The scribes and Pharisees brought unto him a woman taken in adultery" (John 8:3)

ADULTERY[4] IS A HIGHLY SENSITIVE SUBJECT that, in our modern day, is a betrayal of covenants through an unlawful sexual relationship between men and women.[5] But in scripture, *adultery* is typically used to represented a person's general unfaithfulness to gospel covenants (see Jeremiah 3:8, Ezekiel 23:37, Num. 25:1–3; Jer. 3:6–10; Ezek. 16:15–59; Hosea 4).[6]

The Greeks call it *moicheia,*[7] and in Latin, *adulterium*, yet from its etymology we learn "adultery" describes those who alter a path or pervert a pattern of worship (from *ad* "to" and *alterare* "to alter;" the same root as *alter*). Those who become unfaithful to gospel covenants are literally "altering" the divine pattern of faithfulness and covenant keeping. By disobeying the laws of God and breaking (or trying to *alter*) His commandments, we offend Him—yet He is still willing to forgive, repair, and restore our relationship with Him.

"Go, and sin no more." (John 8:11)

IN ONE OF THE MOST PROFOUND scenes of forgiveness in the New Testament, Christ comforts a broken woman on the brink of death by stoning. In John 8, we see the moment between Christ and this woman:

> When Jesus had lifted up himself, and saw none but the woman, he said unto her, Woman, where are those thine accusers? hath no man condemned thee? She said, No man, Lord. And Jesus said unto her, Neither do I condemn thee; go, and sin no more. (John 8:10–11)

---

4. Although adultery generally refers to sexual intercourse between a married person and someone other than his or her spouse, in the scriptures it may also refer to the unmarried.
5. Bible Dictionary, "Adultery."
6. Many of the prophets used sexual immorality as a picture of spiritual unfaithfulness to the Lord to whom the people belonged (Ezekiel 16:32; 23:27; Jeremiah 13:27). In the New Testament, similar language is employed as well (see James 4:4 and Revelation 17:2). The Savior used the word *adultery* when He called the Jews, "An adulterous generation" (see Mathew 16:4 and Matthew 12:39).
7. *Strong's*, 3430.

Her accusers had dispersed, and she was at the mercy of the Savior of the World. He pleaded with her to "Go, and sin no more." Jesus not only called this woman's actions a sin, but told her *not to repeat them.*

Notice that Jesus did not say, "I forgive you." Instead, He said, "Neither do I condemn thee . . ." He was not casting a final judgment on this woman.[8] In granting her time to repent, Jesus let her know that she needed to stop sinning in order to begin the repentance process. President Spencer W. Kimball explained that this is the start of the woman's repentance:

> His command to her was, "Go, and sin no more." He was direct-ing the sinful woman to go her way, abandon her evil life, commit no more sin, transform her life. He was saying, Go, woman, and start your repentance; and he was indicating to her the beginning step—to abandon her transgressions.[9]

Christ understands that we make mistakes; our lives will not be per-fectly sinless while in this life. But if we want to repent, we have to strive to go forward and make humble changes. If there are transgressions or sins that have cunningly slipped into your life, one of the early steps of repen-tance is to abandon the behavior. Take time today to think about the things you could abandon to follow Christ's admonition to "sin no more."

"I am the good shepherd: the good shepherd giveth his life for the sheep." (John 10:11)

THE GREEK WORD FOR "SHEPHERD" IS *poimēn,* and is defined as "the feeder, protector, and ruler of a flock of men."[10] Some of the symbolism in Christ's role as a shepherd and our role as the proverbial sheep may be lost on us, since we're probably not having frequent experiences with sheep like they did in Christ's day! The following points about these animals reveal why, nearly two hundred times, the Lord's people are called sheep in the scriptures:

Sheep are very dirty. They need someone else to clean them. We, too, are in need of our shepherd, Jesus Christ, to cleanse us from sin.

---

8. Of these verses Elder Dallin H. Oaks said, "The Lord obviously did not justify the woman's sin. He simply told her that He did not condemn her—that is, He would not pass final judgment on her at that time. . . . The woman taken in adultery was granted time to repent, time that would have been denied by those who wanted to stone her." ("'Judge Not' and Judging," *Ensign,* Aug. 1999).
9. Spencer W. Kimball, *The Miracle of Forgiveness* (Deseret Book, 1969), 165.
10. *Strong's,* 4166.

Sheep are helpless against predators. We are helpless against the adversary if we don't have help from the Good Shepherd.

Sheep chew without looking up and they become lost very easily. Like sheep, we can easily get lost spiritually if we focus on the world and don't look up enough.

Prompt rescue is necessary when sheep get lost because they can't digest until they lie down. Many varieties of sheep don't have enough sense to lie down, even when they are aching, and a shepherd makes them lie down for their own good. We, too, sometimes must be forced to "lie down" by the Good Shepherd at certain points in our lives.

If sheep fall into moving water, they drown because their coats absorb water rapidly. As well, we are in danger of drowning in the fast-moving world in which we live; staying close to the Good Shepherd provides safety.

Sheep fear moving water and won't drink unless the water is still. Jesus is called "Living Waters" and we have been invited to drink of His waters freely (see Revelation 22:1)

FOR FURTHER STUDY

- A few Biblical scholars have wondered what Jesus wrote on the ground when the woman who was taken in adultery was brought before Him. Search some of their hypothetical suppositions along with the symbolism of what writing on the ground meant to the Jews in Jesus's day. (See "Bible Q&A: What did Jesus write in the sand?" from www.biblesociety.org.uk[11] and "What did Jesus Write in the Sand?" from www.catholicproductions.com to start.[12])

- In John 8:9, the woman's accusers were "convicted by their own conscience." Look up the meanings and applications behind the word conscience using www.biblehub.com and www.blueletterbible.org.

- In John 9, the Savior corrects a misunderstanding about pre-earth life. Do a deep dive into a study about truths regarding our pre-earth estate. (See "Chapter 6: Our Premortal Life" in the *Doctrines of the Gospel Student Manual* on www.churchofjesuschrist.org to start.)

---

11. Link: www.biblesociety.org.uk/explore-the-bible/bible-articles/
bible-qa-what-did-jesus-write-in-the-sand/.

12. Brant Pitre, "What did Jesus Write in the Sand?" *Catholic Productions,* 17 Apr. 2019,
catholicproductions.com/blogs/blog/what-did-jesus-write-in-the-sand.

- In John 10, the Savior teaches about shepherds and hirelings. Look up information about these two professions and compare and contrast them with each other. (See www.biblehub.com and "On the difference between a hireling and a shepherd" from www.mhmcintyre.us to get started.[13])

What other unique or insightful words did you find in your study this week?

_____

_____

_____

_____

_____

Please share with us!
Visit www.ComeFollowMeWOW.com and
share your word discoveries and insights!

---

13. Mark McIntyre, "On the difference between a hireling and a shepherd," *Attempts at Honesty: Reflections on the interplay of the Bible and Culture,* 16 Nov. 2011, www.mhmcintyre.us/on-the-difference-between-a-hireling-and-a-shepherd/.

Chapter 18

Luke 12–17; John 11

Don't miss these Words of the Week

"Strait" (Luke 13:24)
"Prodigal" (Luke 15:11–32)
"Came to himself" (Luke 15:17)
"Compassion" (Luke 15:20)
"Sycamine" (Luke 17:5)

"Strive to enter in at the strait gate." (Luke 13:24)

FOR MOST LATTER-DAY SAINTS, WHEN WE hear the word "strait" we think of the "straight and narrow way" which is reaffirmed from the Greek word for "straight," *stenēs*, which is defined as "narrow."[1]

You may have also noticed the differences in spelling in these two homophones. While the adjective "straight" means "direct," "strait" is from the Latin *strictus* and *stringere* which mean "to bind" or "draw tight" (same root as *stringent* and *strain;* think also of the modern adjective "strait laced" when describing obedient covenant keepers). Relatedly, the Hebrew word for covenant (*akedah*) means "to bind."[2]

Therefore, one way to look at the meaning of the term "strait gate" is "the covenant path" wherein we bind ourselves to our God through covenants. The covenant path is the way home. This path includes being

---

1. *Strong's,* 4728.
2. See "strait," *Online Etymology Dictionary.*

baptized, being confirmed and receiving the gift of the Holy Ghost, being ordained to the priesthood (for men), receiving the temple endowment, and being sealed in the temple. Each covenant is a checkpoint along the strait gate that begins our covenant path. As we faithfully head down the covenant path through binding ourselves with the Lord, we will grow and find true happiness.

"The Prodigal Son" (see Luke 15:11–32)

WHEN WE STUDY THE STORY OF the "prodigal son," we focus heavily on the mercy of the father toward his wayward and rebellious son. We rightly compare this to the mercy of our Heavenly Father who is so quick to forgive our sins. But there's another lesson to be learned from the prodigal son that sits right at the surface of the story. "Prodigal" actually means "extravagant, lavish, or wastefully spendful." The son in Jesus's parable found in Luke 15 asked for the money that had been set aside for his inheritance and, after receiving it, left home. He spent his money on things that he thought would bring him happiness. He probably did not set out to squander his fortune and end up living with pigs. But when all of his money was gone, he knew he had no choice but to return home and hope that his father would forgive him. When the father saw him from "yet a great way off . . . [he] had compassion, and ran, and fell on his neck, and kissed him."[3] Mercy was shown unto one who deserved it least but needed it most.

In our day, we have been commanded to be wise stewards over our money and assets and be self-reliant:

> Self-reliance is the ability, commitment, and effort to provide the spiritual and temporal necessities of life for self and family. As members become self-reliant, they are also better able to serve and care for others.[4]

Even if we've become prodigal (extravagant, lavish, or spendful), the Lord will help us be wiser with the blessings we've been given. And that road begins with a new commitment to be wiser in our stewardship of money and resources.

---

3. Luke 15:20.
4. *Handbook 2: Administering in the Church* (The Church of Jesus Christ of Latter-day Saints, 2010), 6.1.1.

"He came to himself." (Luke 15:17)

AN OLD ADAGE READS, "YOU CANNOT enjoy the things money can buy if you ignore the things money cannot buy." You may have heard this quote used for people rich or poor, but nobody seems to emulate the statement more than the "Prodigal Son" in Luke 15.

After leaving home and wasting his inheritance, this son soon ran out of money and friends. A famine came, and he ended up in a pig pen eating food given to hogs—an embarrassing and culturally inappropriate environment for a Jewish man.

The King James Bible records that he began his journey home after "he came to himself" (Luke 15:17). The New Inspired Version uses the phrase, "When he finally came to his senses." The original Greek implies that the young man had been suffering from a type of mental illness or unfavorable brain health. The Greek word *heauton* means "his senses" is used in place of "himself."[5]

This young man may have seen himself as if he were a separate person—and then one day he emerged from his haze of delusion and sinfulness and saw himself with clear vision. He realized he had made a mess of his life and had failed economically, morally, relationally, and religiously. We wonder what it felt like for him to "come to himself" at that moment!

Though we might never find ourselves living with pigs and wanting to eat their slop, many of us have been blessed to have had a "coming to ourselves" experience, or we've seen this transformation in others. All of a sudden and with crystal clear clarity we understand the results of our choices we have made—and that understanding can lead us back toward our God.

If you've felt your feebleness and failure and feel ready to turn—or to return—to God, please know that He will greet you with arms wide open, just as did the Prodigal's father. Come home. Your Father is eager to receive you back again.

---

5. *Strong's*, 1438.

"When he was yet a great way off, his father saw him, and had compassion, and ran, and fell on his neck, and kissed him." (Luke 15:20)

WE'VE BEEN COMMANDED TO "MOURN WITH those that mourn . . . and comfort those that stand in need of comfort."[6] Many of us excel at the comfort part, offering freezer meals and blessings to those in need, but what does it mean to "mourn with those that mourn"? In other words, what does it mean to have *compassion*?

Many of us define *compassion* as "having an awareness of others' distress" or "having a desire to relieve a burden." However, the etymology of the word compassion goes far beyond simply having awareness of and a desire to relieve a burden.[7]

The Latin root *compassionem* is broken down into two parts of speech: *com*, which means "with," and *pati*, which means "to suffer." The word "compassion" literally means "to suffer with another person." The Greek word for "compassion," *esplanchnisthē*, means "to be moved and to have pity on."[8]

Luke records that the Prodigal Son's father demonstrated this beautiful compassion for his son. Based on the word's origin, the father's compassion could mean that he was suffering alongside his son while he was away from home.

Compassion was a driving force in the Savior's ministry. He could bless people and teach them by discerning their needs and desires. He also sensed and deeply felt the pains that others were feeling. Certainly, the Savior's compassion led to the ultimate act of compassion: His Atonement for the sins and suffering of humankind where He literally "suffered with" every one of God's children. As Elder David A. Bednar wrote, "Jesus, who suffered the most, has the most compassion for all of us who suffer so much less."[9]

This week, consider praying for the gift of a compassionate heart to feel more deeply the sufferings of others. Praying for the gift of compassion can help you "come to feel a sincere concern for the eternal welfare and happiness of other people."[10]

---

6. Mosiah 18:9.

7. See "compassion," *Online Etymology Dictionary.*

8. *Strong's,* 4697.

9. David A. Bednar, "The Character of Christ," Brigham Young University–Idaho Religion Symposium, 25 Jan. 2003, www.byui.edu/devotionals.

10. "How Do I Develop Christlike Attributes?" *Preach My Gospel: A Guide to Missionary Service* (The Church of Jesus Christ of Latter-day Saints, 2004), 124; see also Moroni 7:48.

A couple ideas for getting started are listening intently to others, striving to understand by considering how they might feel, and acting on any nudge you feel from the Spirit to help others. Make your actions meaningful to the unique situations of the people you want to help. Before you make another casserole, think about what that person really needs. As you do these things, your love for others will increase, and it will be easier to recognize ways to show that love and practice the true meaning of *compassion*.

"If ye had faith as a grain of mustard seed, ye might say unto this sycamine tree, Be thou plucked up by the root, and be thou planted in the sea; and it should obey you." (Luke 17:6)

HAVE YOU EVER HAD A TRIAL that feels like it will never go away? Like, despite all the work you've done to remove it, it hasn't budged? These stubborn trials are frustrating and can almost make us want to give up trying to remove it, but the Savior teaches us in the scriptures how these trials can end if we exercise the tiniest speck of faith.

Of all trees available, why did the Savior choose the sycamine tree for this teaching? Consider these facts about the sycamine tree:

The roots of the sycamine tree grow hundreds of feet into the ground, deeper than most any other tree. Hot weather and blistering temperatures have little effect on this tree because its long roots tap into water sources deep under the earth. Of all trees in the area, the sycamine was likely the hardest to move because of its deep root system.

Sycamine wood was used for making caskets. This may point our minds to the idea that faith can help us overcome spiritual death or faith that has gone dormant.

Sycamine fruit is pollinated by wasps because only their stingers can penetrate the sycamine flower. The fruit of the sycamine is almost impenetrable. Likewise, our faith may at times feel impossible.

President Russell M. Nelson taught that, if we start today to increase our faith, Christ will increase our ability to do the impossible. He wrote:

My dear brothers and sister, my call to you . . . is to *start today* to increase your faith. Through your faith, Jesus Christ will increase your ability to move the mountains in your life, even though your personal challenges may loom as large as Mount Everest.

Your mountains may be loneliness, doubt, illness, or other personal problems. Your mountains will vary, and yet the answer to each of your challenges is to increase your faith. That takes work. Lazy learners and lax disciples will always struggle to muster even a particle of faith.[11]

With even a tiny measure of faith, we can command the sycamines of bitterness, unpleasantness, and disappointment to leave. No matter how deep the roots of our troubles are, if we exercise whatever faith we have and humbly ask the Lord to help us remove our challenges, or ask for Him to give us strength to endure as we try to uproot them with His strength, He will help us.

FOR FURTHER STUDY

- There is a fascinating definition of the Greek word for "fool" (see Luke 12:16–21). Consider researching its meaning using www.biblehub.com and www.blueletterbible.org.

- Look up the meaning of the phrase "Make to yourselves friends of the mammon of unrighteousness" (Luke 16:9) using www.biblehub.com and www.blueletterbible.org to see what it meant originally.

- In Luke 16:22, the phrase "Abraham's bosom" is used. Consider looking at commentaries about what that term means using www.blueletterbible.org.

- Luke 17:11–19 is centered in gratitude. Look up the etymology of the word gratitude using www.www.etymonline.com and see what applications are there for you.

- In John 11, Lazarus had been dead for 4 days. The Jews had some interesting beliefs about what "dead" means; do a search for their traditions and beliefs about what "dead" meant to them. (See "Death

---

11. Russell M. Nelson, "Christ Is Risen; Faith in Him Will Move Mountains," *Liahona*, May 2021.

& Bereavement in Judaism: Death and Mourning" on www.jewish-virtuallibrary.org to start.[12])

What other unique or insightful words did you find in your study this week?

_____

_____

_____

_____

_____

_____

Please share with us!
Visit www.ComeFollowMeWOW.com and
share your word discoveries and insights!

12. Site: www.jewishvirtuallibrary.org/death-and-mourning-in-judaism.

Chapter 19

Matthew 19-20; Mark 10; Luke 18

Don't miss these Words of the Week

"Divorce" (Matthew 19:7)
"Possessions" (Matthew 19:22)
"Beholding" (Mark 10:21)
"Treasure" (Luke 18:22)

"Why did Moses then command to give a writing of divorcement, and to put her away?" (Matthew 19:7)

The greatest single factor affecting . . . your eventual destiny . . . is the decision you make that moonlit night when you ask that individual to be your companion for life. That's the most important decision of your entire life![1]

IN OUR CULTURE, THERE IS A great emphasis on marriage and much discussion about divorce. The same was true in Jesus's day. Hillel was a Jewish religious leader that lived shortly before the time of Christ. He was a scholar associated with the development of the Talmud and the founder of the House of Hillel school of tannaim (a Rabbinical school). The Hillel school of thought was a liberal view of marriage, permitting divorce in a variety of circumstances (even if the wife spoiled a meal). A second school of thought was perpetuated by the House of Shammai (a contemporary leader at the

---

1. *The Teachings of Spencer W. Kimball*, 301.

same time as Hillel), which conservatively taught that divorce should be avoided and reserved only for in the case of adultery.[2]

The English word "divorce" comes from the Latin *divortium* which simply means "a dissolution of marriage."[3] The root is *divertere* which is the same root as "divert," which means "a change of direction" or, according to the Greek word, *apostasiou*, "a separation." [4]

When Jesus was asked about His views of marriage and divorce, it's likely that the Pharisees were referencing the current conversation about divorce, and they may have wanted to know which school of thought Jesus ascribed Himself to. Wisely, Jesus responded, "Have ye not read?" (Matthew 19:4). What a reply! Some people in that day (and in our day as well) quickly choose divorce or adamantly support non-Christian marriage because either they don't have a solid understanding of what the scriptures teach on that subject or they don't understand the doctrine of marriage.

Divorce carries many innocent victims. From former spouses who were betrayed, to abandoned children who suffer innocently, those who have been through a divorce can be strengthened by the healing power of the Atonement of Jesus Christ.

Jesus, the Master teacher, points His inquirers to the scriptures for answers in Matthew 19. This is instructive for us! When doctrinal questions arise, we too should look to the word of God for what has been revealed. As President Dallin H. Oaks reminded that reading the scriptures allows us to receive personal inspiration:

> . . . The reading of the scriptures will . . . put us in a position where we can obtain inspiration to answer any doctrinal or personal question, whether or not that question directly concerns the subject we are studying in the scriptures. That is a grand truth not understood by many. . . . [E]ven though the scriptures contain no words to answer our specific personal questions, a prayerful study of the scriptures will help us obtain such answers.[5]

When we have questions, no matter how challenging or simple they are, we can always turn to the scriptures for answers.

---

2. Soloman Schechter and David Werner Amram, "Divorce," *Jewish Encyclopedia: The unedited full-text of the 1906 Jewish Encyclopedia,* www.jewishencyclopedia.com.
3. See "divorce," *Online Etymology Dictionary.*
4. *Strong's,* 647.
5. Dallin H. Oaks, "Studying the Scriptures," Brigham Young University—Hawaii fireside, 14 Mar. 1986, 19–21.

"When the young man heard that saying, he went away sorrowful: for he had great possessions." (Matthew 19:22)

THE GREEK WORD HERE FOR "WEALTH," *ktēmata*, connotes an "acquired estate,"[6] while the Latin for "possessions" is *fortuna*, also meaning "good fortune or property." The story of the rich, young ruler in Matthew 19 has many applications for us today. While we all may not have "great possessions" (see Matthew 19:22), we may be tempted with the same feelings that came to the young man about what we *do* have.

From its etymology, the word "possession" is likely a compound of *potis* "power" and *sedere* "to sit." Sometimes we are tempted to think that we "sit in power" with what we possess in our lives, not realizing that our possessions, be they great or small, might actually be "sitting in power" over us!

Before we judge the rich, young ruler in Matthew 19, notice how many good qualities this young man possessed:

- He was *eager* (he came to Jesus, Matthew 19:16)
- He was *humble* (he wanted to do good things, Matthew 19:17)
- He showed *reverence* (he called Jesus "Good Master" in Matthew 19:16)
- He had a desire for *righteousness* (he wanted eternal life, Matthew 19:16)
- It appears he was a *good, faithful, obedient* young man (he was a commandment keeper, Matthew 19:20).
- He was *successful* (he had great possessions, Matthew 19:22)—and still recognized his spiritual poverty

The pulls and tugs of our world are absolutely real—and absolutely powerful. And if we aren't careful, we can easily be overcome, as Peter counseled: "Of whom a man is overcome, of the same is he brought in bondage" (2 Peter 2:19). Some great people in our world sincerely hope for more possessions in order to do more good in the world, but it seems that only a few are good enough to handle their possessions properly. Too many "spend money for that which is of no worth . . . [and] which cannot satisfy" (2 Nephi 9:51).

It may be wise to take an inventory of your possessions. Give thanks for all you have—and check yourself to ensure that your possessions are not taking possession of you!

---

6. *Strong's*, 2933.

"Then Jesus beholding him loved him." (Mark 10:21)

THE GREEK WORD FOR "BEHOLDING" OR "looking," *emblepsas*, means "to observe fixedly, or to discern clearly."[7] In His interaction with the rich, young ruler—and before correcting and inviting him to change—Mark records that, "Jesus beholding him loved him" (Mark 10:21). Why might Jesus have wanted to *behold* the rich, young ruler before correcting him?

The *Online Etymology Dictionary* reveals that the word "behold" was a common West Germanic compound that meant "to hold" or "to keep." It references the Old Frisian *bihalda* which adds "to possess, keep, protect, save."[8] It appears that before asking this young man to leave his wealth, Jesus wanted to connect with him, showing that He loved him and wanted to protect and save him as His primary mission.

This principle is wonderful: when it comes to helping a wayward child or friend, *connect* before you *correct*. And when it comes to us and our hesitancies to come to Christ, remember that Elder S. Mark Palmer taught we should think of the Lord beholding and loving us:

My dear brothers and sisters, now anytime you feel you are being asked to do something hard—give up a poor habit or an addiction, put aside worldly pursuits, sacrifice a favorite activity because it is the Sabbath, forgive someone who has wronged you—think of the Lord *beholding* you, *loving* you, and inviting you to let it go and *follow Him*. And thank Him for loving you enough to invite you to do more.[9]

Christ loves us, and He will support us in all of our efforts to grow closer to Him and our Father in Heaven.

"Thou shalt have treasure in heaven." (Luke 18:22)

IT SEEMS THAT THE LORD IS very interested in where our focus is in life. In a multitude of scripture passages, the Lord invites us to focus on Him and to treasure things like our covenants, our families, and our standards. And yet it's so easy to be distracted and lose our focus on things that matter most as the world tugs and pulls us in different ways.

The Greek word "treasure" used in Luke 18, as the Savior yet again taught the principle of focus, is *thesauros*.[10] The word "treasure" originally

---

7. *Strong's*, 1689.
8. "Behold," *Online Etymology Dictionary*.
9. S. Mark Palmer, "Then Jesus Beholding Him Loved Him," *Ensign*, May 2017, 116.
10. *Strong's*, 2344.

referred to a storage place in which good and valuable things were stored; over time, the Greek word *thesauros* became a synonym for the treasures that were stored.[11]

As you read that Greek word, you probably noticed that it's where we got our English word "thesaurus" from. In English, a thesaurus is a special "treasure" book that lists words with similar meanings. So, a *thesaurus* is a book full of treasures—and those treasures are words. Like the psalmist penned, "Thy word have I hid in mine heart [treasured], that I might not sin against thee" (Psalm 119:11).

Looking back to what Jesus may have been teaching in Luke 18 about *treasures*, have you ever thought of your mind—full of words—as a treasury? What we treasure—what words fill our vocabularies and what words fill the thoughts of our minds each day—tell us a lot about what we truly treasure in life. Words—our personal treasured thesaurus of vocabulary— can bless or curse (see Matthew 12:35). Words indeed are *treasures*, and they open up whole new treasures in the person who speaks, writes, reads, or hears them.

Today, remember that a good word spoken at the right time is a beautiful *treasure*. Look to share your treasury of words and use them in a way that God bless others with them. Today, seek to treasure your words!

FOR FURTHER STUDY

- Matthew 19:3–12 is rich in doctrine about marriage. Consider reviewing the Lord's definition of marriage and the doctrines surrounding its foundation within these verses.

- Some readers are unfamiliar with what a "eunuch" is (see Mathew 19:21). Several Church manuals provide commentaries on what this term means, so consider looking them up. (See the "Eunuch" entry in the Bible Dictionary and the "Matthew 19:21" section of www. gospeldoctrine.com to get started.[12])

- There is a wonderful cultural implication in Jesus's statement that "It is easier for a camel to go through the eye of a needle, than for a rich man to enter into the kingdom of God" found in Matthew 19:23.

---

11. See "thesaurus," *Online Etymology Dictionary.*
12. Site: www.gospeldoctrine.com/new-testament/matthew/matthew-19.

Research what "the eye of a needle" is. (See the Wikipedia article "Eye of a needle" to get started.[13])

- The mother of James and John asked Jesus an innocent question in Matthew 20:21; she had no idea what she was really asking—and the road her sons would need to take to fulfill her request. Re-read Matthew 20:20–28 looking for how Jesus answered her.

What other unique or insightful words did you find in your study this week?

_____

_____

_____

_____

Please share with us!
Visit www.ComeFollowMeWOW.com and
share your word discoveries and insights!

---

13. Site: en.wikipedia.org/wiki/Eye_of_a_needle

Chapter 20

Matthew 21-23; Mark 11; Luke 19-20; John 12

Don't miss these Words of the Week

"**Hosanna**" (Matthew 21:9)
"**Garment**" (Matthew 22:11)
"**Hypocrite**" (Matthew 23:13)

> **"The multitudes that went before, and that followed, cried, saying, Hosanna to the son of David." (Matthew 21:9)**

THE PRAISE OF *HOSANNA* HAS BECOME a celebration of Jesus Christ as the Deliverer. Its use in adoration of Christ seems to span all ages and continents (1 Nephi 11:6; 3 Nephi 11:14–17). From the Greek *ossana* and the Hebrew *hosha'na,* we get "save, we pray" or, to simplify, "please save us." *Hosanna* can turn our minds to the pre-earthly Council in Heaven "when all the sons of God shouted for joy" (Job 38:7) after Christ offered Himself as the Savior of the world.

We read in the Old Testament that during the Feast of Tabernacles (a celebration to commemorate the Lord's deliverance of the Children of Israel into the promised land), people chanted the words of Psalm 118 and waved palm branches. In a reflection of this tradition during the Savior's ministry,[1]

---

1. "The donkey has been designated in literature as 'the ancient symbol of Jewish royalty,'

the multitudes cried "*Hosanna*" and spread palm branches for Jesus to demonstrate their understanding that He was that same Being that had delivered Israel anciently (Psalms 118:25–26; Matthew 21:9, 15; Mark 11:9–10; John 12:13). These faithful followers were celebrating Christ's divinity and acknowledging His role as Redeemer.[2]

In modern times, the hosanna shout was included in the dedication of the Kirtland Temple (see D&C 109:79) and is now a part of the dedication of modern temples. The Bible Dictionary teaches that this tradition is connected to the Feast of Tabernacles "at our Lord's triumphal entry into Jerusalem."[3]

It appears that this shout will be heard at the Second Coming of Christ (see 1 Thessalonian 4:16).

Figuratively, as we participate in the administration of the sacrament or temple ordinances or make covenants through baptism and other ordinances, we are echoing the same message of what the word "hosanna means:" *Please save us.* As we pray or attend church meetings, we are asking for the Savior's role as Redeemer and Deliverer to change us, purify us, and ultimately, save us.

"He saw there a man which had not on a wedding garment." (Matthew 22:11)

OUR WARDROBES ARE FULL OF DIFFERENT types of clothing for different occasions: boots for rainy days, short sleeves for when it's hot, dresses and suits for church, and the list goes on. It's important to be prepared for whatever awaits us. Otherwise, at best we'll be uncomfortable, and at worst we won't be allowed where we want to go.

In Matthew 22, a guest arrived at a wedding and "had not on a wedding garment" (see Matthew 22:11). Most every endowed Latter-day Saint wears a similar garment[4] under their clothing. Matthew 22 expresses the importance of the garment. Like us, the Israelites in the Old Testament

---

and one riding upon an ass as the type of peaceful progress" (James E. Talmage, *Jesus the Christ*, 3rd ed. [1916], 516–17). The donkey "Riding on a donkey ... showed that Jesus came as a peaceful and 'lowly' Savior, not as a conqueror upon a warhorse" (New Testament Student Manual [Church Educational System manual, 2014], 64).

2. See *Guide to the Scriptures*, "Hosanna," scriptures.ChurchofJesusChrist.org.

3. Bible Dictionary, "Hosanna."

4. The garment is often referred to as the "temple garment" or "garment of the Holy Priesthood." See Gospel Topics, "Garments," topics.churchofjesuschrist.org.

wore their garments as personal reminders of their covenants with God (see Numbers 15:37–41 and Exodus 28:39–43).

In our day, President Russell M. Nelson has emphasized the symbolic significance of temple garments. He said:

Wearing the temple garment has deep symbolic significance. It represents a continuing commitment. Just as the Savior exemplified the need to endure to the end, we wear the garment faithfully as part of the enduring armor of God. Thus we demonstrate our faith in Him and in His eternal covenants with us.[5]

In etymological terms, "garment" means "any article of clothing" or, as the Greek word "*endyma*" defines it, "raiment or apparel."[6] A Germanic source links the word origin of "garment" to the word *garnish*, which means "to cover" (the word origin of "garnish" will be discussed in our study of 1 Corinthians 13:5).

The way temple garments are worn "is an outward expression of an inward commitment to follow the Savior."[7] Elder Carlos E. Asay taught that the garment "strengthens the wearer to resist temptation, fend off evil influences, and stand firmly for the right."[8]

One of the current temple recommend questions asks, "Do you keep the covenants that you made in the temple, including wearing the temple garment as instructed in the endowment?" If you are endowed, consider reviewing the "Wearing the Temple Garment" statement to evaluate yourself and your use of the garment:

The temple garment is a reminder of covenants made in the temple and, when worn properly throughout life, will serve as a protection against temptation and evil. The garment should be worn beneath the outer clothing. It should not be removed for activities that can reasonably be done while wearing the garment, and it should not be modified to accommodate different styles of clothing. Endowed members should seek the guidance of the Holy Spirit to answer personal questions about wearing the garment. It is a sacred privilege to wear the garment and doing so is an outward expression of an inner commitment to follow the Savior Jesus Christ. [9]

5. Russell M. Nelson, "Personal Preparation for Temple Blessings," *Ensign*, May 2001, 33.

6. *Strong's*, 1742.

7. First Presidency letter, 10 Oct. 1988.

8. Carlos E. Asay, "The Temple Garment: 'An Outward Expression of an Inward Commitment,'" *Ensign*, Aug. 1997.

9. "Wearing the Temple Garment," enclosure to the First Presidency letter "Preparing to Enter the Temple," 6 Oct. 2019.

"Woe unto you, scribes and Pharisees, hypocrites!" (Matthew 23:13)

THE WORD "HYPOCRITE" USED BY THE Master is translated from a Greek word meaning "actor," and refers to one who pretends, exaggerates a part, or is deceitfully inconsistent in his or her actions.[10] We read this word first in Matthew 6 and we will read it again at the end of the Savior's life in Matthew 23.

The Savior's sternest rebukes were to hypocrites. Hypocrisy is spiritually destructive, both to the hypocrite and to those who observe the inconsistency.

To understand what *hypocrisy* means, consider it as being the opposite of integrity. When our actions and our motives are not consistent, we stand in danger of falling into the trap of hypocrisy, as seen in the chart below that shows the connection between actions and motives:

	Impure Motives	Pure Motives
Unrighteous Actions	Rebel	Natural Man
Righteous Actions	Hypocrite	Disciple

Are YOU a hypocrite? Most likely so! And that's okay. Why? President Dieter F. Uchtdorf taught that we all fall short of living up to our beliefs sometimes:

> If you define *hypocrite* as someone who fails to live up perfectly to what he or she believes, then we are all hypocrites. None of us is quite as Christlike as we know we should be. But we earnestly desire to overcome our faults and the tendency to sin. With our heart and soul we yearn to become better with the help of the Atonement of Jesus Christ.[11]

As you interact with others, pay attention to your motives and actions and avoid the trap of hypocrisy. And, remember, if you fail, you're just like the rest of us and you can pick yourself up and try again.

---

10. *Strong's*, 5273.
11. Dieter F. Uchtdorf, "Come, Join with Us," *Ensign*, Nov. 2013, 23.

FOR FURTHER STUDY

- The name Zacchaeus (Luke 19:1–10) reveals much about him. Look up the meaning of Zacchaeus's name using *Hitchcock's Bible Name Dictionary.*[12]

- Was Jesus angry when He cleansed the temple in Matthew 21:12–17? Look up a few of the phrases used in that passage using www.biblehub.com and www.blueletterbible.org to learn about the principle of righteous indignation.

- Many prophets and apostles have provided commentary on what the phrase "Render therefore unto Caesar the things which are Caesar's" means in Matthew 22:21. Search this phrase on www.churchofjesuschrist.org under "general conference" to talks that have referenced this scripture.

What other unique or insightful words did you find in your study this week?

_____

_____

_____

_____

**Please share with us!
Visit www.ComeFollowMeWOW.com and
share your word discoveries and insights!**

---

12. Site: www.biblestudytools.com/dictionaries/hitchcocks-bible-names.

Chapter 21

Joseph Smith—Matthew 1; Matthew 25; Mark 12-13; Luke 21

Don't miss these Words of the Week

"**Virgins**" and "**Bridegroom** (Matthew 25:1)
"**I know you not**" (Matthew 25:12)
"**Know**" (Matthew 25:12)
"**Talent**" (Matthew 25:15)

"Then shall the kingdom of heaven be likened unto ten virgins, which took their lamps, and went forth to meet the bridegroom." (Matthew 25:1)

THE TRADITIONAL JEWISH WEDDING DURING CHRIST'S ministry kept everyone on their toes. The process would begin with a contract, which was agreed to after the proposal occurred.[1] From this point on, the man and woman were legally considered married.[2] During the first stage of betrothal, after the contract was established, the bridegroom went to his father's house to build a home on his father's property for the bride, groom, and their

---

1. See Steve Rudd, "Marriage in the Bible and Ancient Marriage and Jewish Wedding Customs: The Three Stage [R]itual of Bible Marriages," accessed 10, Jun. 2017, www.bible.ca/marriage/ancient-jewish-three-stage-weddings-and-marriage-customsceremony-in-the-bible.htm.
2. The Greek word for "virgin" is *parthenois*, meaning "an unmarried daughter," while the Latin word *impubis* defines a virgin as "youthful, unmarried and chaste."

126

future family to live in. Until his father gave his approval that the work was complete, the couple couldn't see each other. Usually, the Hebrew bride did not know the exact day or hour the groom would return to marry her, but only knew the general time as it drew near.

President Joseph Fielding Smith taught, "[A]s the bride is expected to be adorned, so also was the church until His return, when the marriage should take place."[3] The scriptures repeatedly speak of the bridegroom coming at night (likely because of the Mideast desert heat), so after the father approves of the addition to his home, the invitations go out for the wedding feast in the form of trumpets sounding and torches being lit.

On the night of the marriage, the bride and her entourage would hear the trumpets and see the torches lighting the countryside and the grooms-men parading down the street. She would have to immediately arise, make a few final preparations, and then be escorted to the marriage by the wedding party.[4]

The five wise virgins in Matthew's parable understood clearly the necessity of being prepared at all times. When the bridegroom came, they calmly arose, made some last-minute preparations, and were off to the wedding.

Today, we're preparing for Christ to return, and we could learn so much from the brides who did all they could to prepare and then waited with patience. Like the brides, we should be preparing for Christ to come again; each of our days can be filled with sincere prayer, scripture study, and service to others. We should strive to live up to the terms of our marriage contract (or covenant), with the Savior. Let's feel ready when He returns to bring peace to those who are prepared to receive Him.

"I know you not." (Matthew 25:12)

YOU MAY HAVE NOTICED THE JOSEPH Smith Translation of Matthew 25:12 changes the Greek phrase "I know you not" to "Ye know me not." It appears that Joseph was trying to teach us that our entrance to the Lord's kingdom is based on our relationship with Him.

The covenant path seems to be marked with important relationships—from our relationship we had with Heavenly Parents in the pre-earth life, to the relationships between parents and children, to relationships between

---

3. Joseph Fielding Smith, "What Is Babylon?" *Times and Seasons,* vol. 4, Nov.
4. Charles C. Ryrie, *Come Quickly, Lord Jesus* (Eugene: Harvest House Publishers, 1996), 67; Arnold G. Fruchtenbaum, *The Footsteps of Messiah*, Revised edition. (San Antonio: Ariel Ministries, 2003), 162–63.

husband and wife, to the relationship we have with the Holy Ghost after we are confirmed. Consider how focused Satan is on ruining all righteous relationships.

How can we come to know Jesus in such a way that we can enter into the feast like the wise virgins?

Joseph Smith in his *Lectures on Faith* taught that to have true faith in God we must have accurate ideas about the characteristics of God. In other words, the better that we know God, the deeper our faith will become. To have eternal life, we must know God (see John 17:3).

Our English word "know" comes from the Greek word *gnosis*, which means "knowledge." In Spanish and other Latin-based languages, there are companion words for "knowing;" the Greek derived word *conocer* (meaning "to know someone," like a close, intimate, friendly relationship) and *saber* (which means "to know about something in general terms"). Our English word "know" lets us express that we know someone intimately and also know general things about them.[5]

We can probably say with great confidence that these virgins in Matthew 25 *knew about* Jesus; after all, they were invited to a wedding with Him. Yet, at the door, as they frantically knocked after having arrived late, Jesus teaches them a truth that is very sobering. In essence, He may have been saying, "Don't you even know me? You know what I expected of you. You had plenty of time to be ready. I'm so sorry—you just don't know me."

In application, think of a few small things you can do today—maybe even right now—to know God better. Maybe it's a heartfelt prayer. Maybe it's sincerely serving a family member or friend. Maybe it's time for a deep experience in scripture. As you seek to know Him more deeply, one day you will be greeted with open arms with the greeting, "I know you!"

"And unto one he gave five talents, to another two, and to another one." (Matthew 25:15)

WHEN WE HEAR THE WORD "TALENT," we often think of playing the piano or singing or creating art. In the Biblical language, a talent was a measurement of silver containing 3,000 shekels (see Exodus 38:25–26), and was equal to just over 94 lbs. The Greek talent weighed around 82 lbs.

In the Savior's parable of the talents (see Matthew 25:15), three people receive different measurements of talents: the first receives five talents, the

---

5. See "know," *Online Etymology Dictionary*.

second receives two talents, and the third receives one talent. It's interesting to note that each person received their measurement based on their ability (see Matthew 25:15). The word "ability" used here in the Greek is *dynamin* which translates to "miraculous power."[6]

In other words, the Lord may have made an investment into each person based on their unique gift or divine power.

We may feel sad for the fellow who only received one talent, but in working out the math on the value of just one talent, it equates to several hundred thousands of dollars. What an investment the Lord made in that servant!

Even if a single talent were a small amount, Jesus has shown us what He can do with very little. While He was on the Sea of Galilee teaching, food became scarce (see Matthew 14:13–21). The disciples began to scramble to find sustenance for the multitude. In John 6:9, we read that a young boy was among the crowd and had with him five loaves and two fishes. The young boy may have commented to the Master that he had five loaves and two fishes—and we wonder if the disciples may have responded with something like, "Okay, nice try, young man. We've got thousands of people and there's no way that five loaves and two fishes can feed this group. You simply don't have enough . . ." But then the Master breaks that little offering and there is enough to feed everyone and have leftovers!

In the case of the servant with one talent, sadly, in Matthew 25, we read that, "he that had received one went and digged in the earth, and hid his lord's money" (Matthew 25:18). Hence the phrase, "burying one's talent."

Please know this: the Lord has made an investment in you! You have been given gifts with miraculous power! Even if you feel like you only have "five loaves" or "two fishes" worth of talent or ability, it's plenty to be a blessing to others around you!

FOR FURTHER STUDY

- Make a list of events surrounding the Second Coming using Joseph Smith—Matthew.
- There is a mention of a marketplace in Matthew 25:9. Consider researching this symbol using www.biblehub.com and www.blueletterbible.org and liken it to where we go to "fill out lamps."

6. *Strong's*, 1411.

- Study Mark 12 and the meaning of the word "lawful" (see Mark 12:14) using www.biblehub.com and www.blueletterbible.org. Consider ways that you can be more lawful as the Lord directed.

- Study the mite (Mark 12:41) and its unit of measurement using www.biblehub.com and www.blueletterbible.org to help you understand the woman's donation a bit better.

What other unique or insightful words did you find in your study this week?

_____

_____

_____

_____

_____

_____

Please share with us!
Visit www.ComeFollowMeWOW.com and
share your word discoveries and insights!

Chapter 22

John 13-17

Don't miss these Words of the Week

"**Commandment**" (John 13:34)
"**The Way**" (John 14:6)
"**Comfort**" (John 14:18)
"**Abide**" (John 15:4)

"A new commandment I give unto you, That ye love one another." (John 13:34)

IN OUR DAY, THE USE OF "commandment" or "command" in everyday talk is pretty rare. Many in modern culture find this word a bit abrasive or controlling. Yet it is through His "Thou Shalts" and "Thou Shalt Nots" that the Lord demonstrates His love for us.

Wait, what? The Lord shows His love for us by *commanding* us? Yes, indeed!

The word "commandment" comes from Greek *entolēn* and is defined as an "authoritative prescription,"[1] whereas, the Latin *commendare* which means "to recommend" (think of the words "commend" and "recommend," which both share the same root as "command").[2]

Think about that. The word "commandment" might be interpreted as meaning "a recommendation or commendation." A wise Father

---

1. *Strong's*, 1785.
2. See "commandment," *Online Etymology Dictionary*.

communicates to His children that, "If you want to be happy or if you want to show your love for Me, I *highly recommend* that you _____ ."

As the Savior commanded His disciples to love one another, He was inviting each of us to discover happiness and joy. Rather than restricting our agency, commandments open our lives to more freedom (see D&C 82:8–9). President Dieter F. Uchtdorf has said that obedience can help us learn who we are:

> Maybe obedience is not so much the process of bending, twisting, and pounding our souls into something we are not. Instead, it is the process by which we discover what we truly are made of.[3]

If you feel like you are struggling to keep commandments (and many of us wonder why we don't more easily accept the Lord's recommendations for happiness), please take heart. Elder Jeffrey R. Holland taught that the Atonement can help us improve:

> With the gift of the Atonement of Jesus Christ and the strength of heaven to help us, we *can* improve, and the great thing about the gospel is we get credit for *trying,* even if we don't always succeed. . . . Keep trying. Keep trusting. Keep believing. Keep growing. Heaven is cheering you on today, tomorrow, and forever.[4]

Like any good parent, Heavenly Father not only gives us recommendations for how we can live better but He is there to help us as we try.

"I am the way, the truth, and the life." (John 14:6)

EACH DAY, MOST OF US GO several different ways. We walk around our homes. We drive to work or to visit with friends. Every day without fail we navigate our different ways with our feet and with our vehicles and with our minds.

Knowing of the myriads of "ways" in our lives, the Savior reminds us: "I am the way, the truth, and the life" (John 14:16). The Greek word used here for "way" is *hodos* and means "a road, journey, or path."[5]

Some have theorized that the original Greek translated, "I am the way, the truth, and the life" in John 14:6 actually says, "I am *a* way, *a* truth,

---

3. Dieter F. Uchtdorf, "He Will Place You on His Shoulders and Carry You Home," *Ensign,* May 2016, 103–4.
4. Jeffrey R. Holland, "Tomorrow the Lord Will Do Wonders among You," *Ensign,* May 2016, 126–27.
5. *Strong's,* 3598.

and *a* life."[6] In the original Greek, the words translated "way," "truth," and "life" in John 14:6 are each preceded by the definite article, "the"—η (hE). Hence (and truthfully) "I am *the* way, *the* truth, and *the* life" is the correct translation—and the correct application for us as well. As the Old English *weg* implies, this is a "course of life."[7]

Some of us worry that we can't fully follow Him because His standards and commandments are too high or unattainable. We might feel that obedience is beyond our capacity or ability—that it's simply too high or too much. But please do not believe those Satanic lies!

In the October 2008 General Conference, Elder Lawrence Corbridge of the Seventy shed marvelous light on what the Savior meant. Here are a few excerpts that help us understand more clearly Christ's role as "The Way":[8]

- "There is only one way to happiness and fulfillment. He is the Way. Every other way, any other way, whatever other way, is foolishness."

- "Only God can bless us. Only He can sustain us. Only He can cause our hearts to beat and give us breath. Only He can preserve and protect us. Only He can give us strength to bear up the burdens of life. Only He can give us power, knowledge, peace, and joy. Only He can forgive our sins. Only He can heal us. Only He can change us and forge a godly soul. Only He can bring us back into His presence. And He will do all of that and much more if we but remember Him to keep His commandments. What then shall we do? We will remember Him to keep His commandments. It is the only intelligent thing to do."

- "The Lord's way is not hard. Life is hard, not the gospel. . . . Life is hard for all of us, but life is also simple. We have only two choices: We can either follow the Lord and be endowed with His power and have peace, light, strength, knowledge, confidence, love, and joy, or we can go some other way, any other way, whatever other way, and go it alone—without His support, without His power, without guidance, in darkness, turmoil, doubt, grief, and despair. And I ask, which way is easier?"

- "Get on the path and never, ever give up. You never give up. You just keep on going. You don't quit, and you will make it. There is only one way to happiness and fulfillment. Jesus Christ is the Way."

---

6. See www.bibleversestudy.com/johngospel/john14-way-truth-life.htm
7. "Way," *Online Etymology Dictionary.*
8. Lawrence E. Corbridge, "The Way," *Ensign,* Nov. 2008.

As you navigate your different "ways" during your day, remember that The Way is Jesus Christ.

"I will not leave you comfortless: I will come to you." (John 14:18)

ON ONE OCCASION THE PROPHET JOSEPH Smith was asked what made our religion unique. He replied that one of the main differences was the gift of the Holy Ghost by the laying on of hands, and that we believe in the continuing power of the Holy Ghost.[9]

The English word "comfort" means "with power." The Greek word for power is *dumanis*, from which the word "dynamite" comes. It may be fitting to say that the Comforter comforts and teaches with a power like "spiritual dynamite."[10] The Holy Spirit does not simply come to give us a hug or dutifully wipe our tears away, He gives us a dynamic power to cope with life.

Two Comforters are mentioned in scripture: the Holy Ghost (which we are learning about this week in John 14) and also the Lord Jesus Christ Himself (see John 14:16). "When any man obtains this last Comforter," the Prophet Joseph taught, "he will have the personage of Jesus Christ to attend him, or appear unto him from time to time, and even He will manifest the Father unto him."[11] Jesus Christ promised, "I will not leave you comfortless: I will come to you" (John 14:18). He offers "beauty for ashes, the oil of joy for mourning" (Isaiah 61:3).

Because Christ suffered and died and rose again for each of us, He will offer His divine power to comfort us, and He will never forget us (see Isaiah 49:16). Our Savior took upon Himself our pains, trials, and afflictions so that He can know what we feel and how to comfort us.

We also can play a similar role as we seek to comfort others. The first covenant we make with God is our baptismal covenant to mourn with those who are mourning, to comfort those who are in need of comfort, and to represent Christ in all places and at all times (see Mosiah 18:10–18). This invitation sounds much like what the Comforter does for us! As covenant sons and daughters, we indeed have incredible power, as potent as is dynamite, to bless and comfort others around us. We are here to learn how to

---

9. *Documentary History of the Church*, vol. 4, 42.
10. As Nephi taught, "When a man speaketh by the power of the Holy Ghost the power of the Holy Ghost carrieth it unto the hearts of the children of men" (2 Nephi 33:1).
11. See D&C 88:3–4; 130:3; *History of the Church* 3:381.

watch out for one another and care for and comfort one another in a powerful and profound way.

Consider someone that needs your comfort. And if you are needing comfort, pray for His *dumanis*—that dynamite-level of potent power that the Comforter can bring.

"Abide in me, and I in you." (John 15:4)

CONSIDER THE LYRICS OF THIS FAVORITE hymn:

Abide with me; 'tis eventide.
The day is past and gone;
The shadows of the evening fall;
The night is coming on.
Within my heart a welcome guest,
Within my home abide.[12]

Throughout the scriptures, the Lord invites us to *abide* in Him.[13] Abide is from the Old English *abidan* "Remain, wait for" or "to stay with someone or remain in the service of someone."[14] The Hebrew and Greek term for "abide" is *yashabh*, meaning "to dwell or to remain."[15] We might think of our modern-day term "hanging out" or "visiting."

The Lord repeatedly invites us, based on the etymology of the word "abide," to wait for Him, to stay with Him, or remain close with Him. Jesus said, "As the Father hath loved me, so have I loved you: continue ye in my love. If ye keep my commandments, ye shall abide in my love; even as I have kept my Father's commandments, and abide in his love" (John 15:9–10). To abide with the Savior means to seek to spend time within His loving arms.

Elder Jeffrey R. Holland put new light on the abide passages in John 15 when he taught that the Spanish translation of "abide" is connected to "permanence:"

"Abide in me" is an understandable and beautiful enough concept . . ., but "abide" is not a word we use much anymore. . . . In Spanish that familiar phrase is rendered *"permaneced en mi."* Like the English verb "abide," *permanecer* means "to remain, to stay," but even gringos like me can hear the

---

12. "Abide with Me; 'Tis Eventide," *Hymns*, no. 165.
13. See Joel 2:11; Mal. 3:2; Mark 6:10; Luke 9:4; John 1:32; 14:16; 1 Cor. 7:24; 1 John 2:14; 1 Nephi 11:27, D&C 35:18; 88:35.
14. "Abide," *Online Etymology Dictionary*.
15. *Strong's*, 3306.

root cognate there of "permanence." The sense of this then is "stay—but stay *forever.*" That is the call of the gospel message. Come, but come to remain. Come with conviction and endurance. Come permanently.[16]

In your busyness today or this week, look to *abide* with Him. Look for opportunities to visit with Him and enjoy His precious presence.

FOR FURTHER STUDY

- There is a fascinating meaning in the name "Judas Iscariot" in the Greek. Consider looking that up. See Christanity.com's article "Who Was Judas Iscariot?" to get started.[17]

- Elder Jeffrey R. Holland once shared at a speech at BYU that John 14:27 "Let not your heart be troubled, neither let it be afraid" is a commandment that has been broken by many faithful members. Consider reading Elder Holland's full message (see "Come unto Me," Brigham Young University fireside, 2 Mar. 1997, speeches.byu.edu)

- Look up the meanings of the words "vine" and "branch" and "fruit" from John 15 using www.biblehub.com and www.blueletterbible.org.

- Try to define "life eternal" based on John 17:3.

What other unique or insightful words did you find in your study this week?

_____

_____

_____

_____

Please share with us!
Visit www.ComeFollowMeWOW.com and
share your word discoveries and insights!

---

16. Jeffrey R. Holland, "Abide in Me," *Ensign*, May. 2004.
17. Site: www.christianity.com/wiki/people/who-was-judas-iscariot.html.

Chapter 23

Matthew 26; Mark 14; Luke 22; John 18

Don't miss these Words of the Week

"**Sacrament**" (Matthew 26:26, 28)
"**Bless**" (Matthew 26:26)
"**Kiss**" (Matthew 26:49)
"**Agony**" (Luke 22:44)
"**Abba**" (Mark 14:36)

Sacrament (Matthew 26:26–28)

THE WORD "SACRAMENT" DOES NOT APPEAR in the King James Bible, but the ordinance is found in several passages.[1] For Latter-day Saints, *sacrament* usually refers to the ordinance of partaking of bread and water in remembrance of Christ's atoning sacrifice. It is the most important meeting to attend each week.[2] The tangible tokens of the sacrament are reminders of His sacred atonement; the bread representing His body and the water representing His precious blood.

When Church members take the sacrament, they promise to take upon them the name of Christ, to always remember Him, and to keep His commandments (see Moroni 4:5). Members have a sacred moment each week to

---

1. See Matthew 26, Mark 14, Luke 22, 1 Corinthians 10–11.
2. "The ordinance of the sacrament makes the sacrament meeting the most sacred and important meeting in the Church" (see Dallin H. Oaks, "Sacrament Meeting and the Sacrament," *Ensign*, Nov. 2008, 17).

think of Christ's selfless sacrifice and how they'll use the upcoming week to access grace through Christ's Atonement.

In Roman law, the Latin term *sacramentum* was a deeply sacred oath. In particular, it was the oath taken by soldiers, especially by the newly enlisted, to be true and faithful both to their commanding general and, in the days of the Roman Republic, to the Republic itself (as represented by the Roman consul).[3] To violate the oath was desertion, dereliction of duty, and perhaps even treason, because the *sacramentum* was a covenant between the person swearing it and their god(s).

In the Church today, as from the Roman army where the term originated, the *sacrament* is administered reverently and carefully. In gospel etymology, there are two distinct uses of the word "sacrament," not just the one. One use of the word "sacrament" points to the ordinance and emblems of the bread and water presented each Sunday by Aaronic priesthood holders.[4] A second definition of "sacrament" centers in *our* sacrifice and what *we* consider to be sacred.

From Doctrine and Covenants 59:9 we read, "And that thou mayest more fully keep thyself unspotted from the world, thou shalt go to the house of prayer and offer[5] up *thy sacraments* upon my holy day." What are the sacraments that we have been commanded to offer up as we go to the house of prayer? Based on the etymology of the word "sacrament," they may be *our* sacred offerings that *we* offer to the Lord as we worship each week.

Certainly He offers us His sacred sacrament each Sunday, the physical sacrament bread and water, but He also invites each of us to examine our lives and identify a few offerings that we can bring to sacrament meeting to offer to Him.

The next time you participate in a sacrament meeting, ponder on the meaning of the word "sacrament" and what you can do to better "offer up [your] sacraments" to Him.

3. See Daniel Peterson, "The Surprising and Meaningful History Behind the Word 'Sacrament,'" *LDS Living Magazine*, 22 Aug. 2019, www.ldsliving.com.
4. The apostle Paul gave council about what to do when partaking of the sacrament in 1 Corinthians 11:27–29: "Let a man examine himself, and so let him eat of that bread, and drink of that cup." He warned, "whosoever shall eat this bread, and drink this cup of the Lord, unworthily, shall be guilty of the body and blood of the Lord."
5. Any offering is a gift to the Lord. In Old Testament times, offerings referred to sacrifices or burnt offerings. The Church today uses sacred offerings, such as fast offerings and other freewill offerings (including time, talents, and possessions), as a sign of our love and devotion to God and our fellowmen.

"Jesus took bread, and blessed it."
(Matthew 26:26–28)

IN DIFFERENT VARIETIES OF ENGLISH IN the southern states, you might hear someone say "bless their heart"; it's a phrase full of gospel goodness. Just as "bless their heart" can have meanings that range from genuine sympathy to a phrase that softens the blow of an insult, the word "bless" as used in the New Testament has a deeper and more profound meaning than supposed.

The Greek word for "bless" is *eulogēsas* and it means "to speak well of."[6] The Latin meaning of "bless" goes a bit deeper. It means "to hallow with blood; consecrate; make holy."[7] This idea can apply to any priesthood blessing or any blessing from our Father in Heaven.

It is noteworthy that we hear the word "bless" twice each week while the sacrament is being administered. As priesthood holders carefully read the prayer for the bread and then the prayer for the water, using the word "bless" each time, they are literally making these emblems holy, hallowing each through the atoning blood of Jesus Christ. In return, as members of The Church of Jesus Christ of Latter-day Saints partake of these emblems, they are inviting the Lord to make *themselves* hallowed and holy through the Atonement of Jesus Christ as well.[8]

Elder Don R. Clark of the Seventy shared an experience that helped him make the sacrament a more holy experience:

> When I was a teenager, Brother Jacobs, my teacher, asked that we write down on a card what we had thought about during the sacrament. I took my card and began to write. First on the list was a basketball game we had won the night before. And then came a date after the game, and so went my list. Far removed and certainly not in bold letters was the name of Jesus Christ.
>
> Each Sunday the card was filled out. For a young Aaronic Priesthood holder, the sacrament and sacrament meeting took on a new, expanded, and spiritual meaning. I anxiously looked forward to Sundays and to the opportunity to partake of the sacrament, as understanding the Savior's Atonement was changing me. Every

---

6. *Strong's*, 2127.
7. "Bless," *Online Etymology Dictionary*.
8. The sacrament prayers are one of very few set prayers the Lord has revealed. Because of this, each word is sacred, yet many of us often hear them without really listening to their meaning; indeed, familiarity may breed complacency; see John S. Tanner, "Reflections on the Sacrament Prayers," *Ensign*, Apr. 1986.

Sunday to this day, as I partake of the sacrament, I can see my card and review my list. Always on my list now, first of all, is the Savior of mankind.[9]

Elder Melvin J. Ballard testified, "I am a witness that there is a spirit attending the administration of the sacrament that warms the soul from head to foot; you feel the wounds of the spirit being healed, and the load being lifted."[10] Partaking of the blessed bread and water opens the door for us to achieve a new level of holiness. The sacrament bread and water literally feeds our soul because they are blessed and sanctified for this very purpose.

The next time you participate in a sacrament service, remember that the etymology for the word "bless" means "to hallow with blood or mark with blood" and "to consecrate and make holy." Allow Christ's sacrifice to consecrate your efforts and literally bless your heart.

"And forthwith he came to Jesus, and said, Hail, master; and kissed him." (Matthew 26:49)

WHEN WE KISS SOMEONE, IT MEANS something. Whether it's kissing our significant other on the lips, our child on the forehead, or our friend on the cheek, every kiss is a sign of affection and love. It's hard to imagine kissing someone we love to cause them harm.

Matthew, Mark, and Luke each relate that Judas Iscariot identified Jesus as the one the Romans should arrest by the sign of a *kiss* (Matthew 26:48; Mark 14:44; Luke 22:47). This *kiss*[11] was to be the way for the Roman soldiers to be sure they had the right man; this kiss, given in the Garden of Gethsemane, led directly to the arrest of Jesus by the Sanhedrin police force.

Many films that portray this exchange show a simple kiss on the cheek. Certainly, the kiss could have occurred in this manner. However, the Greek word for "kiss" used by the Greek writers and translators here is *kataphileo*. This type of kiss is much more than a simple kiss on the cheek. *Katafileo* means, "to kiss much, kiss again and again, kiss tenderly."[12] Lutheran theologian Johann Bengel suggests that Judas kissed Him repeatedly: "He kissed Him more than once in opposition to what He had said in the preceding

---

9. Don R. Clark, "Blessings of the Sacrament," *Ensign*, Nov. 2012, 104.

10. Melvin J. Ballard, "The Sacramental Covenant," *Improvement Era*, Oct. 1919, 1027.

11. Today, a "Judas kiss" refers to an act appearing to be an act of friendship, but ultimately brings some type of harm to the recipient.

12. *Strong's*, 2705.

verse, and did so as if from kindly feeling."[13] This term literally means Judas smothered Jesus with kisses.

Why did Judas betray Him with that type of a kiss? The scriptures are silent as to why, but the use of the word *katafileo* begs the question: why a kiss and why not just a gesture like pointing at Jesus?

One idea is that Judas was acting in complete hypocrisy. Even in this, his hour of ultimate betrayal, he wanted to appear to be loyal to Jesus, just like when he falsely accused Mary for anointing Jesus's feet with expensive perfume that could have been sold to help the poor.[14]

But why would the writers include this detail of a "smothering of kisses" and not a single kiss on the cheek? While we aren't sure, recall that this *katafileo* kiss exchange occurred immediately after Jesus suffered and bled from every pore in the Garden of Gethsemane. Luke 22:44 teaches that Jesus's "sweat was as it were great drops of blood falling down to the ground." In the light of the full moon of Passover, Judas could see Jesus clearly. He must have been able to see Jesus's clothing stained red with blood. I wonder if, upon seeing the blood-dyed garments of Jesus, Judas realized that He was indeed the Christ, for the next act of Judas was to take his own life (see Matthew 27:3–5).

When Jesus emerged from the Garden and Judas approached the bloodied Savior, was Judas overcome with emotion as he realized that Jesus had fulfilled prophecy and had suffered for all sin? Did this revelation cause Judas to kiss Jesus on the cheek over and over and over again (*katafileo*) as he was engulfed in a moment of anguish, realizing that he had just mockingly sold Jesus for a tawdry 30 pieces of silver? While we may never know how this kiss played out, there is a truth that resonates from this story: when people truly "see" Jesus and recognize that He is the Christ, they are never the same thereafter.

As President Ezra Taft Benson taught, "When you choose to follow Christ, you choose to be changed."[15] And because Judas employed a *katafileo* kiss after seeing the bloodied Jesus, we can draw an application of changing our hearts once we see Jesus through new eyes.

13. "Mathew 26:49," Bengel's Gnomon of the New Testament, *Bible Hub*, www.biblehub.comcommentaries/bengel/matthew/26.htm, accessed 27 Feb. 2020.

14. Hypocrisy is like a sickness, wanting to look good on the outside when disease rages on the inside. Because he may have sensed Judas's hypocrisy, it is possible that Peter took out his sword and cut off the ear of the arresting guard, Malchus (Luke 22:49–50).

15. Ezra Taft Benson, "Born of God," *Ensign*, Nov. 1985, 5; See also Thomas S Monson, "Be a Light to the World," Brigham Young University devotional, 1 Nov 2011.

"Being in an agony he prayed more earnestly." (Luke 22:44)

FOR A MOMENT, THINK OF THE most painful experience you have endured. Maybe it was an injury or an illness or a heart-wrenching emotional episode. Whatever the degree of pain we feel, our doctrine teaches that Jesus felt it all (see Alma 7:11–13). In times of pain or heavy—and if it feels as though nobody could possibly understand what we are feeling—we are never completely alone. Why? Jesus fully understands how we feel because of the *agony* He felt in Gethsemane.

The word "agony" was used by Luke to describe Jesus's suffering. The Greek and Latin word for "agony" is the same—*agonia,* meaning a "struggle for victory."[16] "Anguish," in contrast, means "pain or evil that has already passed." Fittingly, the word "agony" was chosen by Luke.

For Latter-day Saints, Jesus's time in Gethsemane marked the greatest moment of agony (possibly surpassing the Savior's torture on the cross—see Mark 14:33–39[17]).

Following the Last Supper, Jesus left Peter, James, and John to wait near the Garden's gate while He ventured into the Garden of Gethsemane alone to wrestle with the adversary alone. Kneeling and ultimately falling forward on His face, He cried with agony, "O my Father, if it be possible, let this cup pass from me" (Matt. 26:39). But he knew that it could not pass and that he must drink that bitter cup. It is interesting to note that the "bitter cup" is mentioned more often by the Savior than the cross in scripture when He speaks of His suffering.

A beloved sacrament hymn reads, "Although in *agony* he hung, No murmuring word escaped his tongue" (*Hymns,* no. 191). As Jesus went through agony (again, "a mental struggle for victory") while in Gethsemane, we are eternally grateful for His victory! Surely, because of what He endured in Gethsemane, we can have perfect faith in Him and His power to empathize and succor us (see Alma 7:12).

---

16. "Agony," *Online Etymology Dictionary.*

17. While the cross at Calvary was the place He bore a tremendous amount of physical pain and suffering, it seems that Gethsemane is where He may have borne the psychological trauma of taking upon Himself our sins. The handbook *True to the Faith* records, "Jesus's atoning sacrifice took place in the Garden of Gethsemane and on the cross at Calvary. In Gethsemane, He began to take upon himself the sins of the world. . . . The Savior continued to suffer for our sins when He allowed Himself to be crucified" ("Atonement of Jesus Christ," *True to the Faith* [The Church of Jesus Christ of Latter-day Saints, 2004]).

FOR FURTHER STUDY

- There is rich symbolism in what the woman did for Jesus in Matthew 26:6–13. Do some research about her actions using www.biblehub.com and www.blueletterbible.org to discover some wonderful applications.

- Matthew 26:15 mentions the price that Judas arranged for to disclose Jesus's location. There is a purpose behind that price point. Consider digging into that point of Jewish and Hebrew history using www.biblehub.com and www.blueletterbible.org.

- In Gethsemane, Mark records, "And he said, Abba, Father" (Mark 14:36). Look up the meaning of the word "abba" using www.biblehub.com and www.blueletterbible.org to learn its beautiful, personal meaning.

- We read this week of Peter's "denial" during the final hours of Jesus's life, following His arrest. Several scholars and also Church leaders have shared ideas on why Peter denied his association with Christ, based on the Greek wording of Matthew 26:34. Consider researching a few of these theories. See Eric D. Huntsman's article "The Accounts of Peter's Denial: Understanding the Texts and Motifs" on the BYU Religious Studies Center site to get started;[18] it's a long read but it's worth it.

---

18. Site: rsc.byu.edu/ministry-peter-chief-apostle/accounts-peters-denial-understanding-texts-motifs.

- Mark 14:51 records that there was a "young man" that witnessed these events. Consider researching who he was—you may be surprised! See the www.gotquestions.org article "Who was the young man who fled naked in Mark 14:51–52?" to get started.[19]

What other unique or insightful words did you find in your study this week?

_____

_____

_____

_____

_____

_____

_____

Please share with us!
Visit www.ComeFollowMeWOW.com and
share your word discoveries and insights!

---

19. Site: www.gotquestions.org/Mark-fled-naked.html.

Chapter 24

Matthew 27; Mark 15; Luke 23; John 19

Don't miss these Words of the Week

"Offend" (Mark 14:27)
"Barabbas" (Matthew 27:17)
"Scourge" (Matthew 27:26)
"It is finished" (John 19:30)

"All ye shall be offended because of me." (Mark 14:27)

EVERYBODY AT SOME POINT HAS PROBABLY been offended by another person—and probably many times. In some cases, many, many times.

The Greek word most frequently translated into the English word "offend" in the King James Version is *skandalizo.*[1] *Skandalon* means "a bent stick on which bait is fastened that an animal strikes against to spring a trap."[2] Thus "offend" came to denote a snare, or anything that one strikes against injuriously. The Hebrew word *moqesh* echoes the Greek meaning of "offend" as it means a "noose" or "snare." Meanwhile, the Latin

---

1. See Matthew 5:29, "if thy right eye offend thee"; Matthew 5:30; 11:6; 18:6, "Whoso shall offend one of these little ones"; Matthew 13:41, "all things that offend"; Luke 17:1, "It is impossible but that offenses will come," Romans 14:21; 16:17, "Mark them which cause .... offenses"; 1 Co 8:13, "if meat make my brother to offend."
2. See "Offense," *Net Bible*, classic.net.bible.org/dictionary.php?word=Offence.

offendere means "to strike against" or, more figuratively, "to commit a fault or displease."[3]

The Savior taught that in the latter days, it will be impossible for us to not hear or see offending messages (Luke 17:1). The scriptures do not deny the fact that offenses will come, but they give us tools to combat the feelings associated with offense.

At such times, our first impulse may be to react with irritation, revenge, or contention. But we can choose to react instead with charity and not be "easily provoked" (Moroni 7:45). We can turn the other cheek (see Matt. 5:38–39) and respond with patience and kindness. Psalm 119:165 reads, "Great peace have they which love Thy law; and nothing shall offend them." Some modern translations will replace the last phrase with something akin to "nothing can make them stumble."

Elder David A. Bendar taught that the only actions that we can control are our own:

> [I]t ultimately is impossible for another person to offend you or to offend me. Indeed, believing that another person offended us is fundamentally false. To be offended is a *choice* we make; . . . You and I cannot control the intentions or behavior of other people. However, we do determine how we will act. Please remember that you and I are agents endowed with moral agency, and we can choose not to be offended.[4]

We must always remember that becoming angry is a secondary feeling; when we feel offended—or misunderstood, undervalued, unappreciated (primary emotions)—we often cope with those negative sentiments with anger (a secondary emotion). In other words, we often feel negativity and try to mask it by becoming angry. When feelings of offense well up inside, our admonition as covenant keepers is to "not take the bait."

"Whom will ye that I release unto you? Barabbas, or Jesus which is called Christ?" (Matthew 27:17)

TRADITIONS ARE WONDERFUL. FROM THINGS WE do at Christmas each year to little things we do annually for a person's birthday, traditions bring excitement and the joyous and nostalgic feelings of reminiscence. According

---

3. "Offend," *Online Etymology Dictionary*.
4. David A. Bednar, "And Nothing Shall Offend Them," *Ensign*, Nov. 2006, 90–91.

to the Bible, the yearly Passover custom in Jerusalem in Jesus's time allowed the governor of Judea to release one prisoner (see Leviticus 16:8–10).

After Jesus was arrested and accused of blasphemy, the crowd was given a choice to release *Barabbas* or *Jesus* from Roman custody.[5] Barabbas had been imprisoned for committing murder (see Mark 15:7; Luke 23:19) and Jesus, ironically, was sent to earth to free people from death. In this moment, the crowd chose Barabbas to be released—and Jesus to be crucified (see Mark 15:6–15). Pilate reluctantly acquiesced to their insistence.

In a bit of New Testament irony, the Greek name Barabbas literally means "Son of the father."[6] While Christ would rescue *all* mankind, the cry from the crowd to release Barabbas was an appeal to rescue a life-taking murderer instead of the ever-life-giving Jesus (see Mark 15:7–15). Barabbas, the "son of the father" was set free while Jesus, "The Son of The Father," was condemned to crucifixion.

Elder Neal A. Maxwell of the Quorum of Twelve Apostles described irony as "the hard crust on the bread of adversity."[7]

What was this moment like for Barabbas? Put yourself in his sandals for a minute. You are condemned to die and might be executed today (literally). And then all of a sudden, when you least expect it, you are freed. As you run away from your captors, echoes of "Crucify him, crucify him!" ring out behind you. Then you see a bloodied stranger dragging a cross toward death's mountainside. It's the same cross you had imagined yourself carrying only moments earlier. And then it hits you: he's dying my death.

Jesus took away death from Barabbas. Jesus bore the guilt and shame that Barabbas deserved. Jesus gave the release and freedom to Barabbas. Just as the apostle Paul wrote, "For he hath made him to be sin for us, who knew no sin; that we might be made the righteousness of God in him" (2 Corinthians 5:21).

It's no secret that you and I are sinners. We sit in a spiritual prison, bound and waiting for the punishment we deserve. But the good news is that when we repent, Jesus offers to suffer for us (see Doctrine and Covenants 19:16–19). Jesus receives what we deserve; and we receive what He truly deserves.

---

5. The custom of releasing prisoners in Jerusalem at Passover is known as the Paschal Pardon.
6. "Barabbas : Facts & Significance," *Encyclopedia Britannica,* www.britannica.com/topic/Barabbas-biblical-figure.
7. Neal A. Maxwell, "Irony," *Ensign*, May 1989.

It is the greatest exchange in all of history. Jesus gives up His life so we, Barabbas, can have eternal life.

"When he had scourged Jesus, he delivered him to be crucified." (Matthew 27:26)

As we study the final hours of Jesus's mortal life, we might miss one of the most agonizing moments in the life of Christ: His *scourging*.

The verb "scourge" originates with the same root as "excoriate," which means "to flay" or "strip off the skin."[8] Here are some facts about scourging:[9]

Only women and Roman senators or soldiers (except in cases of desertion) were exempt.

The usual instrument was a short whip with several single or braided leather thongs of variable lengths to which small iron balls or sharp pieces of sheep bones were tied at intervals.

For scourging, the man was stripped of his clothing, and his hands were tied to an upright post. The back, buttocks, and legs were flogged either by two soldiers (lictors) or by one who alternated positions.

As the Roman soldiers repeatedly struck the victim's back with full force, the iron balls would cause deep contusions, and the leather thongs and sheep bones would cut into the skin and subcutaneous tissues.

The lacerations would tear into the underlying skeletal muscles and produce quivering ribbons of bleeding flesh.

Pain and blood loss generally set the stage for circulatory shock.

The extent of blood loss may well have determined how long the victim would survive on the cross.

As strange as this next sentence may sound, it might be true: Pilate commanded that Jesus be scourged as an act of mercy. *Scourging? As* an act of *mercy?* Possibly yes. Hoping to appease the Jews bloodthirst for Jesus's life, by ordering Jesus's scourging (and knowing that it may not lead to death) might have been an attempt to save Jesus from crucifixion. As Pilot brought the broken body of Christ in front of the angry crowd, he might have been saying, "Hasn't he had enough? I find no fault in this man. Please let this scourging be sufficient punishment!"[10]

---

8. "Scourge," *Online Etymology Dictionary*.
9. William D. Edwards, Wesley J. Gabel, and Floyd E. Hosmer, "On The Physical Death of Jesus Christ," *JAMA Network*, 255 (11): 1455–1463, 21 Mar. 1986, jamanetwork. com/journals/jama/article-abstract/403315.
10. Elder F. Whitney Clayton taught, "Pilate concluded that Jesus had done nothing that

The stamina that Christ displayed in the Garden, on the cross, and during His being scourged all show the diligence with which He fulfilled His mission. During all of the abuse and torture, He humbly submitted Himself to His Father's will. As you close your prayers or complete your ordinances in His name, consider the words of Elder Jeffrey R. Holland:

> His solitary journey brought great company for our little version of that path . . ... Trumpeted from the summit of Calvary is the truth that we will never be left alone nor unaided, even if sometimes we may feel that we are. Truly the Redeemer of us all said: "I will not leave you comfortless: [My Father and] I will come to you [and abide with you]."[11]

Christ suffered so He could comfort us.

"It is finished." (John 19:30)

ONE OF THE BEST FEELINGS IN mortality is the feeling of accomplishment. Checking important things off of a list brings satisfaction and fulfillment. But nothing quite compares to when the Savior declared on the cross, "It is finished" (John 19:30).

The phrase "It is finished" is the English translation of the Greek word *Tetelestai*, which was the last word to escape Jesus's mouth before He died on the cross of Calvary. *Tetelestai* comes from the Greek verb *teleo*, which means "to bring to an end" or "to accomplish."[12]

It's the word a climber would use after ascending a difficult mountain after days of climbing. It's the word for when a student turns in their final copy of a thesis. It's the word for when a family submits their final payment on their home mortgage. And it's the word used when a runner crosses the finish line of their first triathlon.

Tetelestai goes much deeper than "Phew, I survived!" It means "I accomplished exactly what I had determined to do." In fact, *tetelestai* is not past tense, which looks back to an event and says, "This happened," or future

---

merited crucifixion. He ordered that Jesus be scourged, a form of extreme but normally not-fatal physical punishment. Perhaps Pilate hoped that by thus torturing and humiliating the Savior, he would persuade the leaders of the Jews that Jesus had been taught a terribly painful lesson and been made a public example. Perhaps he hoped to awaken some sense of mercy in them. Thus, following the scourging, Pilate ordered that Jesus be brought into public view" ("Rooted in Christ," *Ensign*, Aug. 2016).

11. Jeffrey R. Holland, "None Were with Him," *Ensign*, May 2009.
12. *Strong's*, 5055.

tense, which looks forward and says, "This will happen." It is in the perfect tense, which means, "It happened—and it is still in effect today;" it's an action which was completed in the past with results continuing into the present.

Elder Tad R. Callister's *The Infinite Atonement* describes what exactly Christ paid for in the moment He finished His mortal mission on the cross:

> What weight is thrown on the scales of pain when calculating the hurt of innumerable patients in countless hospitals? Now, add to that the loneliness of the elderly who are forgotten in the rest homes of society, desperately yearning for a card, a visit, a call—just some recognition from the outside world.
>
> Keep on adding the hurt of hungry children, the suffering caused by famine, drought, and pestilence. Pile on the heartache of parents who tearfully plead on a daily basis for a wayward son or daughter to come back home. Factor in the trauma of every divorce and the tragedy of every abortion.
>
> Add the remorse that comes with each child lost in the dawn of life, each spouse taken in the prime of marriage. Compound that with the misery of overflowing prisons, bulging halfway houses and institutions for the mentally disadvantaged. Multiply all this by century after century of history, and creation after creation without end. Such is but an awful glimpse of the Savior's load. Who can bear such a burden or scale such a mountain as this? No one, absolutely no one, save Jesus Christ, the Redeemer of us all.[13]

The moment that Christ died on the cross is arguably the most sublime moment in all of eternity. This moment inspires reverence and eternal awe. Consider taking time today to ponder on Christ's eternal payment finished on Calvary.

FOR FURTHER STUDY

- Much occurred following the death of Judas Iscariot and the field in which he took his life (see Matthew 27:5–10). Consider a study of the aftermath of that field following his passing. See the Wikipedia article "Akeldama" (en.wikipedia.org/wiki/Akeldama) to get started.

---

13. Tad R. Callister, *The Infinite Atonement* (Deseret Book, 2000), 105.

- As Jesus hung on the cross, why did He choose John as His mother's caretaker? (see John 19:25–27). Of all disciples, why John? Think about John's nature and the answer will reveal a simple principle of love between a son and his mother. See the www.gotquestions.org article "Why did Jesus entrust Mary to the apostle John instead of to His brothers?" (www.gotquestions.org/Jesus-Mary-John.html) to get started.

- There are wonderful conversations throughout recent history about "It is finished" being translated as "Paid in full." Search those terms and see what is being said. See the www.gotquestions.org article "What did Jesus mean when He said, 'It is finished'?" (www.gotquestions.org/it-is-finished.html) to get started.

- Consider the meaning of the word "blasphemy" (see Mark 14:64) using www.biblehub.com and www.blueletterbible.org. Why is it ironic that Jesus was accused of this particular crime?

What other unique or insightful words did you find in your study this week?

_____

_____

_____

_____

_____

Please share with us!
Visit www.ComeFollowMeWOW.com and
share your word discoveries and insights!

Chapter 25

Matthew 28; Mark 16; Luke 24; John 20–21

Don't miss these Words of the Week

"Resurrection" (Matthew 28)
"Simon Peter" (John 21:16)
"Love" (John 21:15)

"He is risen from the dead." (Matthew 27:64)

EASTER TIME IS A BEAUTIFUL DAY of reflection for Christians around the world. Because Christ rose from the dead, Christianity is centered and rooted around Christ's resurrection. The word "resurrection" occurs over 40 times in the New Testament.

Resurrection means that a dead body can be and will be restored to full activity with the spirit and the body permanently reunited and perfected.

The Greek word for resurrection is *anástasis* and combines *aná* ("up, again") and *hístēmi* ("to stand"); it literally means "to stand up again."[1]

The English word "resurrection" comes from two Latin terms —*re*, meaning "again"; and *surgere*, "to rise." A root word for "resurrection" is *surge*, meaning to "rise with power."[2]

Can you imagine the moment Jesus died? While we think of the horrific scenes on the cross as Jesus was tortured to death, we often

---

1. *Strong's*, 386.
2. "Resurrection," *Online Etymology Dictionary*.

overlook Matthew's insertion of beautiful reunions that occurred after Jesus's resurrection:

> The graves were opened; and many bodies of the saints which slept arose, And came out of the graves after his resurrection, and went into the holy city, and appeared unto many. (Matthew 27:52–53)

Picture parents reuniting with children and children who died in infancy reunited with loving parents. Picture resurrected grandparents knocking on the doors of their grandchildren and reuniting with them and husbands resurrecting and sharing a warm embrace with their sweethearts. This day must have been one of the most tender and sweet days in history.

What does Jesus's *resurgence* through *resurrection* mean for us today? It means there is hope! All will die, but not all will experience the second death. This is because of Jesus. Because of Him, bodies can be reclaimed and reframed, and families can be together forever. We can "stand up" with our loved ones again, all thanks to the Atonement of Jesus Christ.

"Simon, son of Jonas, lovest thou me?" (John 21:16)

EARLIER THIS YEAR, WE LEARNED THAT a man named Simon was invited to follow Christ and to be a "fisher of men" (see Matthew 4:19). Later, Jesus changed Simon's name to Peter (see John 1:42). Recall that the name Peter in Greek means "rock" (*Petros*).[3] In fact, you can probably hear the root cognate and reflect the word *petrify*.

Don't forget that Peter's given name was *Simon,* a Greek transliteration of the Hebrew name Shimon, possibly taken from one of the sons of Jacob (see Genesis 29:33). Simon means "to hear" or "he that hears."[4]

Following the resurrection, as Christ appeared on the shore and then conversed with His disciples following a fishing trip, the name/title that Jesus used with His lead apostle was Simon, not Peter. While we don't know exactly why He used Peter's given name, given the rebuke given, we wonder if the Master was reminding Peter of his original name: Simon ("he that hears"). In this moment on the shore, Peter didn't appear to be acting as "the rock" that Jesus had asked him to be. Using some literary license, Elder Jeffrey R. Holland helps us picture what this exchange may have sounded like:[5]

---

3. See footnote a on "rock" in Matthew 16:18.
4. Leah named her son "hearer" because YHWH "heard" her.
5. Jeffrey R. Holland, "The First Great Commandment," *Ensign,* Nov. 2012, 84.

"Then Peter, why are you here? Why are we back on this same shore, by these same nets, having this same conversation? Wasn't it obvious then and isn't it obvious now that if I want fish, I can get fish? What I need, Peter, are disciples—and I need them forever. I need someone to feed my sheep and save my lambs. . . . I am asking you to leave all this and to go teach and testify, labor and serve loyally until the day in which they will do to you exactly what they did to me."

Now where are we in this account? Well, given the meaning of Simon's name—are we trying to hear the voice of God in our lives? Are we active listeners when it comes to what God is saying? Seek to be both a Peter (a rock-solid disciple) and also a Simon (one that seeks to hear the voice of the Lord). Be a modern-day Simon Peter.

"After these things Jesus shewed himself again to the disciples at the sea of Tiberias." (John 21:1)

THE ENGLISH WORD "DISCIPLE" COMES FROM the Latin word *discipulus* which means "student or follower."[6] The Greek word for disciple, *mathētais*, is similarly, "a learner or pupil."[7] What a blessing we have in our lives to be led by a First Presidency, living disciples of Christ. These three men, each called of God, are led by Him—and we are in good hands as we are led by them.

Anciently, Peter, James, and John were the key leaders in the New Testament Church. It is assumed that they functioned in a similar First Presidency role in their day. He promised Peter, "I will give unto thee the keys of the kingdom of heaven" (Matthew 16:19.) And all three accompanied Jesus to a "high mountain apart," where Moses and Elias appeared in glory before them (see Matthew 17:1–3).

There are some fascinating symbols that point our minds to the possibility of Peter, James, and John being a symbol of the Godhead:

---

6. "Disciple," *Online Etymology Dictionary.*
7. *Strong's,* 3101.

Apostle	Characteristic
Peter	Peter has a resurrected body,[8] as does God the Father (D&C 130:20–21).
	His original name, Simon, means "He that hears."[9] God hears us and our prayers.[10]
	He denies Christ (Matt. 26:33–35, 58, 69–75) just before Jesus cries, "My God, my God, why hast thou forsaken me?"
	Jesus's first appearance after Mary is to Peter (Luke 24:32–34) just before His ascension to His father.
James	James has a resurrected body, as does Jesus Christ.
	The name James means "Supplanter"; Jesus was the ultimate "supplanter" as He suffered in our stead.
	Jesus's only recorded brother's name was James; Jesus is our elder Brother.
	James was beheaded; when the disciples entered Jesus's tomb, the head napkin was separated from the body linens (see John 20:6–7).
	James is not invited to prepare the Passover meal (Luke 22:7–8); James does not come to the tomb (John 20:2–4); James is not mentioned at the sea following the resurrection (John 21:6–8). In each of these moments, Jesus was represented symbolically by the roasted lamb at the Passover, the resurrected being from the tomb, and at the sea of Galilee.

8. See Bible Dictionary, "Peter."

9. "Peter," *Bible Study Tools*, www.biblestudytools.com/dictionary/peter/.

10. "25 Powerful Bible Scriptures on God Hearing Our Prayers," *ConnectUS*, 7 Spet. 2020, connectusfund.org.

John	John does not have a resurrected body, nor does the Holy Ghost
	John was a brother to James; the Holy Ghost is a spirit brother to Jesus Christ.
	John never shares his name; we do not know the name of the Holy Ghost.
	John's nickname is "The Revelator," one of the key roles of the Holy Ghost.
	John's mission is to tarry on the earth until the Second Coming (John 21:20–24); the Holy Ghost's mission is to testify of Christ in preparation for the Second Coming.
	John was banished (Revelation 1:9) and the Holy Ghost is being banished and rejected in our later day.

"Lovest thou me more than these?" (John 21:15)

SEVEN OF JESUS'S DISCIPLES SPENT THE night fishing in the Sea of Galilee and had not caught anything. From the beach, the resurrected Jesus beckoned to try the right side of the boat; they did and struggled to haul in the net full of fish (see John 21:1–6).

After serving them a meal, Jesus turned to Simon Peter and said: "Simon son of John, do you love me more than these?" To what was Jesus referring? Peter was quite attached to fishing. So it seems that Jesus was asking him where his true affection lay: in following Jesus, or in finding fish. In answer, Peter declared his love for Jesus (see John 21:15)

There are so many terms for *love* in the beautiful Greek language, and much is lost in the translation of the John 21 passage from Greek into English about Peter's love. In this passage, there are three different words that are translated into English from Greek as the word "love": *eros* (romantic love); *phileo* (brotherly love); and *agapao* (pure love).[11]

Peter counted 153 large fish from his haul according to John 21:11. Maybe it was the time Peter took to count his 153 fish instead of running to the Lord at the small fire that caused Jesus's litany of questions; but looking at John 21 using the original Greek terms, we read more deeply into their conversation of love and loyalty:

---

11. See "Powerful Greek Words for Love & Their Meanings," *Your Dictionary*, reference. yourdictionary.com/other-languages/powerful-greek-words-love-their-meanings, accessed 10 Oct. 2021.

So when they had dined, Jesus saith to Simon Peter, Simon, son of Jonas, lovest [*agapao*] thou me more than these? He saith unto him, Yea, Lord; thou knowest that I love [*phileo*] thee.

He saith to him again the second time, Simon, son of Jonas, lovest [*agapeo*] thou me? He saith unto him, Yea, Lord; thou knowest that I love [*phileo*] thee.

Peter is replying that he loves Jesus as a friend, so the Savior asks ask Peter if he truly loves him as a friend:

He saith unto him the third time, Simon, son of Jonas, lovest [*phileo*] thou me? Peter was grieved because he said unto him the third time, Lovest [*phileo*] thou me? And he said unto him, Lord, thou knowest all things; thou knowest that I love [*phileo*] thee.

Elder Jeffrey R. Holland asked us to picture ourselves being asked the same question in a future day:

And if at such a moment we can stammer out, "Yea, Lord, thou knowest that I love thee," then He may remind us that the crowning characteristic of love is always loyalty.[12]

Do you have any "fishes" in your life (maybe even 153 of them!) that might confuse your love and loyalty for Jesus? As you seek to remove the distractions from your life, your love and your loyalty will be on full display and you can, through word and deed, declare, "Yeah Lord, thou knowest that I love thee!"

---

12. Jeffrey R. Holland, "The First Great Commandment," *Ensign*, Nov. 2012, 84.

FOR FURTHER STUDY

- How long was Jesus in the tomb of Joseph of Arimathea? The "easy" answer is "3 days" but through a deeper look you can determine the number of hours He laid in rest. See the "Chronology" section of the Wikipedia article "Crucifixion of Jesus" (en.wikipedia.org/wiki/Crucifixion_of_Jesus) to get started.

- Consider researching Mary Magdalene's name and what it means—and what it implies. See the Wikipedia articles "Mary (name)" (en.wikipedia.org/wiki/Mary_(name)) and "Mary Magdalane" (en.wikipedia.org/wiki/Mary_Magdalene) to get started.

- The word "Peace" is used three time in Matthew 28 following the resurrection of Jesus Christ. Do a study of that word using www.biblehub.com and www.blueletterbible.org and consider how it applies to the resurrection of Christ.

What other unique or insightful words did you find in your study this week?

_____

_____

_____

_____

_____

_____

_____

Please share with us!
Visit www.ComeFollowMeWOW.com and
share your word discoveries and insights!

Chapter 26

Acts 1-5

Don't miss these Words of the Week

"Infallible proofs" (Acts 1:3)
"Sincere—Singleness of Heart" (Acts 2:46-47)
"Ninth Hour" (Acts 3:1)
"Honesty" (Acts 5:1-11)

"[Jesus] shewed himself alive after his passion by many infallible proofs." (Acts 1:3)

TODAY, APPROXIMATELY ONE-THIRD OF THE EARTH gathers to celebrate Christ's resurrection at Easter; nearly half the world celebrates His birth at Christmas. Despite the opposition to the early church following the death of Jesus Christ, the small group of early believers were remarkably able to help the early church survive, despite having very limited access to scriptures or manuals.

What was the cause of that early church's survival? The answer is found in the book of Acts: the reality of Jesus's death and resurrection (after all, if someone can predict his death and also predict his being raised from the dead—and then have the power to accomplish it—would not that convince many of his power?).

The King James Bible reads that Christ taught for forty days following His marvelous resurrection, using "infallible proofs" (Acts 1:3). The English word "infallible" is taken from Latin's *infallibilis* meaning, "exempt from

159

error in judgment."[1] Looking at the Greek text from which the verse was translated, the word translated as "infallible proofs" is *tekmēriois*, meaning literally "to show by sure signs or tokens."[2] It appears that Jesus was using physical signs or tangible tokens to witness His resurrection from the dead.

Upon hearing of Christ's post-mortal appearance among His fellow Apostles, John wrote that Thomas immediately questioned the veracity of Christ's resurrection. Having likely witnessed the crucifixion personally, Thomas expressed his skepticism:

> Except I shall see in his hands the print of the nails, and put my finger into the print of the nails, and thrust my hand into his side, I will not believe. (John 20:25)

A week later, as John's account stated, Christ miraculously appeared in a home where the disciples had gathered. There, Jesus asks Thomas to come forward. Offering His hand and sides as tangible evidence (an *infallible proof*) of His resurrection, Christ invited Thomas to feel His wounds:

> Reach hither thy finger, and behold my hands; and reach hither thy hand, and thrust it into my side: and be not faithless, but believing. (John 20:27)

By requesting that Thomas feel the tangible wounds of the crucifixion, the proof of Christ's resurrection was made evident to the doubting disciple. Jesus persuaded Thomas and others to believe through the sure signs and tokens by which he "shewed himself alive after his passion" (Acts 1:3).

It is difficult to discern from the Gospels how much these early disciples understood before the crucifixion (after all, it appears that the first thing Peter wanted to do after the crucifixion was go fishing). It wasn't until this group of early followers saw the empty tomb that they believed unequivocally. It appears that it may not have been Jesus's teaching, suffering, or death that converted this special group. His disciples reengaged because they saw Him and felt Him and knew firsthand that He was indeed a resurrected being.

From this point on, these men (and, presumably, women) preached and taught in the streets boldly and with unabashed confidence. Interestingly, the record shows that they weren't too focused on preaching and teaching His sermons or His parables: they preached and taught almost exclusively about His resurrection.

---

1. "Infalliable," *Online Etymology Dictionary.*
2. *Strong's,* 5039.

Tens of thousands of people believe the testimony of Peter, James, John, Matthew, Mark, Andrew, and many others as they testified of the risen Lord; many ultimately gave their lives because they were so convinced of the miraculous resurrection and what they saw firsthand.

So how did the early church survive? How did the gospel continue? Why does one third of the earth's population call Him Lord? It is because of His resurrection. It was because of the *"infallible proofs"* that Jesus showed them following His death and resurrection.

"And they . . . did eat their meat with gladness and singleness of heart, Praising God." (Acts 2:46–47)

WE LOVE *SINCERITY*. WE CRAVE IT. It makes us love and trust on a much deeper level. And yet it's a virtue that seems to elude us in our day of quick responses and fast-paced living.

Thanks to modern lexicons, we have learned that the phrase *"singleness of heart"* found in the King James translation of Acts 2:46 is most likely better rendered as "sincere hearts." In fact, the New Inspired Version of the Bible reads:

> Every day they continued to meet together in the temple courts. They broke bread in their homes and ate together with glad and *sincere* hearts, praising God and enjoying the favor of all the people. (Acts 2:46, NIV)

The Greek word used here, *aphelotēti*, meaning "simplicity and sincerity,"[3] reiterates this interpretation.

A common unsubstantiated etymology for the word "sincere" proposes that it is derived from the Latin *sine* ("without") and cera ("wax"). According to one account, dishonest sculptors in Rome or Greece would cover flaws in their work with wax to deceive the viewer; therefore, a sculpture "without wax" (sincere) would mean honesty in its perfection.[4] The Oxford English Dictionary states, however, that "there is no probability in the old explanation from sine cera 'without wax.'"

Many scripture passages teach the principle of *sincerity*:

King Benjamin taught his people to "ask in *sincerity* of heart that he [God] would forgive you" (Mosiah 4:10)

---

3. *Strong's*, 858.
4. "Sincerity," *Online Etymology Dictionary*.

Alma later testified that he who "repenteth in the *sincerity* of his heart," shall be forgiven (Mosiah 26:29)

Zenos taught that God "didst hear me because of . . . my *sincerity*" (Alma 33:11)

The prophet Helaman shared that "the Lord is merciful unto all who will, in the *sincerity* of their hearts, call upon his holy name" (Helaman 3:27)

Moroni assures readers that "if ye shall ask with a *sincere* heart, . . . [God] will manifest the truth of it unto you" (Moroni 10:4)

Looking at the true etymology of the word "sincere," we learn that it means "one growth" or "not mixed." This definition points our minds to passages like Matthew 6:22, "The light of the body is the eye: if therefore thine eye be single, thy whole body shall be full of light," and John 17:21 "That they all may be one; as thou, Father, art in me, and I in thee, that they also may be one in us."

Sincerity and striving to be one with God are companion principles. Those with sincere faith and sincere hearts are genuine and authentic in the way they live their faith. Sincerity means honesty of intention and freedom from hypocrisy for those who strive to unite their hearts with God.

When we allow our Savior to strip pretense away, we discover our authentic selves and then begin to serve others with "glad and sincere hearts" (Acts 2:46) and become closer to being one with Christ.

In our world of instant messages and superficial speech, seek for the virtue of sincerity. As you text and talk and instant message with sincerity, you will see yourself grow in a singleness of heart.

"Now Peter and John went up into the temple at the ninth hour of prayer." (Acts 3:1)

IN SCRIPTURE, HOURS AND DAYS OFTEN offer us deeper significance than just ways to tell time: six days of work and a day of rest, three days from crucifixion to resurrection. *"Ninth hour"* holds a meaning that might otherwise be lost to us without a dive into the word. The English word "noon" has roots in the Latin *nona hora* which means "ninth hour of daylight." By Roman and ecclesiastical reckoning (which began at midnight), noon (or *nona hora*—ninth hour) began at 3 p.m.

It was at this *noon* time (or ninth hour) that Elijah prayed to God against the prophets of Baal on Mount Carmel to prove that Elijah was a prophet for the true God of Israel (see 1 Kings 18:36–39). This was also the hour of Ezra's great prayer (Ezra 9:5). When Daniel uttered his own prayer of faith, it was "about the time of the evening oblation" (Daniel 9:21). In the New Testament, the first Gentile convert was Cornelius, who was praying "about the ninth hour of the day" (Acts 10:3) when he received a visit from an angel. The Apostles respected these customary hours of prayer according to Acts 3:1: "Now Peter and John went up into the temple at the ninth hour of prayer."

Even more importantly, it was also at this *noon* time (or ninth hour) that Matthew records, "And about the ninth hour Jesus cried out with a loud voice, saying, Eli, Eli, lama sabachthani? that is to say, My God, my God, why hast thou forsaken me?" (Matthew 27:46). While on the cross, Jesus offered His prayer at exactly the ninth hour of the day, keeping in custom with the Jewish traditional prayer time; at the apex of His suffering, it was fitting that He should utter this desolate cry at the ninth hour (the time of the regular evening prayer and sacrifice).

We know that prayer is meaningful at any hour of the day; our loving Father really just wants to hear from us. And while the Jews' observance of these hours of prayer was not a saving practice, they did feel added strength by scheduling their petitions at certain points of the day. We rejoice in latter-day scripture that invites us to pray morning, midday, and evening (see Alma 34:21).

We can use the symbol of the ninth hour when we notice the clock strike three as a reminder to communicate with our loving God.

"[Ananias] kept back part of the price, his wife also being privy to it." (Acts 5:2)

HONESTY EMBRACES MANY MEANINGS, SUCH AS integrity, sincerity, according to the truth, just, virtuous, purity of life, moral character, and uprightness in mutual dealings (in contrast, a *lie*—the opposite of honesty—is any form of communication with the *intent* to deceive[5]). And at the root of the word honest we have *honor*. Simply put, those who are honest in their dealings bring honor to themselves and their families.[6] We all want truthfulness and sincerity from others and it's important that we develop those attributes ourselves as well.

In contrast, Ananias and his wife, Sapphira, were dishonest with the Lord. They held back a portion of money they had consecrated to the

---

5. See Marvin J. Ashton, "There Is No Harm," *Ensign*, May 1982, 9–11.
6. We read in Proverbs 20:7: "The just man walketh in his integrity: his children are blessed after him."

Church, and when Peter confronted them, they both fell to the ground and died (see Acts 5:1–11). A dramatic death like Ananias and Sapphira's isn't in our future based on our honesty, but dishonesty can chip away at our spiritual strength and *could* contribute to a spiritual death.

Karl G. Maeser taught about the meaning of honor with an illustrative example:

> My young friends, I have been asked what I mean by word of honor. I will tell you. Place me behind prison walls—walls of stone ever so high, ever so thick, reaching ever so far into the ground—there is a possibility that in some way or another I may be able to escape, but stand me on that floor and draw a chalk line around me and have me give my word of honor never to cross it. Can I get out of that circle? No, never! I'd die first![7]

Think of a few ways that honesty is manifested today. As parents, are we honest with our children? Have you fallen into the trap of telling little white lies to protect yourself? Husbands and wives, are you faithful and true to your spouse and living a transparent life? Children, are you being honest at school? (When you forget to complete your homework, do you turn in a blank assignment or do you choose to borrow the completed assignment from a friend and copy their work, turning it in—dishonestly—as your own work?).

So many lives, families, and marriages have been ruined and dishonored because of a disregard for honesty. As one author wrote, "Sin has many tools, but a lie is the handle which fits them all."[8]

Lies and even seemingly small mistruths drive a wedge between us and God that only becomes harder to repair as time goes on. Strive to be honest in your actions, words, and deeds, and you will honor both your life and your loving Heavenly Father.

---

7. In Alma P. Burton, *Karl G. Maeser: Mormon Educator* (Deseret Book, 1953), 71; see also Dallin H. Oaks, "Be Honest in All Behavior," Brigham Young University devotional, 30 Jan. 1973, speeches.byu.edu.

8. O. W. Holmes, in Burton Stevenson, *The Home Book of Quotations* (Dodd, Mead & Co, 1934), 1111.

FOR FURTHER STUDY

- In Acts 1:9, the apostles "looked stedfastly" toward heaven after the ascension of Jesus. Consider looking up the Greek word for 'stedfastly' using www.biblehub.com and www.blueletterbible.org and see what principles of application you find.

- Casting lots (Acts 1:26) seems like an unusual way to choose a new apostle. Consider researching this phrase using www.biblehub.com and www.blueletterbible.org and compare its meaning to how apostles are called today.

- As the Holy Ghost is poured out in Acts 2, a great supplemental study would be to list the characteristics of the Holy Ghost, or compare the roles of the Spirit and the gift of the Holy Ghost. See the *True to the Faith* entry "Holy Ghost" (www.churchofjesuschrist.org) to get started.

- Consider researching the word "pricked" as found in Acts 2:37 using www.biblehub.com and www.blueletterbible.org and look for an application to understanding the Holy Ghost.

- When the lame man was healed in Acts 3, it says that the disciples were "greatly wondering." Consider looking up what that phrase meant and what their true reaction may have been based on the original Greek, using www.biblehub.com and www.blueletterbible.org.

- Consider looking up the meaning of Gamaliel's name in Acts 5 and see how it relates to his story in Acts 5:34–41. See the Wikipedia article "Gamaliel (disambiguation)" (en.wikipedia.org/wiki/Gamaliel_(disambiguation)) to get started.

What other unique or insightful words did you find in your study this week?

_____

_____

_____

_____

_____

_____

Please share with us!
Visit www.ComeFollowMeWOW.com and
share your word discoveries and insights!

Chapter 27

Acts 6-9

Don't miss these Words of the Week

"Martyr" (Acts 7:59-60)
"Right" (Acts 8:21
"Resist" (Acts 7:51)

"And they stoned Stephen . . ." (Acts 7:59)

THE SCRIPTURES LIST HUNDREDS AND HUNDREDS of believers as *martyrs* ("martyr" in Greek means "witness"[1]) for the gospel. From valiant individuals like Stephen, Abel, Zaccarias, Abinadi, and Joseph Smith, to groups of stalwarts like the Anti-Nephi-Lehi's who wanted to suffer death rather than fight (see Alma 24) and the early Christians who were stoned, cut in half, and killed with swords (see Hebrews 11:37–40). Each of these "obtained a good report through faith" (Hebrews 11:39). Sadly, many Christians are killed in our day because of their testimony of Jesus.

As we study the lives of these martyrs, we may feel a surge of feelings and have many thoughts run through our minds, pinned with memories for each person and each story. Just as when we lose loved ones and we try to honor them by sharing their stories and the lessons they taught with friends and family, we would do well to remember the history behind the word "martyr."

---

1. "Martyr," *Online Etymology Dictionary.*

"Martyr" came from Latin's *memor* and means simply, "to be mindful."[2] Keeping the legacy and teachings of those who have died for their faith close to our hearts is a key to being mindful of their sacrifice. There is nothing better than hearing an inspiring story, a beautiful life lesson, or a heartfelt memory about someone we love, and when that person died for the cause of Christianity, their stories can create a legacy of belief as we valiantly share them.

Brooke Anderson, a writer for Church Magazines, has a unique way to remember those who have passed. She, like most of us, grew up celebrating Easter with colored eggs, Easter baskets, and candy. But one Easter morning while living away from home, she decided to put herself in the shoes of the women who came to Christ's tomb by going to the cemetery near her house just before sunrise. She wrote:

> As I read the words of the angel to the women, "He is not here: for he is risen" (Matthew 28:6), a sweet spirit settled over me, and I saw what a truly remarkable and wonderful gift His sacrifice was. I looked at all the gravestones and realized the immense magnitude of His gift. Each gravestone represented a person for whom Christ had suffered—and who, because of His suffering, would rise again.
>
> I thought of my deceased grandfather, who had been paralyzed for most of his life, and the joy I would feel not only to see him again but also to see him standing and running and to feel his arms around me. I thought of all the tears that had been shed here for loved ones lost and of the joy that would come with future tender reunions. I thought of Mary Magdalene seeing her resurrected Lord (see John 20:15–17)—of the wonder, the joy, the hope of His glorious gift.
>
> Now each Easter morning, before I eat my bunny-shaped chocolates and boiled Easter eggs, I walk to the cemetery and sit and read the story of His Resurrection.[3]

Without action, memories of our loved ones (and the valiant *martyrs* of our faith) tend to fade. Consider pondering a few ways to keep those who have passed on close to your mind and heart. Study the lives of those amazing martyrs and let their legacies live on, not only in your hearts and mind, but in the hearts of others who may not have had the pleasure of knowing their remarkable stories from the scriptures.

---

2. Ibid.
3. Brooke Anderson, "My Not-So-Traditional Easter Tradition," *Ensign*, Apr. 2020.

"Ye do always resist the Holy Ghost." (Acts 7:51)

SOME THINGS IN OUR WORLD FEEL *irresistible*. From the decadence of chocolate to just eating a single potato chip or even trying to resist looking at a police car's lights when they are illuminated (they are practically irresistible to look at!).

In Acts 7:51, as Stephen is being stoned to death, he mentions that his assassins "do always *resist* the Holy Ghost" (Acts 7:51). The only time that the Greek word *antipiptete* for "resist" or "oppose"[4] is used in the New Testament is in Acts 7. While we aren't fully sure of the nature of the group that killed the disciple Stephen, we can derive that they must have been a spiritually insensitive group based on Stephen's assessment of their lack of inclination toward things of the Spirit.

The Latin word *resistere* means "to stand against" (from *re-* "against" and *sistere* "stand."[5]) Using this definition, those stoning Stephen were "standing against" the Holy Ghost. What a dangerous stance to take!

Rather than resisting the Holy Ghost, children of God should seek to resist temptation. When we are faced with temptation, we should recall the Savior's example of resisting: "He suffered temptations but gave no heed unto them."[6]

Each week as we worthily partake of the sacrament, we are promised that we may always have His Spirit to be with us (see D&C 20:77). To invite (rather than resist) the Holy Ghost, the standard is clear:

> If something we think, see, hear, or do distances us from the Holy Ghost, then we should stop thinking, seeing, hearing, or doing that thing. If that which is intended to entertain, for example, alienates us from the Holy Spirit, then certainly that type of entertainment is not for us.[7]

Look to do things that invite the Spirit into your life. Never resist the Holy Ghost.

---

4. *Strong's*, 496.
5. "Resist," *Online Etymology Dictionary*.
6. D&C 20:22; see also Hebrews 4:15.
7. David A. Bednar, "That We May Always Have His Spirit to Be with Us," *Ensign*, May 2006, 30.

"Thy heart is not right in the sight of God." (Acts 8:21)

TAKE OUT A SHEET OF PAPER and try to draw a straight line without using a ruler. Even the most practiced artist will never be able to draw a perfectly straight line without some help. The line may be straight enough, but without a ruler or some other tool, it will never be perfectly *right*.

When we think about the word "right," most Latter-day Saints are familiar with the words to the hymn "Choose the Right" penned by Joseph L. Townsend (1849–1942) and it's music as written by Henry A. Tuckett (1852–1918):

> Choose the right when a choice is placed before you.
> In the right the Holy Spirit guides;
> And its light is forever shining o'er you,
> When in the right your heart confides.
> Choose the right! Choose the right!
> Let wisdom mark the way before.
> In its light, choose the right!
> And God will bless you evermore.

"Right" can mean something good or correct (as in right versus wrong) and right can also mean "appropriate" (as in, "do what is right").

The Greek word for "right" used in Acts 8:21, in speaking of Saul's wayward ways leading up to his remarkable conversion is *eutheia,* which means "straight"[8] with the Latin word *rectus* holding the same meaning.[9] Think of that: Saul's heart was not *straight*—it was misaligned and needed correction from heaven.

There's another layer of right that has wonderful applications. Have you noticed that the root word for "righteous" is "right"? That is, to determine righteousness, one only needs to examine their heart to see if it is right or straight (aligned) with God's commandments. Righteous means aligned (with God); wickedness (or from Acts 8:21, "not right"), simply means not aligned with God.

The next time you sing beloved Hymn no. 239, ponder on your heart and see if it's aligned with God. If there's a misalignment, seek to more fully "choose the right."

---

8. *Strong's,* 2117.
9. "Right," *Online Etymology Dictionary.*

FOR FURTHER STUDY

- When Stephen is stoned, the response of his assassins is remarkable: "When they heard these things, they were cut to the heart, and they gnashed on him with their teeth" (Acts 7:54). Research the Greek meaning of "cut to the heart" and "gnash" using www.biblehub.com and www.blueletterbible.org and see what principles are there for modern-day application.

- The word "lamentation" is found in Acts 8:2. It has a rich meaning. Consider researching its etymology using www.etymonline.com.

- Several names are found in Acts 8–9; consider looking up each one using *Hitchcock's Bible Names Dictionary* (www.biblestudytools.com/dictionaries/hitchcocks-bible-names/) and see how each name's meaning relates to the truths Stephen is teaching.

What other unique or insightful words did you find in your study this week?

_____

_____

_____

_____

_____

Please share with us!
Visit www.ComeFollowMeWOW.com and
share your word discoveries and insights!

Chapter 28

Acts 10–15

Don't miss these Words of the Week

"**Christian**" (Acts 11:26)
"**Easter**" (Acts 12:4)
"**Ward**" (Acts 12:12)

"The disciples were called Christians." (Acts 11:26)

WHEN WE ARE BAPTIZED, WE TAKE upon ourselves the name of Christ. How different our world might be if we called each other by that new name-title: Christ! Can you imagine greeting your friends with His name? Do you think you would act differently if people greeted you with a title associated with Jesus's name?

Most scholars agree that the formation of the word "Christian" is Latin in origin. *Christianus* from *Christus* (Christ). When the Latin *Christianus* or the Greek *Christianos* terms were formed from the word *Christ*, it linked the name of Christ to His followers—those who belong to, or are devoted to, Christ.[1] When the disciple Barnabas left Antioch to search for Saul, he found that the disciples were called *Christians* in Antioch (see Acts 11:26). Some records show that in the earliest days of the church, "Christian" was a term of ridicule

---

1. Other terms were used for "Christians" before that title was given: "Jews," "disciples," "believers," "the Lord's disciples," those "who belonged to the Way" (Acts 1:15; 2:44; 6:1; 9:1, 2).

the pagans gave to the followers of Christ.[2] Over time, Jesus's followers came to love and adopt this name, wearing it as a badge of honor.[3]

The suffix *-ianus* in *Christianus* is fascinating. It was a common practice of the 1st century for identifying people by attaching suffixes with the name of their leader[4] (for example, Pompeiani, Augustiani, Ceasariani, Herodianoi (see Matthew 22:16; Mark 3:6; 12:13).[5] These suffixes can be translated as "little" or "a miniature version of" or "belonging to" (much like a slave is owned by their master). Thus *Christianus* may have been used to call people "Little Christ" (much like the term "Mormon" was used to describe people who followed the principles in the Book of Mormon).

We, as members of The Church of Jesus Christ of Latter-day Saints, are Christians. We worship God the Eternal Father in the name of Jesus Christ. Joseph Smith declared this when he said:

> The fundamental principles of our religion is the testimony of the apostles and prophets concerning Jesus Christ, . . . "that he died, was buried, and rose again the third day, and ascended up into heaven;" and all other things are only appendages to these, which pertain to our religion.[6]

And if you take the meaning of "Christ" ("anointed one") and apply it to "Christian," those who follow Jesus are literally "little anointed ones." Think of that principle! As a follower and believer, your life has been anointed for greatness!

"After Easter to bring him forth to the people." (Acts 12:4)

That Easter morn, a grave that burst
Proclaimed to man that "Last and First"
Had ris'n again

2. Christine Trevett, *Christian Women and the Time of the Apostolic Fathers* (Cardiff: University of Wales Press, 2006).
3. Kenneth S. Wuest, *Wuest's Word Studies from the Greek New Testament*, vol. 1 (William B. Eerdmans Publishing Co., 1973).
4. Elias J. Bickerman, "The Name of Christians," *The Harvard Theological Review* (April 1949), 42 (2).
5. D. N. Freedman, *The Anchor Bible Dictionary* (New York: Doubleday, 1992).
6. Joseph Smith, *Teachings of Presidents of the Church: Joseph Smith* (The Church of Jesus Christ of Latter-day Saints, 2007), 49.

And conquered pain.
("That Easter Morn," *Hymns*, no. 198)

EASTER IS THE CHRISTIAN HOLIDAY CELEBRATING the Resurrection of Jesus Christ. Almost all neighboring languages use a variant of the Latin *pascha* to name this holiday, referring to the *paschal—the passover.*[7] It is a celebration not only of the Resurrection of Jesus Christ and His victory over death and hell, but also of the universal resurrection of all:

> But now is Christ risen from the dead, and become the firstfruits of them that slept. . . . For as in Adam all die, even so in Christ shall all be made alive" (1 Corinthians 15:20, 22; see also Alma 11:42–45).[8]

The term "Easter" is first found in Acts 12:4 as Paul is recounting one of his many missions along the Mediterranean rim.

The prophet Malachi wrote that "The Sun of righteousness [shall] arise with healing in his wings" (Malachi 4:2). According to Kent Jackson, the term "Sun of righteousness" is an allusion to the Lord and His resurrection (because of the use of the capital letter in the word "Sun").[9] The "Sun of Righteousness" reflects his *solar* role, the vernal equinox truly represents the resurrection of the "Light of the World"—the *sun*—bringing with it life and birth found in the Spring.

Hence, each "East"er, Christians remind themselves that Jesus will return from the East (see Joseph Smith—Matthew 1:26), just as the sun rises. This symbol of the sun rising after a period of "death" during the night can point our minds to Jesus and His great victory over death, which we celebrate most poignantly on Easter.

"Many were gathered together praying." (Acts 12:12)

HAVE YOU EVER WONDERED WHY WE call congregations of The Church of Jesus Christ of Latter-day Saints *wards*? Each member in the world,

---

7. "Easter," *Online Etymology Dictioanry.*
8. For Latter-day Saints, Easter is a celebration of the promise of eternal life through Christ. They share the conviction of Job: "For I know that my redeemer liveth, and that he shall stand at the latter day upon the earth: and though after my skin worms destroy this body, yet in my flesh shall I see God" (Job 19:25–26).
9. Kent P. Jackson, "Teaching From the Words of the Prophets," *Studies in Scripture: Book of Mormon*, Part 2 (Deseret Book, 1999), 201.

regardless of location, belongs to a ward (or branch) where they attend worship services near their home, but why the word "ward"?

In the New Testament, we read of early Saints gathering together in groups to strengthen each other, pray, and fast. While it is unlikely that they used the term "ward," it is comforting to know that there was a structure to their meetings.

The term "ward" originally referred to political boundaries in the United States. The use of the term "ward" first began in Nauvoo, Illinois, in the 1840s where bishops were assigned duties and responsibility over specific ward boundaries and over time individual congregations were defined by these boundaries, using the word "ward."[10]

"Ward" comes from the Old English word *weard* and it means "to guard, protect, watch out for."[11] Supporting this word's root, Sister Virginia H. Pearce, who served in the Young Women's General Presidency, taught that wards are like families:

> Learning in groups is so important that Heavenly Father planned for us to be born into a group—the most basic, most hallowed, and most powerful group on earth: the family. . . . Wards are not designed to replace the family unit, but to support the family and its righteous teachings. A ward is another place where there is enough commitment and energy to form a sort of "safety net" family for each of us when our families cannot or do not provide all of the teaching and growing experiences we need to return to Heavenly Father.[12]

Elder Robert D. Hales added that we are all part of a ward family:

> We are all members of a ward family in the community of Saints, where we may all contribute with our individual gifts and talents. . . . [We] should focus our concern on caring for the needs of others. Reaching out and helping somebody who is in need can dispel feelings of loneliness and imperfection—and replace them with feelings of hope, love, and encouragement.[13]

---

10. See "Ward," *Encyclopedia of Mormonism* (New York: Macmillan, 1992), 1541–1543.
11. "Ward," *Online Etymology Dictionary*.
12. Virginia H. Pearce, "Ward and Branch Families: Part of Heavenly Father's Plan for Us," *Ensign*, Nov. 1993, 79.
13. Robert D. Hales, "Belonging to a Ward Family," *Ensign*, Mar. 1996, 15.

As we, like the New Testament Saints, "gather together" in our ward family, we should watch out for one another, encourage one another, and find ways to help one another. Rather than asking, "What is in it for me if I choose to attend Sacrament meeting or a ward activity," we should instead seek to be a blessing to others as we attend. We may be the key to touching the life of someone who is quietly struggling. Indeed, a ward is a wonderful place where individuals and families can guard, protect, and watch out for one another.

FOR FURTHER STUDY

- Cornelius is described as being "devout" in Acts 10:2. Look up the word "devout" using www.biblehub.com and www.blueletterbible. org and see what it says about Cornelius.

- The practice of circumcision is discussed in Acts 11. Consider research-ing the meaning of that word and how it relates to covenant keeping. See the www.bibleodyssey.org article "Circumcision" (www.bibleod-yssey.org/en/passages/main-articles/circumcision) to get started).

- Acts 12:1 mentions the word "vex" to describe the assault on early believers. Consider looking up the meaning of this word using www. biblehub.com and www.blueletterbible.org to better understand the mindset of early Christians during this time in history.

- The act of shaking off the dust from one's feet was used anciently (see Acts 13:51)—and also in our early modern-day church. To find out what it means or what it implies, spend some time looking up its use over time. See the www.gotquestions.org article "What does it mean to shake the dust off your feet?" (www.gotquestions.org/shake-dust-off-feet.html) to get started.

- In Acts 15:1–12, we read of a council in Jerusalem. Consider review-ing our modern-day process of Church councils and the blessings that come from them. Compare and contrast with the council in Acts 15. See the Gospel Topics entry "Church Councils" on topics. churchofjesuschrist.org to get started.

What other unique or insightful words did you find in your study this week?

_____

_____

_____

_____

_____

_____

Please share with us!
Visit www.ComeFollowMeWOW.com and
share your word discoveries and insights!

Chapter 29

Acts 16–21

Don't miss these Words of the Week

"Noble" (Acts 17:11)
"Stirred" (Acts 17:16)
"Apostasy" (Acts 20:30)

"These were more noble." (Acts 17:11)

When we read the word "noble," we might think immediately of kings and queens, world leaders and valiant warriors. How often do we think of those around us who serve with a willing heart and learn with an open mind? This section may open your eyes to a new definition of *nobility*. We read in Acts 17:11 that believers living in the city of Berea were described as noble. Why? Because "they received the word with all readiness of mind, and searched the scriptures daily, whether those things were so" (Acts 17:11).

The well-known definition of "noble" most likely comes from both the Latin and Greek roots. From Latin, we learn that "noble" means to be "well-known; excellent, superior, splendid; of superior birth; having lofty character, having high moral qualities."[1] In Greek, the word *eugenesteroi* is used for "noble minded" and describes one who is "well-born, high in rank, generous, or noble in nature."[2] Based on its etymology, those who possess the

---

1. "Noble," *Online Etymology Dictionary.*
2. *Strong's,* 2104.

attribute of being noble show unique personal qualities and are renowned for possessing high moral principles and ideals.

These definitions of root words, along with the description of the people of Berea, help us to better understand Abraham's vision described in the Pearl of Great Price. We read that Abraham saw "the intelligences that were organized before the world was; and among all these there were many of the noble and great ones" (Abraham 3:22). Authors Michelle Wilson and Dennis Gaunt reflected on this vision by writing:[3]

> Whenever I think of this moment, I imagine the following exchange taking place between God and Abraham:
>
> "These are my noble and great ones, Abraham," God says. "What do you think?"
>
> "They are wonderful," Abraham says. "Truly wonderful people."
>
> "But Abraham," God says with a smile, "Don't you see? Don't you recognize that man right there, with the dark hair? That's *you*, Abraham! You are one of my noble and great ones. I chose you before you were even born" (see Abraham 3:23).

Those who were seen as being noble, both in the pre-earth life and those who "received the word with all readiness of mind, and searched the scriptures daily" have *a lofty character and high moral qualities* and were chosen to come to earth to fulfill specific missions. The Bible Dictionary speaks to this doctrine:

> An "election of grace" spoken of in D&C 84:98–102 and Rom. 11:1–5 has reference to one's situation in mortality; that is, being born at a time, at a place, and in circumstances where one will come in favorable contact with the gospel. This election took place in the premortal existence.[4]

Jesus Christ taught this doctrine of divine nobility in 3 Nephi 20:25:

> And behold, ye are the children of the prophets; and ye are of the house of Israel; and ye are of the covenant which the Father made with your fathers, saying unto Abraham: And in thy seed shall all the kindreds of the earth be blessed.

---

3. Michelle Wilson and Dennis Gaunt, "Youth Theme Insight: What It Means to Be a 'Noble and Great One,'" *LDS Living*, 19 July 2019.

4. Bible Dictionary, "Election," www.churchofjesuschrist.org/study/scriptures/bd.

By reading passages like the one found in Acts 17, and others like Abraham 3, we learn so much about the noble and great ones, in other words, we learn so much about *ourselves*. Through these verses, we can be reminded of who we are and who we have always been—and who we might become. Remember that you stood by our Savior faithfully (*nobly*) despite Satanic opposition in the pre-earth life. You were known and chosen in the pre-earth life and were reserved for this day and age because you had *a lofty character and high moral qualities*. By virtue of being born into the house of Israel, you are noble—with potential to inherit all our Father has. You are the daughter or son of a King!

"His spirit was stirred in him." (Acts 17:16)

Most of us have had feelings of being unsettled—or *stirred*. Whether it was through a prompting, a premonition, or a time we saw something unsettling or disturbing, most know the feeling of being stirred that Paul described in Acts 17:16.

As Paul approached Athens, "his spirit was stirred in him, when he saw the city wholly given to idolatry" (Acts 17:16). This word in Greek (*parōxyneto*) means, "To arouse anger, provoke, irritate."[5] In other words, Paul was upset—and on the borders of anger.

The English word "stir" is derived from a number of Hebrew and Greek verbs, each of which has its different shade of meaning. In Psalms 39:2, the Hebrew translation of "stir" is *akhar*, "to be troubled." In Song of Solomon 2:7, the verb used for "stir" is *ur*, "to awake or disturb." In 2 Timothy 1:6, the Greek work for "stir" is *anazopureo*, relating to the resuscitation of a flame. In Acts 21:27, the Greek word used for "stir" is *sugcheo* and means "to commingle," vividly portraying the confusion and tumult that resulted when Paul was arrested in the temple.

The original Greek word for "stir" is *storan*, which means "to scatter, destroy, disturb." It has been noted that the words "stir" and "storm" probably share the same root. Elder Lynn G. Robbins said that "stir" "sounds like a recipe for disaster":

> Put tempers on medium heat, stir in a few choice words, and bring to a boil; continue stirring until thick; cool off; let feelings chill for several days; serve cold; lots of leftovers.[6]

5. *Strong's*, 3947.
6. Lynn G. Robbins, "Agency and Anger," *Ensign*, May 1998, 80.

The Savior said that the devil can stir our hearts to anger:

> For verily, verily I say unto you, he that hath the spirit of contention is not of me, but is of the devil, who is the father of contention, and he stirreth up the hearts of men to contend with anger, one with another. (3 Nephi 11:29)

Using the Savior's teaching to the Nephites, we see that being "stirred up" is a secondary emotion. That is, we don't feel anger initially. Anger is often called a secondary emotion because we tend to resort to anger in order to protect ourselves from or cover up other feelings. We almost always feel a feeling of vulnerability first before we get angry; feelings such as being afraid, attacked, offended, disrespected, forced, trapped, or pressured all precede the secondary emotion of anger.

So what is Satan's methodology when it comes to anger? According to the Savior, the devil loves to stir us up when we feel the initial feelings of being afraid, attacked, offended, disrespected, forced, trapped, or pressured so that we are tempted to contend and retaliate with anger.

By way of application, when we, as Christians, feel the initial stirrings (the "storm" of emotion, similar to what Paul felt in Acts 17 upon witnessing pure wickedness), our responsibility is to manage those feelings and not let them drift into the arena of anger and contention. When we feel "stirred up," this is a defining moment for us: will we act and respond with Christlike attributes—or will we allow our stirring up to transfer into anger and contention?

"Men [shall] arise, speaking perverse things, to draw away disciples after them." (Acts 20:30)

MANY PEOPLE STRUGGLE WITH COMMITMENT. ALL big, life-changing decisions carry some fear, even for the most committed among us. What if things don't work out? What if something bad happens? What if I feel stuck? We may all ask ourselves these questions, but if we dwell on them, doubt can creep in and lead us away from what we know and stop our God-given decision-making powers in their tracks.

Early on, following the crucifixion of Jesus, Paul began warning the people that an *apostasy* would occur. When people or groups turn from the gospel, they are in a state of apostasy. Apostasies have occurred several times throughout history. One example is the Great Apostasy, which happened shortly after the Savior's death when men corrupted the principles of the gospel. In consequence of this turning away, the Lord withdrew the authority of the priesthood from the earth. During the Great Apostasy, people were without divine direction from living prophets. Many other churches were established, parts of the scriptures were corrupted or lost, and no priesthood ordinances were performed.

The English word "apostasy" is from the Greek and Latin words *apostasia* or *apostasis*, which mean an "abandonment of what one has professed," "to revolt," or "*to defect*"; it literally means, "to stand" (*apo*) and "*away*" (*stenai*).[7] That is, when people *apo-stenai* (when they don't take a stand for things or when they're *standoff-ish* about convictions), the Lord withholds blessings.

We now live in a time when the gospel of Jesus Christ has been restored. Although there will not be another general apostasy from the truth, we must each guard against personal apostasy by keeping our covenants and fully committing to the gospel. We must realize we are at war. The war began before the world was and will continue. As we demonstrate our devotion to God by our daily acts of righteousness, we (and He) will know where we stand. In our world where many see evil as good and good as evil, and we must take a *stand* for good.

Consider ways that you can take a stand for truth and righteousness today, and avoid the *apo-stenai* that leads to person apostasy.

---

7. "Apostasy," *Online Etymology Dictionary.*

FOR FURTHER STUDY

- There is great symbolism and a bit of etymology with colors. Acts 16:14 mentions the color purple and it is significant. Take some time to do a deep dive into the symbolism of colors. See the www.biblestudytools.com commentary on Acts 16:14 to get started.[8]

- In Acts 19:12, a handkerchief is mentioned and was associated with healings. A similar account is found in modern Church history as well with a red silk handkerchief that belonged to the Prophet Joseph. Consider looking into this story. See "A Day of God's Power" on www.churchofjesuschrist.org to get started.[9]

- In Acts 21:8, Phillip is called an "evangelist." Consider looking up this work and study its meaning in Greek using www.biblehub.com and www.blueletterbible.org.

What other unique or insightful words did you find in your study this week?

_____

_____

_____

_____

_____

Please share with us!
Visit www.ComeFollowMeWOW.com and
share your word discoveries and insights!

---

8. Site: www.biblestudytools.com/commentaries/gills-exposition-of-the-bible/acts -16-14.html.
9. Site: history.churchofjesuschrist.org/content/museum/ museum-treasure-a-day-of-gods-power?lang=eng.

Chapter 30

Acts 22-28

Don't miss these Words of the Week

"**Profane**" (Acts 24:6)
"**Courage**" (Acts 28:15)
"**Wax Gross**" (Acts 28:27)

"Who also hath gone about to profane the temple: whom we took, and would have judged according to our law." (Acts 24:6)

Our world is sprinkled with evidence of *profanity*. From language used in entertainment to websites containing profane messages, it's tough to avoid this impurity.

As you probably know, *profanity* is disrespect, vulgarity, or behavior that shows contempt for sacred things, including the irreverent use of the name of any member of the Godhead. The Greek translation here uses the word *bebēlōsai* meaning "to desecrate."[1] Certainly, all Christians should always use the names of Heavenly Father, Jesus Christ, and the Holy Ghost with reverence. Profanity and vulgarity (including gestures and jokes) are offensive to the Lord and to others. As President Joseph Fielding Smith once taught, "Profanity is filthiness . . . Filthiness in any form is degrading and soul-destroying and should be avoided."[2]

---

1. *Strong's,* 953.
2. Joseph Fielding Smith, *Doctrines of Salvation* (Salt Lake City: Bookcraft, 1956), 1:13;

Because the root word for "profane" (*profano*) means, "not admitted into the temple with the initiates," and quite literally "out in front of the temple" (*pro* "in front of" + *fano* "temple"),[3] a principle of temple preparation and temple worship stemming from good, clean speech is easy to extract.

The Lord admonished, "Therefore, strengthen your brethren in all your conversation, in all your prayers, in all your exhortations, and in all your doings" (D&C 108:7). Our language should be used to enlighten, edify, lift, motivate, elevate, build, uplift, and inspire.

Standards for Youth teaches that our language reflects who we are:

> How you communicate should reflect who you are as a son or daughter of God. Clean and intelligent language is evidence of a bright and wholesome mind. Good language that uplifts, encourages, and compliments others invites the Spirit to be with you. Our words, like our deeds, should be filled with faith, hope, and charity.[4]

As you prepare to enter or re-enter the temple, keep this principle in mind: profanity should not be found among those that have been to the temple or those preparing to enter therein. If you've found yourself dabbling in the arena of profanity, consider making goals to overcome so you are better prepared to make and keep sacred temple covenants.

"He thanked God, and took courage." (Acts 28:15)

TODAY, *COURAGE* IS MORE SYNONYMOUS WITH being *heroic* or *brave*. While these are important characteristics and bravery and heroics are needed and applauded, the original meaning of the word "courage" has great value.

The root of the English word "courage" is *cor* or *kerd*,[5] the Latin word for "heart."[6] Courage once was derived to mean, "to speak from one's heart."

Gospel Topics, under "Profanity," teaches that, "Foul language is both degrading and harmful to the spirit. We should not let others influence us to use foul language. Instead, we should use clean language that uplifts and edifies others, and we should choose friends who use good language."

3. See "profane," *Online Etymology Dictionary.*
4. Standards for Youth, "Language," www.churchofjesuschrist.org.
5. "Courage," *Online Etymology Dictionary.*
6. The root *cor* or *kerd* is found in many other words that describe actions associated with the heart: accord; cardiac; cardio; core; cordial; credible; credit. Each of these words speak to the heart of human behavior. Being of "one accord" requires an individual surrender for the greater good; "cardiac" and "cardio" speak to the heart organ. "Core" points directly to the center of beings, our heart. Being "cordial" and "credible" and having "credit" each speak to having a pure heart with pure desires.

The Greek word used here is *tharsos* meaning "confidence or boldness."[7] Indeed, courage originally meant more about being *vulnerable* than about performing brave deeds.

Several scriptural passages speak about courage and point us to the fact that courage originates with the heart and culminates in speaking or acting in truth with true bravery:

- Be strong and of a good *courage* (Deut. 31:6; Josh. 1:6; 23:6–8; 1 Chr. 22:13; 28:20).
- Be thou strong and very *courageous* (Josh. 1:7; 23:6–8).
- Deal *courageously*, and the Lord shall be with the good (2 Chr. 19:11).
- He thanked God, and took *courage* (Acts 28:15).
- His heart began to take *courage* (Alma 15:4).
- [They were] exceedingly valiant for courage (Alma 53:20) . . . never had I seen so great courage (Alma 56:45).[8]

Speaking on a principle of courage, Elder Lynn G. Robbins once said that we must choose a single master to serve:

> When people try to *save face* with men, they can unwittingly *lose face* with God. Thinking one can please God and at the same time condone the disobedience of men isn't neutrality but duplicity, or being *two-faced* or trying to "serve two masters."[9]

It takes courage to speak from the heart, and the badge of honor for demonstrating courage is given when we bravely express heartfelt feelings. As we overcome the fear of men and courageously speak from the heart, mutual trust and respect will grow. Whether it is the courage of a missionary speaking to a disobedient companion about inappropriate behavior, or a wife courageously speaking with her husband about the way she feels when she is mistreated, or even the courage it takes to speak from the heart about the gospel with a colleague or boss, speaking from the heart is a true measure of Christian courage.

---

7. *Strong's*, 2294.
8. Topical Guide, "Courage, Courageous," www.churchofjesuschrist.org.
9. Lynn G. Robbins, "Which Way Do You Face?" *Ensign*, Nov. 2014, 10.

"For the heart of this people is waxed gross." (Acts 28:27)

AT TWO DIFFERENT TIMES IN THE King James Bible, the heart of the people are described as having *waxed gross,10* a perfect way to describe the collective heart of many in the first century AD. The ESV Bible reads, "For this people's heart has grown dull" and the NIV Bible reads, "For this people's heart has become calloused." The Book of Mormon sheds more light on the use of the word "gross" as well. Those in the city of Ammonihah are described as people who "wax more gross in iniquities" (Alma 8:28). In modern revelation, the Lord described the conditions of the world as having "gross darkness [covers] the minds of the people" (D&C 112:23).

The Oxford English Dictionary defines the word "gross" as being "overfed, bloated with excess, unwholesomely or repulsively fat or corpulent." The Greek word for "gross" (*epachynthē*) means "to thicken; to become stupid, dull, unfeeling.11* In almost every instance of the word "gross," a reference to the heart or mind is used.

Why are the heart and mind referenced when describing people that wax gross? Because they are a synonym for one's spiritual condition.[12] We describe people as being "big-hearted" or "goodhearted" or having a "heart of gold."[13] A heart that has *waxed gross* represents an inflexible person that is unwilling to receive direction; those with hardened, *gross* (thickened and calloused) hearts are typically insensitive to the gentle stirrings of the Holy Ghost.

Throughout the Book of Mormon, there are many examples of softening hearts. In Mosiah 21, when the people of Limhi are in bondage, the Lord "began to soften the hearts of the Lamanites" (Mosiah 21:15). In Alma 24 when the Anti-Nephi-Lehis were converted, they thanked God "that he has given us a portion of his Spirit to soften our hearts" (Alma 24:8). In 1 Nephi 7, "the Lord did soften the heart of Ishmael."

---

10. Each time that it is used, once by Jesus Christ and once by the Apostle Paul, they make it plain that they are making reference to Isaiah 6:10, "Make the heart of this people fat, and make their ears heavy, and shut their eyes."

11. *Strong's*, 3975.

12. The Lamanites in Mosiah 23 did not choose to soften their hearts or have their hearts softened; Ishmael did not choose to have his heart softened; Laman and Lemuel did not choose to soften their hearts; yet hardening a heart appears to be a choice: King Noah chose to harden his heart, as did Zeezrom, along with the people in 1 Nephi 17:30.

13. Marvin J Ashton, "The Measure of our Heart," *Ensign*, Oct. 1988.

Those with soft, supple hearts use their agency to initiate a change of heart through the Atonement of Jesus Christ.[14]

FOR FURTHER STUDY

- Gamalalel has a rich history in ancient Jerusalem (Acts 22:3). Consider a study of his life and history (and the meaning of his name). See the www.gotquestions.org article "Who was Gamaliel in the Bible?" to get started.

- The Church is referred to as a "sect" in Acts 28:22. Consider looking up what that word means using www.biblehub.com and www.blueletterbible.org.

- Acts 27:14 speaks of "a tempestuous wind, called Euroclydon." The meaning of these words shed light on this mission that Paul was on, so consider looking up their etymology. See the www.abarim-publications.com article "Euroclydon meaning" to get started.

What other unique or insightful words did you find in your study this week?

_____

_____

_____

_____

_____

Please share with us!
Visit www.ComeFollowMeWOW.com and
share your word discoveries and insights!

---

14. Paul, one who we may safely describe as having a heart that had waxed gross as he was torturing Christians, has a moment of softening: "Immediately there fell from his eyes as it had been scales: and he received sight forthwith, and arose, and was baptized" (Acts 9:18).

Chapter 31

Romans 1-6

Don't miss these Words of the Week

"**Saint**" (Romans 1:7-8)
"**Ashamed**" (Romans 1:16)
"**Virtue**" (Romans 1:24-27)
"**Justified**" (Romans 3:24)
"**Atonement**" (Romans 5:11)

"Beloved of God, called to be saints." (Romans 1:7)

MANY OF US KNOW SOMEONE WE love who hasn't stepped inside a chapel in years. Some because they have been offended and others because they just don't feel like they are "worthy" to associate with others who appear to be the definition of what a "Saint" is.

The Greek word for "saints" used in Romans 1:7 is *hagiois*. It simply means "set apart by (or for) God."[1] It also connotes "holy" and "sacred."

Nelson Mandela was imprisoned for almost three decades for his role in the antiapartheid struggle, but he remarkably forgave those who had imprisoned him. Deflecting praise for his saintly approach to his plight, said, "I'm no saint—that is, unless you think a saint is a sinner who keeps on trying."[2] What a definition of *saint* that is!

---

1. *Strong's* 40.
2. See Nelson Mandela's address at Rice University's Baker Institute on Oct. 26, 1999, bakerinstitute.org/events/1221. He was likely paraphrasing the well-known statement attributed to Robert Louis Stevenson: "The saints are the sinners who keep on trying."

Adding even more richness to what it means to be a saint, President Dieter F. Uchtdorf pointed out:

> The Church is not an automobile showroom—a place to put ourselves on display so that others can admire our spirituality, capacity, or prosperity. It is more like a service center, where vehicles in need of repair come for maintenance and rehabilitation.[3]

The Lord can (and will) change our desires and our hearts so that we can become better saints. We will ultimately see mighty changes. The next time you meet someone who feels that they're just not keeping "enough" of the commandments to associate with "saints," consider looking them lovingly in the eyes and saying, "Awesome! Guess what? The Church is for sinners as much as it is for 'saints'!" And that's what being a "saint" is all about.

"I am not ashamed of the gospel of Christ." (Romans 1:16)

THERE MAY HAVE BEEN MOMENTS IN your life where you shied away from speaking up against wrongs being said about the Savior or the gospel. You may have avoided confrontation when you might have been more bold. The verse found in Romans 1:16 may echo in our minds: "I am not ashamed of the gospel of Christ" (Romans 1:16).

But what does the word "ashamed" mean?

The Greek word for "ashamed" used here by Paul is *epaischynomai* which simply means, "feeling of guilt or disgrace; confusion; disgrace, dishonor."[4] The Old English word for "shame," *scamu*, is defined in nearly identical terms as the Greek with the addition of "a loss of esteem or reputation."[5] Interestingly, the root for the word ashamed is not completely clear; the best guess is that this is from *skem*, which means "to cover" (think back to Adam and Eve feeling ashamed when they saw their nakedness in Genesis 3:7).

One element of our baptismal covenant that reverberates with Paul's message of being "not ashamed" is "to stand as witnesses of God at all times and in all things, and in all places that [we] may be in" (see Mosiah 18:9). As

---

Over the years many have expressed similar sentiments. For instance, Confucius is credited with saying, "Our greatest glory lies not in never falling but in getting up every time we fall."

3. Dieter F. Uchtdorf, "On Being Genuine," *Ensign*, May 2015, 83.

4. *Strong's*, 1870.

5. "Shame," *Online Etymology Dictionary*.

Christians, we may at times feel nervous, uncomfortable—or even unpopular—as we defend or articulate our beliefs. In those moments, remember the words of President Thomas S. Monson:

> We will all face fear, experience ridicule, and meet opposition. Let us—all of us—have the courage to defy the consensus, the courage to stand for principle. Courage, not compromise, brings the smile of God's approval.[6]

As you live your life, look for small ways to live a life that is unashamed. Even when you feel *naked* and *not covered* in those moments of opposition, stand tall and seek to never be ashamed of the gospel of Jesus Christ knowing that you are "clothed with purity, yea, even with the robe of righteousness" (see 2 Nephi 9:14).

"Uncleanness through the lusts of their own hearts, to dishonour their own bodies between themselves." (Romans 1:24)

CHASTITY AND VIRTUE—ESSENTIAL TOPICS IN THE Church and society—are often tough to articulate to children and youth. Many in Paul's day were overtaken by the world and were found having "uncleanness through the lusts of their own hearts, to dishonour their own bodies between themselves" (Romans 1:24).

The word "virtue" (meaning modesty and morality in conduct) is from the Latin *virtutem,* meaning "high character; valor, bravery, courage (in war); excellence, worth." Sometimes we instinctively associate virtue with chastity or women, but it actually was derived from *vir* which means "man" (what an amazing image to picture *virtue* as being *manly*!). In both Latin and Greek, virtue means *"strength"* or *"power."*[7]

Keeping the covenants of virtue and chastity puts us in a position of power. Sadly, those in Rome during Paul's ministry were lacking these Christlike attributes.

Each time you choose to live a life of virtue—whether it's dressing modestly or staying away from impure things in life—you have greater access to God's strength and power, all through your obedience to the principle of virtue.

---

6. Thomas S. Monson, "Be Strong and of a Good Courage," *Ensign,* May 2014, 69.
7. "Virtue," *Online Etymology Dictionary.*

"Being justified freely by his grace through the redemption that is in Christ Jesus." (Romans 3:24)

WHEN WE WANT TO BETTER UNDERSTAND the differences between the words "sanctification" and "justification," it's important for us to recognize just what happens when we sin. We've been taught that "no unclean thing can dwell with God" (1 Nephi 10:21) and when we disobey God's commandments, we are unclean. When we repent and are cleansed through Christ's Atonement, we have been *sanctified*. When we sin, we are also breaking a divine law, which requires a punishment. But again, because of Christ's Atonement, we are pardoned, or *justified*, through repentance. Throughout the book of Romans, we read several messages from the apostle Paul about justification and sanctification.[8]

As you study the words *justification* and *sanctification* this week, keep in mind these truths:

Justification	Sanctification
An event	A process
We become guiltless	We become spotless
We return to the path	We begin progressing along the path
We've repented	We are reborn
We are free from the taint of sin	We are free from sin's tyranny
The inner vessel has been cleansed	We are now filling the inner vessel
We have had a true change of mind	We truly have had a change of heart
We now experience a change of behavior	We now experience a change of nature

---

8. Here's a way to understand both. As we know, sin is both polluting—and it's criminal. That is, sin dirties us—and it also puts us in a position to restore a broken law. To overcome the dirtiness that sin brings, cleansing is needed. To overcome the breaking of the law, a punishment is required. Once we have been cleansed, we are pronounced cleaned, or sanctified. And once a criminal pays his dues to society, he or she is considered pardoned, or justified.

"We also joy in God through our Lord Jesus Christ, by whom we have received the atonement." (Romans 5:11)

THOUGH IT STANDS AT THE CORE of all we believe, the word "atonement" can be found in only one passage of Biblical scripture: Romans 5:10–11. The additional translations for the word to describe Christ's atoning sacrifice can offer so much to our gospel study. President Russell M. Nelson wrote, "Rich meaning is found in study of the word *atonement* in the Semitic languages of Old Testament times. . . . I weep for joy when I contemplate the significance of it all."[9]

Everywhere else in the New Testament the same Greek word is translated as "reconciliation" rather than "atonement."[10] When the Biblical scriptures speak of *atonement,* it is always with the words "reconciliation," "redemption," or "release."[11] Of the redemptive nature of the Atonement of Jesus Christ, Hugh Nibley wrote:

> It was the custom for one fleeing for his life in the desert to seek protection in the tent of a great sheik, crying out, *"Ana dakhiluka,"* meaning "I am thy suppliant," whereupon the host would place the hem of his robe over the guest's shoulder and declare him under his protection. In one instance in the Book of Mormon we [read] . . . "O Lord, wilt thou encircle me around in the robe of thy righteousness! O Lord, wilt thou make a way for mine escape before mine enemies!" (2 Nephi 4:33.) In reply, according to the ancient custom, the Master would then place the hem of his robe protectively over the kneeling man's shoulder (*kafata*). This puts him under the Lord's protection from all enemies. They embrace in a close hug, as Arab chiefs still do; the Lord makes a place for him (see Alma 5:24) and invites him to sit down beside him—they are at-one.[12]

In the English language, *atonement* is a compound of three words: at-one-ment, suggesting that a person is *at one* with God. We owe the creation

---

9. Russell M. Nelson, "The Atonement," *Ensign,* Nov. 1996, 34.
10. "Romans 5:11," *Bible Hub,* www.biblehub.com.
11. The word "atonement" appears 35 times in the Book of Mormon and 127 times in the Old Testament. 122 of the biblical uses occur in the books of Exodus, Leviticus, and Numbers, describing temple rites on the Day of Atonement (see H. W. Nibley, "The meaning of the Atonement," in *Approaching Zion,* edited by Don E. Norton. The Collected Works of Hugh Nibley 9 [Salt Lake City: Deseret Book, 1989], 566).
12. Hugh W. Nibley, "The Atonement of Jesus Christ, Part 1," *Ensign,* July 1990.

of the term "atonement" to William Tyndale. In his 1526 translation of the New Testament, he gave an English translation of Romans 5:10–11 (with modern spelling):

> For if when we were enemies, we were reconciled to God by the death of his Son: much more, seeing we are reconciled, we shall be preserved by his life. Not only so, but we also joy in God by the means of our Lord Jesus Christ, by whom we have received this atonement.

In writing about the Atonement of Jesus Christ, Charles H. Gabriel penned:

> I stand all amazed at the love Jesus offers me,
> Confused at the grace that so fully he proffers me.
> I tremble to know that for me he was crucified,
> That for me, a sinner, he suffered, He bled and died.
> Oh, it is wonderful that he should care for me Enough to die for me!
> Oh, it is wonderful, wonderful to me![13]

The Atonement is truly a wonderful gift that shows God's care for us.

---

13. "I Stand All Amazed," *Hymns*, no. 193.

FOR FURTHER STUDY

- In Romans 1:1, Paul uses the phrase "gospel of God." We are more familiar with the term "Gospel of Jesus Christ." Consider the implications of the term "gospel of God" and applications for us today.

- Romans 1:27 speaks of lust, which has a rich etymology. Consider a study of lust's word origin using www.etymonline.com.

- Romans 1:29–31 lists several words about chastity that we don't use much in our day. Consider a study of several of them using www.biblehub.com and www.blueletterbible.org, looking for modern-day applications of each definition.

- Romans 5:3–5 mentions Paul's tribulations. Look up the Greek meaning of the word "tribulation" using www.biblehub.com and www.blueletterbible.org and look for personal applications.

What other unique or insightful words did you find in your study this week?

_____

_____

_____

_____

_____

_____

Please share with us!
Visit www.ComeFollowMeWOW.com and
share your word discoveries and insights!

Chapter 32

Romans 7-16

Don't miss these Words of the Week

"Warrings" (Romans 7:23)
"Election" (Romans 8:29-30; 9-11)
"Instant" (Romans 12:12)

"I see another law in my members, warring against the law of my mind." (Romans 7:23)

MANY HAVE HEARD THE PHRASE, "THE struggle is real," used to describe a small, everyday frustrating situation or setback. Paul used a similar expression in Romans 7 as he described some of the struggles relating to Roman law. In Romans 7:23, he writes that he described a "warring" in his mind (see Romans 7:23).

The Greek word for "warring" used here is *antistrateuomenon*, which means, "to campaign or war against" (from *anti*, against, and *strateuomai*, to attack or destroy).[1]

Looking at our day—including the warring that happens in many minds due to mental-health issues—many people have described their episodes of mental illness or imbalance as feeling like their minds were at war. Mental health challenges can impact anyone, regardless of their level of education, where they live, the level of their faith, or the calling they hold. The latter-day *antistrateuomenon*s are real and should be nothing to be ashamed of. As people's

---

1. *Strong's*, 497.

196

minds war against their bodies (as Paul described in Romans 7:23), those who are in a good state should meet their struggling brothers and sisters with love.

As you read Romans 7 and learn about the struggles that Paul and other believers faced in that day, look around. Who is having a "war" of their mind? What can you do to help sustain them through their battle?

"There is a remnant according to the election of grace." (Romans 11:5)

FEW TOPICS DIVIDE NATIONS, COMMUNITIES, AND even families like politics and elections. Throughout Romans 8–11, Paul addresses another type of election as he addresses the doctrine of grace (see Romans 11:5).

Our English word "election" is rooted in the Latin *electionem* meaning "a choice."[2] The Greek word, *eklegomai*,[3] simply means "a choosing out or selection."[4] In the Doctrine and Covenants, we read that many are called, but few are chosen (see Doctrine and Covenants 121:40). This doctrine of choosing and election begs the question: who is the one that chooses, selects, or "elects" people in a gospel sense? Some have wondered if God plays favorites, selecting or choosing certain people for exaltation while disregarding others. Would the Lord do this? Certainly not.

So what does "election" mean? Well, we get some help from Elder Bruce R. McConkie. He wrote that the house of Israel was known and divided before we came to earth: "During the long expanse of life which then was, an infinite variety of talents and abilities came into being. . . . The whole house of Israel, known and segregated out from their fellows, was inclined toward spiritual things."[5]

Elder Melvin J. Ballard added that Israel is "a group of souls tested, tried, and proven before they were born into the world. . . . Through this lineage were to come the true and tried souls that had demonstrated their righteousness in the spirit world before they came here."[6]

---

2. "Election," *Online Etymology Dictionary*.
3. *Strong's*, 1589.
4. The Bible Dictionary adds even more to this doctrine: "An 'election of grace' spoken of in D&C 84:98–102 and Rom. 11:1–5 has reference to one's situation in mortality; that is, being born at a time, at a place, and in circumstances where one will come in favorable contact with the gospel. This election took place in the premortal existence."
5. Bruce R. McConkie, *The Mortal Messiah*, 4 vols. (Salt Lake City: Deseret Book Co., 1979–81), 1:23.
6. Melvin J. Ballard, "The Three Degrees of Glory," *Crusader for Righteousness* (Salt Lake City: Bookcraft, 1966), 218–19.

Although one-third of our Heavenly Parents' spirit children rebelled, the more diligent among the rest were chosen to be rulers in the kingdom (Abraham 3:22–23).

Since we know that God is no respecter of persons (see Acts 10:34), it is safe to conclude that the answer as to who elected the House of Israel in the pre-earth life is very clear: we each individually chose to be elected— through our obedience, faithfulness, and diligent righteousness.

Think of that! As the Lord presented the Plan of Salvation and as you progressed in the pre-earth life, you may have "volunteered yourself" to come to earth to take on extra responsibilities, choosing yourself as one to help save Heavenly Father's children. You elected yourself through your obedience, faithfulness, and diligence.

Remember these words from President Russell M. Nelson as you read Romans 8–11 this week:

> My beloved younger brothers and sisters, you are among the best the Lord has *ever* sent to this world. You have the capacity to be smarter and wiser and have more impact on the world than any previous generation![7]

"Rejoicing in hope; patient in tribulation; continuing instant in prayer." (Romans 12:12)

WE TRULY LIVE IN AN "INSTANT" world. From "instant oatmeal" to "instant rice" to "instant pudding," and even the lure of instant gratification and the blessing of having instant answers to questions, thanks to the World Wide Web. The Apostle Paul gives us one more "instant" to add to our list: being "*instant* in prayer" (see Romans 12:12).

Prayer is sacred communication to Heavenly Father from His sons and daughters on earth.[8] We are commanded to pray always to the Father in the name of the Son (see 3 Nephi 18:19–20). In the New Testament, the apostle Paul noted that believers were ones who would be found, "Rejoicing in hope; patient in tribulation; continuing *instant* in prayer" (see Romans 12:12).

The phrase "continuing instant in" in English is rendered with just one Greek word, *instantem*, which literally means "ever enduring in" or

---

7. Russell M. Nelson and Wendy W. Nelson, "Hope of Israel," Worldwide Youth Devotional, Conference Center, Salt Lake City, Utah, 3 June 2018.
8. See Bible Dictionary, "Prayer."

"standing near." In Latin, the word is the same and means "present, pressing, urgent."[9] The picture is one of being always ready to pray—and always standing near the Lord. The same urgent readiness and closeness is implied in Paul's exhortation to "pray without ceasing" (see 1 Thessalonians 5:17; see also Philippians 4:6).

During the course of the day, we should keep a prayer in our heart, as Alma suggested, "Let all thy thoughts be directed unto the Lord" (Alma 37:36):

> Yea, and cry unto God for all thy support; yea, let all thy doings be unto the Lord, and whithersoever thou goest let it be in the Lord; yea, let all thy thoughts be directed unto the Lord; yea, let the affections of thy heart be placed upon the Lord forever.
>
> Counsel with the Lord in all thy doings, and he will direct thee for good; yea, when thou liest down at night lie down unto the Lord, that he may watch over you in your sleep; and when thou risest in the morning let thy heart be full of thanks unto God; and if ye do these things, ye shall be lifted up at the last day. (Alma 37:36–37)

Elder David A. Bednar taught a principle associated with the concept of being "instant" in prayer (urgently praying, or praying with a desired closeness to the Lord):

> Morning and evening prayers—and all of the prayers in between—are not unrelated, discrete events; rather, they are linked together each day and across days, weeks, months, and even years. This is in part how we fulfill the scriptural admonition to "pray always" (Luke 21:36; 3 Nephi 18:15, 18; D&C 31:12). Such meaningful prayers are instrumental in obtaining the highest blessings God holds in store for His faithful children.[10]

As you go throughout your day, seek to be '*instant* in prayer' by having a sincere prayer in your heart and as you seek to feel closer to the Lord.

---

9. See "instant," *Online Etymology Dictionary*.
10. David A. Bednar, "Pray Always," *Ensign*, Nov. 2008, 42.

FOR FURTHER STUDY

- Paul described himself as "wretched" in Romans 7:24. Look up the etymology of this word using www.etymonline.com to find insights to what he meant and what Nephi may have meant when he lamented with the same expression (see 2 Nephi 4:17).

- Romans 8:9 teaches that "ye are not in the flesh, but in the Spirit, if so be that the Spirit of God dwell in you." Consider looking up the meaning of the word "dwell" in the Greek using www.biblehub.com and www.blueletterbible.org and see how it relates to one of the promises of the sacrament prayer.

- Romans 12 is filled with wonderful words with unique origins. Among them is the word "overcome" (Romans 12:21). Consider a search for its meaning and application using www.biblehub.com and www.blueletterbible.org.

What other unique or insightful words did you find in your study this week?

_____

_____

_____

_____

_____

_____

Please share with us!
Visit www.ComeFollowMeWOW.com and
share your word discoveries and insights!

Chapter 33

1 Corinthians 1-7

Don't miss these Words of the Week

"**Carnal**" (1 Corinthians 3:1-3)
"**Puffed Up**" (1 Corinthians 4:6, 18-19)
"**Temple**" (1 Corinthians 6:13-20)
"**Fasting**" (1 Corinthians 7:5)
"**Care**" (1 Corinthians 7:32)

"Ye are yet carnal." (1 Corinthians 3:3)

WHEN YOU THINK OF BEING HUMAN, what words come to mind? Words like "weak" or "fallen" or "mortal" are often used to describe our situation in mortality. Scripturally, one of the Lord's favorite words to describe our fallen state is "carnal" (it's found 74 times in the scriptures!).

The Greek word used in 1 Corinthians 3:3 for "carnal" (*sarkikoi*) means "physical, human, mortal."[1] Directly from Latin *carnalis*, "fleshly" (think of *carne asada* or *chili con carne*).[2]

Following the fall of Adam and Eve, we read, "men began from that time forth to be carnal, sensual, and devilish" (see Moses 5:13; Mosiah 3:19). The Book of Mormon Student Institute Manual teaches further about the meanings of "fallen" and "natural":

---

1. *Strong's*, 4559.
2. "Carnal," *Online Etymology Dictionary*.

In the scriptures, . . . *natural* means fallen or sinful. Though born innocent, all men, through the Fall of Adam, come into a fallen world . . . and experience a resultant "fall" of their own. In other words, it is through transgression of God's law that one becomes a "natural man."[3]

What a thought! Being *fallen* is different from being *natural* (carnal). Many of the mistakes and sins we commit might be caused more by the condition of living in a fallen state and having a fallen nature than by our natural, calculated, or carnal choices. In other words, we are weak and we make mistakes. And when we do, those errors and transgressions are viewed very differently by the Lord than those sins we commit as we consciously choose to rebel against God:

Fallen Man—Weak, Mortal (Jacob 4:7; Alma 12:22–37; 22:14; Ether 12:27; D&C 66:3)	Carnal Man—An Enemy to God (Mosiah 3:19; 16:2–5; Alma 22:14; 41:11; 42:6–12)
• Mistakes/Foolish choices • Influence of Biology • Influence of Psychology • Influence by Environment • Influenced by our families and relationships	• Sin (a conscious fall of our own) • Which cause us to be: • Carnal: temporal, worldly, lack spirituality • Sensual: gratification of the senses, indulgence of appetite • Devilish: excessive, extreme, unmerciful

When you find yourself in the midst of carnality because of choices you've made that contradict God's commandments, remember that you have agency and can decide what to do with your situation and your feelings. The natural and carnal side of yourself will inevitably want you to stay sinful. To combat that, seek counsel from priesthood leaders and faithful friends, family, and professionals, if necessary. Pray for peace. Seek insight as to what caused your slip up. Avoid the "blame game" (the carnal self loves to blame others for mistakes!).

While we are all living in a fallen world, we don't have to let our fallen natures become carnal.

---

3. "Mosiah 3:19—The Natural Man," *Book of Mormon Student Institute Manual* (The Church of Jesus Christ of Latter-day Saints, 2009), 139–40.

"Some are puffed up." (1 Corinthians 4:18)

No, PAUL WAS NOT SPEAKING ABOUT being bloated or swollen or physically inflated in this verse. The Greek word used in 1 Corinthians 4:18 for "puffed up" is *ephysiōthēsan* and it means "to blow up" or "arrogant."[4] It comes from the word *phusa* which means "bellows." This Greek word for "puffed up" only appears seven times in the New Testament; it occurs five times in Paul's First Epistle to the Corinthians.[5]

A simple synonym for being "puffed up" is "pride."[6] Other idiomatic expressions for being "puffed up" are "having a big head," being "high about one's self," or being "full of one's self." Those in the scriptures that don't repent from being puffed up, or prideful, invariably leave their discipleship and reject the Savior's voice (see Alma 5:37, for example).

How can we avoid the temptation to become "puffed up" when we see success or have accomplishments in our lives? When Dieter F. Uchtdorf was called as a General Authority, he had the opportunity to drive President James E. Faust to a stake conference. President Faust talked about how gracious the members of the Church are, especially to General Authorities. Then he said something that resonated within young Elder Uchtdorf: "'They will treat you very kindly. They will say nice things about you.'" He laughed a little and then said, "'Dieter, be thankful for this. But don't you ever inhale it.'"[7]

As you find success and accomplishments or encounter blessings of money or nice clothing or accomplishment with your children or grandchildren, take note of what President Uchtdorf taught: enjoy the moment, but don't let it "puff you up" by inhaling it.

"Know ye not that your body is the temple of the Holy Ghost which is in you?" (1 Corinthians 6:19)

A PLUMB BOB (OR PLUMMET) IS a weight suspended from a string and used as a vertical reference line. It's been used since at least the time of ancient

---

4. *Strong's*, 5448.
5. In other translations of the Bible, the words "arrogant" or "boastful" are used. The term "puffed up" appears nine times in the Book of Mormon.
6. Sometimes wisdom leads to pride; other times, its precursor is riches (see 2 Nephi 9:42 or 2 Nephi 28:15)—and sometimes it's even clothing! (see 2 Nephi 28:13).
7. Dieter F. Uchtdorf, "Pride and the Priesthood," *Ensign*, Nov. 2010, 56.

Egypt to ensure that constructions are "plumb," or vertical.[8] The plumb bob is a wonderful and simple tool to ensure perfect vertical measurements.

The Apostle Paul used the word "temple" as a metaphor for our physical body. The word "temple" originates from the Latin *templum*[9] and has two parts: *tem* "to cut" and *plum* "vertical."[10] It shares the same root with the plumb bob; indeed, physical temples are places of measurement—and how we treat our physical bodies is also an indication of measurement.[11]

An application of this principle of temples and measurements is the process of measuring our lives against the standards the Lord has established to enter His holy temple. Each time we participate in a temple recommend interview, we are examining our lives and measuring ourselves against the Lord's standards for temple worthiness. We can apply the teachings of the Apostle Paul when he said, "Know ye not that ye are the temple of God, and that the Spirit of God dwelleth in you? If any man defile the temple of God, him shall God destroy; for the temple of God is holy, which temple ye are" (see 1 Cor. 3:16–17).

Elder Scott D. Whiting of the Seventy wrote that we cannot hide our imperfections from God:

> [W]hen we become aware of elements in our own lives that are inconsistent with the teachings of the Lord, when our efforts have been less than our very best, we should move quickly to correct anything that is amiss, recognizing that we cannot hide our sins from the Lord. We need to remember that "when we undertake to cover our sins, . . . behold, the heavens withdraw themselves; [and] the Spirit of the Lord is grieved."[12]

Gratefully, the measurement that the Lord uses regarding the care of our physical bodies is not one of perfection. As we live our lives, using the "celestial plumb bobs" of standards to help us discern what we take into our bodies and how we treat our physical temples, may we make the necessary

---

8. Denys A. Stocks, *Experiments in Egyptian Archaeology: Stoneworking Technology in Ancient Egypt* (Routledge, 2003), 180.

9. "Temple," *Online Etymology Dictionary*.

10. A pattern of temple construction was established by King Solomon in the Old Testament when he built a temple unto the Lord using only the finest materials and workmanship (see 1 Kings 6–7) and today we continue to follow this pattern as we build the temples of the Church. See Elder Scott D. Whiting, "Temple Standard," *Ensign*, Nov. 2012.

11. The Greek word *naos* means "A temple, a shrine, that part of the temple where God himself resides." See *Strong's,* 3485.

12. Scott D. Whiting, "Temple Standard," *Ensign*, Nov. 2012, 38–39.

improvements and realign our will with His—all so we can have the Holy Ghost as our companion.

"Give yourselves to fasting." (1 Corinthians 7:5)

THROUGHOUT HISTORY, GOD'S PEOPLE HAVE FASTED to draw near to Him and to worship Him. Jesus showed the importance of fasting (see Luke 4:1–4) and in modern-day revelation, we learn that the Lord still expects His people to fast (see D&C 88:76).[13]

When we *fast* properly, we learn to control our appetites and passions and we gain strength, because we are exercising our self-control over something really difficult: refraining from all our favorite foods!

The origin of the word "fast" is Germanic: *fastuz*, which means "firm." Words like "fasten" and "steadfast" also come from *fastuz*. As the word entered Old English, we got *fæst*, which meant "firmly fixed" or the Old Norse *festr*, "a mooring rope."[14] Both have the connotation of something restrained or immovable. And such is our state when we fast properly: we strive to become more restrained and immovable against sin and temptation.

Church members are encouraged to fast one Sunday each month (fast Sunday) and at other times as needed or desired. A *true* fast should be accompanied by prayer and with a purpose. Fasting allows an individual's spirit to subdue "the natural man," and this invites the Spirit to be with us.

There are so many beautiful promises that come from fasting! Paul taught that when we give ourselves to fasting and prayer and come together again "Satan [will] tempt you not for your incontinency" (1 Corinthians 7:5). Through the prophet Isaiah, the Lord promised peace, improved health, and spiritual guidance as we fast properly:

> Then shall thy light break forth as the morning, and thine health shall spring forth speedily: and thy righteousness shall go before thee; the glory of the Lord shall be thy rearward. Then shalt thou call, and the Lord shall answer; thou shalt cry, and he shall say, Here I am. (Isaiah 58:8–9)

Elder Shayne M. Bowen of the Seventy offered an 11-step plan to claim the promised blessings of strength that comes from fasting:[15]

---

13. As a reminder, mothers that are nursing and those with compromised health and also little children should use wisdom when it comes to participating in fasting.

14. "Fasting," *Online Etymology Dictionary*.

15. Shayne M. Bowen, "Fasting with Power," Ensign College devotional, 28 May 2019, as

1. Plan for each upcoming fast by meditating on the purpose of the fast.
2. Begin each fast with a kneeling prayer. Tell God the purpose of the fast.
3. Go 24 hours without food or drink.
4. Use hunger pains as a reminder to pray again about the purpose of the fast.
5. Express more gratitude through prayer.
6. Give a generous fast offering.
7. When prompted, bear a brief testimony in a fast and testimony meeting.
8. Focus on reverent contemplation while fasting.
9. Study the scriptures in the time that would have been spent eating.
10. End each fast with a kneeling prayer.
11. Commit to be a better person and make plans with God for how to improve.

Fasting helps us to become firmly fixed, secure, and fortified. It is a principle of power and allows us to find strength to "break every yoke" and return home to our beloved Father in Heaven.

"He that is unmarried careth for the things that belong to the Lord." (1 Corinthians 7:32)

YOU'RE PROBABLY FAMILIAR WITH THE TALENTED plate spinners that perform at circuses, variety shows on TV, or at halftimes of basketball games. They are amazing! Some can spin dozens of plates at the same time, using different rods and poles. Using great skill, when one plate begins to lose momentum, the performer will add more spin so the plate can pick up speed and continue. It appears that the apostle Paul understood a principle about the balancing act of marriage and family (and being single).

As you've read this week, his messages remind us of balance in our relationships and balance in our service to the Lord. He wrote, "He that is unmarried careth for the things that belong to the Lord, how he may please the Lord: But he that is married careth for the things that are of the world, how he may please his wife" (see 1 Corithians 7:32–33).

---

recorded by Spencer Williams, *Church News*, 5 June 2019. See also, Shayne M. Bowen, "Fasting with Power," *Ensign*, Apr. 2009.

The word "care" used here by Paul is *merimna* in Greek; it's beyond a simple concern or attention. *Merimna* means "to be over-anxious; distracted."[16] Another translation of 1 Corinthians 7:32–33 helps clarify Paul's message:

> I want all of you to be free from worry. An unmarried man worries about how to please the Lord. But a married man has more worries. He must worry about the things of this world, because he wants to please his wife. So he is pulled in two directions. . . . But a married woman worries about the things of this world, because she wants to please her husband. What I am saying is for your own good—it isn't to limit your freedom. I want to help you to live right and to love the Lord above all else.[17]

If you've ever served in a time-demanding calling while married with children, you know the complexities of balancing these important duties. Paul reminds all married people that it's important to balance our focus at home with our duties at Church (and to not get too overanxious or distracted by our callings).

Notice as well, he teaches that single members of the Church have a wonderful opportunity to spend more time serving the Lord than those that are married. Rather than feeling too "overanxious" or "distracted" by marital status, serving the Lord as a single Saint is a unique opportunity and blessing.

For those who are married or have families, family should certainly come first, but on occasion, time spent ministering in a calling might be needed. Elder Ballard taught about the importance of this balance:

> As a result of their focusing too much time and energy on their Church service, eternal family relationships can deteriorate. Employment performance can suffer. This is not healthy, spiritually or otherwise. While there may be times when our Church callings require more intense effort and unusual focus, we need to strive to keep things in proper balance. We should never allow our service to replace the attention needed by other important priorities in our lives. Remember King Benjamin's counsel: "And see that all these

---

16. *Strong's*, 3309.
17. See Contemporary English Version, 1 Corinthians 7:32–35.

things are done in wisdom and order; for it is not requisite that a man should run faster than he has strength" (Mosiah 4:27).[18]

Just like the plate spinners that entertain and amaze us with their skill of balance, you too can find balance in your life and be free of feeling "over-anxious" or "distracted" as you ask for the Lord's help.

FOR FURTHER STUDY

- There is a wonderful message of *unity* in this week's study of 1 Corinthians 1:10–17; 3:1–11. Consider looking up the Greek definition of "unity" using www.biblehub.com and www.blueletterbible.org to see what implications you discover (be sure to note the root word for "unity" using www.etymonline.com as well!)

- The word "fear" has several definitions, but look at the use of the word fear in 1 Corinthians 2:3 using www.biblehub.com and www.blueletterbible.org and look for application.

- 1 Corinthians 7 is a type of marriage council, full of New Testament rituals and traditions and customs. A study of the seemingly confusing phrases in this chapter using www.biblehub.com and www.blueletterbible.org will open a world of relevancy.

What other unique or insightful words did you find in your study this week?

_____

_____

_____

Please share with us!
Visit www.ComeFollowMeWOW.com and
share your word discoveries and insights!

---

18. M. Russell Ballard, "O Be Wise," *Ensign*, Nov. 2006, 18.

Chapter 34

1 Corinthians 8-13

Don't miss these Words of the Week

"**Head**" (1 Corinthians 11:3)
"**Communion**" (1 Corinthians 11:26)
"**Member**" (1 Corinthians 12:14)
"**Charity**" (1 Corinthians 13:4-8)

"The head of the woman is the man." (1 Corinthians 11:3)

AT A GLANCE, THIS PASSAGE FROM Paul in his first letter to the believers in Corinth can sound infuriating and misogynistic. When we read passages that confuse (or enrage), there usually is something we are not seeing and seeking answers can lead us on a wonderful journey.

To be clear, the word "head" used in 1 Corinthians 11:3 literally is a cranium type *head* (Greek *kephalé*).[1] Paul must have used this word symbolically as we don't know of any women walking around with male heads today!

A glance through multiple scriptures about the Lord's teaching involving husband and wife can give us a much clearer understanding of this doctrine and the principles of marital leadership.

Following the partaking of the forbidden fruit from the tree of knowledge of good and evil, the Lord told Eve that her "*desire* shall be to thy husband, and he shall rule over thee" (Genesis 3:16). Later, in Genesis 4:6–7, in speaking to Cain, the Lord said, "And if thou doest not well, sin lieth at the

---

1. *Strong's*, 2776.

door. And unto thee shall be [its] desire . . ." The English word "desire" is from the Latin *desiderare* and means "to long for, wish for; *demand*." That is, sin would want to dominate her life and rule over her throughout her life.[2]

The Lord may have been telling Eve (and all wives and husbands) that, as a result of the Fall, she and many of her posterity would have a deep desire to dominate and rule over their husbands. Because of her choice in the Garden,[3] in place of the family structure established scripturally by God, there would now be a power struggle: a struggle and battle over who should dominate and lead. Undoubtedly, headship in marriage is being addressed in this passage from Genesis and it's addressed again by Paul in his letter to the saints in Corinth. Elder Bruce C. Hafen, formerly of the Seventy, and his wife, Marie, explained:

> Genesis 3:16 states that Adam is to "rule over" Eve, but this doesn't make Adam a dictator. . . . Also, *over* in "rule over" uses the Hebrew *bet*, which means ruling *with*, not ruling *over*.[4]

The New Testament makes it clear that God's design for marriage is to have a husband become a self-sacrificing head who actively seeks to receive counsel from God (see 1 Corinthians 11:4; Ephesians 5:22–33).

Similar conflicts occur in any marriage when a spouse chooses to make marriage-altering decisions without counseling with their partner beforehand. Ultimately, for a marriage to be strong and free of transgression, each partner must seek council from the other. Marriage is intended to be a

---

2. While Eve transgressed the law in the Garden of Eden regarding partaking of the fruit of the tree of knowledge (and note that it indeed was a transgression and not a sin), this partaking was needed to open the doorway toward eternal life for all of God's children. Yet her choice to partake of the fruit independent of and without counseling with her husband prior to the partaking may have been the basis for the Lord's curse and consequent council about marital leadership in Genesis 3:16. Biblical scholars have offered various interpretations of this subtle Hebrew phrasing about Eve's *desire* and most interpret this passage to mean that the woman would desire to be in control of her husband, abandoning the structure for him to be her partner and to make decisions in concert with her as an equal partner, counselor, and companion. Other scholars see this as implying that the woman's desire for her husband would be frustrated by his role as an authority in her life.

3. Elder Dallin H. Oaks declared: "Some Christians condemn Eve for her act, concluding that she and her daughters are somehow flawed by it. Not the Latter-day Saints! Informed by revelation, we celebrate Eve's act and honor her wisdom and courage in the great episode called the Fall" (see Dallin H. Oaks, "The Great Plan of Happiness," *Ensign,* Nov. 1993, 73).

4. Bruce C. and Marie K. Hafen, "Crossing Thresholds and Becoming Equal Partners," *Ensign,* Aug. 2007, 27.

partnership with husband and wife equally yoked together, sharing in decision making. As Elder L. Tom Perry of the Quorum of the Twelve Apostles eloquently said: "There is not a president or a vice president in a family. The couple works together eternally for the good of the family. . . . They are on equal footing."[5]

It is important to note that the term "equal" is all too often mistaken to mean that if two things are equal, they must be identical to each other. Equality does not mean sameness, however. While both men and women have equal access to priesthood power, men are given responsibility over priesthood ordinances; while both men and women have been given responsibility over bestowing and nurturing life, women provide a unique role in this arena that only they can perform.

Family stewardships are equally sacred—yet they do not include any ideas about domination. Sadly, in some traditions, husbands are authorized and even encouraged to dominate, control, and regulate all family affairs, independent of influence from or accountability to his wife. That is not the way of the Lord, and nothing could be farther from the eternal truth when it comes to equal partnership in marriage. In a poignant teaching, Elder Jeffrey R. Holland taught:

> I would not have you spend five minutes with someone who belittles you, who is constantly critical of you, who is cruel at your expense and may even call it humor. Life is tough enough without having the person who is supposed to love you leading the assault on your self-esteem, your sense of dignity, your confidence, and your joy. In this person's care you deserve to feel physically safe and emotionally secure.[6]

As we come to better understand Paul's use of the word "head" through the story of Adam and Eve and in the marvelous light of the restored gospel, we will recognize our innate (natural man) *desire* to rule over our spouse— and choose to put off that desire and replace it with a desire to council with our companion. We will more easily enjoy the blessing that comes from having an equal partnership between spouses as we use our heads to love each other rather than to rule over each other.

---

5. L. Tom Perry, "Fatherhood, an Eternal Calling," *Ensign*, May 2004, 71.
6. Jeffrey R. Holland, "How do I love thee?" Brigham Young University devotional, 15 Feb. 2000, speeches.byu.edu.

"For as often as ye eat this bread, and drink this cup, ye do shew the Lord's death." (1 Corinthians 11:26)

WE ALL BELONG AT SACRAMENT MEETING. Whether we have crazy kids who make it hard to concentrate, or we didn't get our Sunday laundry done in time, or we just have a second before we have to show up for our shift at work, we all belong, because the point of sacrament meeting, otherwise known as *communion* in other faiths, is to *commune*.

For some, there are moments where despite good intentions, we mindlessly partake of the sacrament or lose focus during Sunday worship. Oftentimes the repeated ordinance can grow to become a bit stale, despite its sacredness. A look at the word "communion" may help to reinvigorate your sacrament experience next Sunday.

The etymological meaning of the word "commune" is sweet and empowering. While we, as Latter-day Saints, use the word "sacrament" to describe the break and water administration each Sunday at church, many other Christian faiths refer to the sacrament as *communion*.

"Commune" comes from *koinonia*, a Greek word which means "joint participation."[7] This idea is presented in 1 Corinthians 11:26 when the Apostle Paul wrote, "For as often as ye eat this bread, and drink this cup, ye do shew the Lord's death." In another passage, Acts 2:42 reads, "And they continued steadfastly in the apostles' doctrine and fellowship [*koinonia*], and in breaking of bread." Used here, the word "fellowship" (which has the same root as the word "communion") literally means, "The right hand as a sign of fellowship." Obvious intonations of our use of our right hand for covenants abound in this definition and other derivatives of the word *koinonia*.[8]

Each week, as we participate in the *communion* of the sacrament, we should realize the Lord's intent with having us "commune" together as brothers and sisters on Sundays. If our temple worship or sacrament worship is approached with the principles of *koinonia* in mind, we should also realize that we are attending church and partaking of the emblems of the Savior to *commune* with Him. As we extend the hand of *communion* to our brothers and sisters with a determination to lovingly and charitably assist them and serve them and love them, the spirit of sharing and caring and connecting and giving becomes tangible.

---

7. See "koinonia," *Online Etymology Dictionary*.

8. *Koinonia* has a second connotation that means "a companion, or a joint-owner." In a marital sense, *koinonia* means that a covenant is shared jointly by a husband and a wife with a common goal to be with God together; the married couple will serve and love and champion each other, and in the process grow together back to God's presence.

As we participate in worship services each week, we would be wise to foster a spirit of *koinonia* within our hearts and attend our meetings no matter where our lives are at with a deep desire to connect and become unified with our fellow brothers and sisters in Christ.

"For the body is not one member, but many." (1 Corinthians 12:14)

HAVE YOU EVER WONDERED WHY WE call people that belong to our church, "members"? Well, it actually comes from the New Testament.

Our physical body is composed of many parts: hands, feet, arms, legs, ears, eyes, etc. Body parts are referred to as *members*; the word "member" comes from the Latin *membrum* and means "limb" or "body part."[9]

It is the distinctiveness of each part of the body that enables our entire body to function correctly. Hence, in the New Testament, the Apostle Paul often referred to Church *members* as being a part of the "body of Christ":

> For as the body is one, and hath many members, and all the members of that one body, being many, are one body: so also is Christ. For by one Spirit are we all baptized into one body . . . For the body is not one member, but many. (1 Corinthians 12:12–14)

Paul went on to teach the critical need for each member of the Church:

> If the foot shall say, Because I am not the hand, I am not of the body; is it therefore not of the body? And if the ear shall say, Because I am not the eye, I am not of the body; is it therefore not of the body? If the whole body were an eye, where were the hearing? If the whole were hearing, where were the smelling? But now hath God set the members every one of them in the body, as it hath pleased him. (1 Corinthians 12:15–18)

Thus, the "body of Christ" with its "members" (body parts) is analogous for how church members are to function together—interdependently, depending upon one another—so that we function properly as the organizational embodiment of Christ.

The Church of Jesus Christ of Latter Day Saints defines church membership as (1) those who have been baptized and confirmed; (2) those under age nine who have been blessed but not baptized; (3) those who are born to members but are not accountable because of intellectual disabilities, regardless of age; (4) unblessed children under age eight when two member

---

9. "Membrum," *Online Etymology Dictionary.*

parents request it or one member parent requests it and the nonmember parent gives permission.[10]

God has granted to each church member gifts, talents, and abilities, with the hope and expectation that we will increase and use them—not for selfish purposes, but for the benefit of others. Just as our body parts (members) differ from each other, our individual talents also differ. Each member has a unique contribution to make to the body of Christ; some members are gifted as teachers, others have a gift for organization, others are gifted at caring for those in need, others are gifted with wisdom and discernment or leadership, etc. Every member has something to offer to the edification of the church (see 1 Peter 4:10 and Ephesians 4:16).

Even if you feel like you are only a "pinky toe" or only an "ankle bone" or the "appendix" within the Church or body of Christ, remember that every member is critical to help everything function properly.

"Charity never faileth." (1 Corinthians 13:8)

THE WORD "CHARITY" HAS MANY CONNOTATIONS these days—from simply giving donations or alms to the poor, to a more divine, selfless way of giving. "Charity" entered the English language derived from the Latin *caritas* which was translated as "a state of benevolence towards the poor."[11] It is manifested when a person or group esteems and values another person or group of people. Charity is a translation of the Greek word *agapē*, which simply means "love."[12] It is the highest form of love: the reciprocated love between God and man and the unselfish love of other people.

The Bible Dictionary says that charity is the pure love of Christ. It is the love that Christ has for the children of men and that the children of men should have for one another. It is "the highest, noblest, and strongest kind of love" and the most joyous to the soul.[13] Paul tells us that charity that is

---

10. "Membership record," *Tech Wiki*, tech.churchofjesuschrist.org/wiki/Membership_record, retrieved 1 June 2021.

11. "Charity," *Online Etymology Dictionary*.

12. *Strong's*, 26.

13. An important principle regarding charity and charitable giving was shared by Elder Wilford W. Andersen of the Seventy. In speaking about helping Saints who live in poverty, he commented to Elder Dale G. Renlund: "The greater the distance between the giver and the receiver, the more the receiver develops a sense of entitlement" (Dale G. Renlund, "'That I Might Draw All Men unto Me,'" *Ensign*, May 2016, 39). Hence, The Church of Jesus Christ of Latter-day Saints actively tries to narrow the gap between the giver and the receiver of goods within its charitable organizations.

feigned and therefore done wrong is as annoying as "sounding brass" or a "tinkling cymbal" (1 Corinthians 13:1–2). Pretending to have charity—without feeling charitable—is simply empty and hollow and a bit annoying.

Elder Marvin J Ashton provided a wonderfully rich definition of the word "charity" when he wrote,

> Real charity is not something you give away; it is something that you acquire and make a part of yourself. . . . Perhaps the greatest charity comes when we are kind to each other, when we don't judge or categorize someone else, when we simply give each other the benefit of the doubt or remain quiet. Charity is accepting someone's differences, weaknesses, and shortcomings; having patience with someone who has let us down; or resisting the impulse to become offended when someone doesn't handle something the way we might have hoped. Charity is refusing to take advantage of another's weakness and being willing to forgive someone who has hurt us. Charity is expecting the best of each other.[14]

There's another side of charity that deserves our attention: receiving charity. Because charity (*agápē*) typically refers to *divine love*, a reminder of the importance of receiving charity is rich. Being truly warm and gracious, and expressing and feeling true gratitude for the acts of service we receive helps us to draw us closer to the Savior (1 Corinthians 13:2). How? Well, recall that Christ both performed—and received—many acts of kindness.[15]

The Savior provided a perfect example for us in giving—and also receiving. And we would be wise to follow Him and His many examples of what charity truly looks like.

FOR FURTHER STUDY

- Paul used the word "common" regarding our temptations and also taught that we can "escape" each of them with God's help (see 1 Corinthians 10:13). Consider looking up those words using www.biblehub.com and www.blueletterbible.org and look for applications.

---

14. Marvin J. Ashton, "The Tongue Can Be a Sharp Sword," *Ensign*, May 1992, 18–19.
15. For example, when Christ's feet were anointed and washed by a poor woman (at great expense) He allowed it to happen (see Luke 7:38; John 12:3–8). It also appears that He frequently was the recipient of acts of kindness from others when He was a guest (see Luke 9:58). Even His tomb was offered— and accepted (see Matthew 27:57–60).

- Paul begins to teach the gifts of the Spirit in 1 Corinthians 12:31. Look up the word "gift" in Greek using www.biblehub.com and www.blueletterbible.org and see what implications there are to gifts of the Spirit.

- There is a wonderful metaphor used by Paul regarding charity in 1 Corinthians 13:1–3. Consider looking up a few of the items listed in that passage using www.biblehub.com and www.blueletterbible.org to see what Paul was trying to teach with each use.

What other unique or insightful words did you find in your study this week?

_____

_____

_____

_____

_____

_____

Please share with us!
Visit www.ComeFollowMeWOW.com and
share your word discoveries and insights!

Chapter 35

1 Corinthians 14–16

Don't miss these Words of the Week

"**Vain**" (1 Corinthians 15:14)

"**Celestial**," "**Terrestrial**," "**Telestial**" (1 Corinthians 15:40–42)

"**Baptism for the dead**" (1 Corinthians 15:29)

"Then is our preaching vain, and your faith is also vain." (1 Corinthians 15:14)

FROM "VANITY" LICENSE PLATES ON CARS to being "vain as a peacock" or the "vain janglings" mentioned in 1 Timothy 1:6, the word "vain" meets us in several places in life and in scripture.

As far as we can tell, the first use of this word in scripture is from the Old Testament. The Lord, through the prophet Moses, commanded us to not take the name of God in vain.[1] Other translations of this Old Testament passage read as follows: "You must not make wrong use of the name of the Lord your God" (Revised English Bible); "You shall not make wrongful use of the name of the Lord your God" (New Revised Standard Version); "You shall not misuse the name of the Lord your God" (New International Version).

---

1. This is a rare commandment that finds itself repeated in the standard works: "Thou shalt not take the name of the Lord thy God in vain" (Exodus 20:7); "Thou shalt not take the name of the Lord thy God in vain; for the Lord will not hold him guiltless that taketh his name in vain" (Mosiah 13:15); "Keep yourselves from evil to take the name of the Lord in vain, for I am the Lord your God, even the God of your fathers, the God of Abraham and of Isaac and of Jacob" (Doctrine and Covenants 136:21).

In the New Testament, the apostle Paul reminded us that if Christ was not resurrected, "then is our preaching vain, and your faith is also vain" (1 Corinthians 15:13–14). That is, if Christ had not been resurrected, our faith would be vain.

But what does "vain" mean?

The Greek word for "vain" (*kenon*) used by Paul in 1 Corinthians comes from Latin and means "void, empty or fruitless."[2] As one biblical scholar has observed, vain implies "emptiness—a wandering in shadows without substance, a life without the possibility of satisfaction."[3] Indeed, without the empty tomb in Jerusalem, our lives and our discipleship would be vain (empty).

Always live your life fully, free of emptiness. When you teach or testify or talk of Christ, do so with depth and fullness. Avoid the trap of being empty in your discipleship. Avoid being vain.

"There are also celestial bodies, and bodies terrestrial." (1 Corinthians 15:40)

MOST LATTER-DAY SAINTS ARE FAMILIAR WITH the words "Celestial," "Terrestrial," and "Telestial" but not everyone has considered each word's origin.

"Celestial" and "terrestrial" are words derived from Latin. The word *caelum* (from the word *Celestial*) means "sky, heaven." "Terrestrial" comes from *terra* and means "earth."[4]

Telestial is a neologistic term,[5] first appearing in Doctrine and Covenants 76 in the Lord's vision to Joseph Smith about the degrees of glory. *Telestial* may have been formed through a combination of *terrestrial* and *celestial*. Although the word "telestial" appears to have a Latin formation, the root may be taken from Greek. One possibility is *telos* (which means "an end" or "to complete").[6] This infers that the mortals who became telestial are the last to be resurrected into a degree of glory, bringing that phase to an end, completing the resurrection of man into a degree of glory.

---

2. "Vain," *Online Etymology Dictionary.*
3. Lawrence O. Richards, *Expository Dictionary of Bible Words* (Grand Rapids, Mich.: Zondervan Publishers, 1985), 608.
4. See "celestial," *Online Etymology Dictionary.*
5. *Neologistic* means "new word."
6. "Telos," *Online Etymology Dictionary.*

Another etymological possibility for the origin of "telestial" is based on the Greek adverb *tele*, which means "far away, distant"[7] with the connotation that the stars are far away.[8] Telestial may be rooted in the Latin *tellus*, which means "earth, ground" since this earth is currently in a *telestial* state.[9]

Regardless of the root of each of these words for the degrees of glory— and rather than a focus on their origin—it might be better for us to focus on our future outcome. Remember, our final station will ultimately depend on what we've become:

[T]he Final Judgment is not just an evaluation of a sum total of good and evil acts—what we have *done*. It is an acknowledgment of the final effect of our acts and thoughts—what we have *become*.[10]

Each celestial choice you make helps you become more celestial; each terrestrial decision will more qualify you for the terrestrial kingdom; and telestial choices will lead to the telestial kingdom. So, choose wisely. You are becoming.

"Why are they then baptized for the dead?" (1 Corinthians 15:29)

For most Latter-day Saints, a first visit to a temple involves the sacred ordinance of baptism for the dead, helping deceased ancestors follow Jesus Christ's invitation: "Except a man be born of water and of the Spirit, he cannot enter into the kingdom of God" (John 3:5). As Joseph Smith explained, "It is no more incredible that God should save the dead, than that he should raise the dead."[11]

This beautiful and saving practice of offering this ordinance vicariously to the deceased did not originate within The Church of Jesus Christ of Latter-day Saints. Theologian Richard Kugelman wrote about this practice:

---

7. Think of telephone, telescope, and television.
8. There may be a natural tie within celestial, terrestrial, and telestial. *Caelum* meaning heaven or sky, *terra* meaning earth, and therefore *telestial* implying something in the underworld. In Philemon 2:10, we read about things "in heaven" (*epouranios* in Greek), things "on earth" (*epigeios* in Greek), and things "under the earth." The Greek word used here by Paul is *katachthono* (*kata* meaning "under" and *chthon* meaning "earth").
9. See "tellus," *Online Etymology Dictionary*.
10. Dallin H. Oaks, "The Challenge to Become," *Ensign*, Nov. 2000, 32.
11. Joseph Smith, *Teachings of the Prophet Joseph Smith*, 191.

It seems that in Corinth some Christians would undergo baptism in the name of their deceased non-Christian relatives and friends, hoping that this vicarious baptism might assure them a share in the redemption of Christ.[12]

Later in the New Testament, after first addressing the topic of baptism for the dead, Paul wrote in his letter to the Hebrews that "they without us should not be made perfect" (Hebrews 11:40). Sometime after Joseph Smith's vision of the celestial kingdom (D&C 137), the Prophet penned, "All those who have not had an opportunity of hearing the gospel, and being administered to by an inspired man in the flesh, must have it hereafter, before they can be finally judged."[13]

There doesn't seem to be anything contradictory in the New Testament wording of "baptism for the dead." The Greek word for "baptism" in 1 Corinthians 15:29 is *baptizomenoi*[14] (you can probably hear the root cognate of *baptism*) and the Greek word for "dead" is *nekrōn* (meaning *deceased, lifeless*).[15]

A non-Latter-day Saint British defender of our practice cleverly wrote:

Why are the Catholic bishops so concerned about Mormons baptizing dead parishioners? The Mormons didn't invent baptism of the dead. The practice has a significant history within mainstream Christianity. . . .

What's the difference between baptizing the dead and baptizing babies? . . . Indeed, given that all Christian Churches believe that the soul lives on after death and retains understanding and consciousness of self, doesn't it make more sense to baptize dead adults than live babies? . . .

The key point is, surely, that all religions believe that the soul, after death, at last knows what's what—whether Hinduism, Free Presbyterian, Jainism, Judaism, Islam, Catholicism or whatever is the true religion. What if it's Mormonism? What if it's an everyday occurrence on the other side that Catholics and Protestants are left standing dumbstruck at the Gates, gasping: "Mormons! Who'd

12. Richard Kugelman, "The First Letter to the Corinthians," *The Jerome Biblical Commentary*, ed. Raymond E. Brown, Joseph A. Fitzmyer, and Roland E. Murphy, 2 vols. (Englewood Cliffs, N.J.: Prentice-Hall, 1968), 2:273.
13. In Elders' Journal 1, no. 2 (July 1838), 43; Smith, *Teachings of the Prophet Joseph Smith*, 121.
14. *Strong's*, 907.
15. *Strong's*, 3498.

have believed it?" And maybe a wife berating her husband: "There! I told you it would be the Mormons! But would you listen?! Now it's an eternal hellfire for the two of us, I hope you're satisfied!"

In that scenario, shouldn't all members of all other religions be literally eternally grateful to the Mormons for sharing their saving grace even unto and after death?[16]

The doctrine of baptism for the dead brings hope to our souls, to "bind up the brokenhearted, to proclaim liberty to the captives, and the opening of the prison to them that are bound" (Isaiah 61:1). Once again, through the Restoration, God reveals His mercy to all of His children.

As you plan your weeks and your months, be sure to include time to participate in this ordinance. The eternal implications are simply immeasurable!

---

16. Eamonn McCann, "What if Mormons are right and Catholics and Protestants wrong?" *Belfast Telegraph*, 28 Aug. 2008, www.belfasttelegraph.co.uk/opinion/columnists/archive/eamonn-mccann/article28532064.ece.

FOR FURTHER STUDY

- There is a wonderful passage addressing "confusion" in the world (see 1 Corinthians 14:33). The word "confusion" has a wonderful root and meaning, so consider digging into it using www.etymonline.com.

- Why would Paul encourage us to "covet to prophesy"? (see 1 Corinthians 14:39). A dive into the words "covet" and "prophesy" using www.biblehub.com and www.blueletterbible.org is a fun journey to take!

- The phrase "stand fast in the faith" is found in 1 Corinthians 16:13. The Greek word for "stand fast" is enlightening, so consider a study of it using www.biblehub.com and www.blueletterbible.org.

- 1 Corinthians 15 is full of wonderful words. Consider a look at the Greek words for "corruptible" and "incorruptible" (see verses 52–54) using www.biblehub.com and www.blueletterbible.org.

What other unique or insightful words did you find in your study this week?

_____

_____

_____

_____

_____

_____

**Please share with us!
Visit www.ComeFollowMeWOW.com and
share your word discoveries and insights!**

Chapter 36

2 Corinthians 1-7

Don't miss these Words of the Week

"Troubled" and **"Perplexed"** (2 Corinthians 4:8)
"Judgment Seat of Christ" (2 Corinthians 5:10)
"Reconciled" (2 Corinthians 5:14-21)
"Godly sorrow" (2 Corinthians 7:10)

"We are troubled on every side, yet not distressed; we are perplexed, but not in despair." (2 Corinthians 4:8)

"CHRISTIANITY IS COMFORTING, BUT IT IS often not comfortable."[1] These words from Elder Holland are inspiring—and yet daunting. So many of us seek rest and comfort from our faith, and yet Paul reminds us in 2 Corinthians 4:8 that followers of Christ will be both "troubled" and "perplexed." Yikes! What do these words imply?

The Greek word for "troubled" is *thlibomenoi*, which means "make narrow by pressure; press hard, or to crowd."[2] With so many parts of the gospel tugging at our schedules each day, from doing family history work to magnifying our callings to being good ministering brothers and sisters, certainly we at times can feel troubled and feel pressured to perform.

---

1. Jeffrey R. Holland, "Waiting on the Lord," *Ensign*, Nov. 2020, 116–17.
2. *Strong's*, 2346.

The Greek word for "perplexed" is *aporoumenoi,* which means, "to be at a loss."[3] And, yes, sometimes while following Christ, who offers victory over so many mortal ailments, we can at times feel *at a loss* trying to understand God's eternal perspective.

Remember that a key to faith is understanding the nature and character of God. It is vital that we don't try to understand God on our own terms, but on His:

> Sadly enough, . . . it is a characteristic of our age that if people want any gods at all, they want them to be gods who do not demand much, comfortable gods, smooth gods who not only don't rock the boat but don't even row it, gods who pat us on the head, make us giggle, then tell us to run along and pick marigolds.[4]

Paul understood the doctrine of God as a God who challenges us—and he added hope. He wrote, "We are troubled on every side, yet not distressed; we are perplexed, but not in despair" (2 Cor. 4:8). What a message of hope! Yes, we will indeed be troubled and feel perplexed as we courageously stand up for our beliefs and strive to do all that we are asked to do, but through it all, we will be strengthened by our God.

If you are at a moment in your life feeling "troubled" (feeling the natural pressure of the gospel) or "perplexed" (at a loss as to what to do next in your discipleship), take courage in Paul's hope provided in 2 Corinthians 4:16–17:

> For which cause we faint not; but though our outward man perish, yet the inward man is renewed day by day. For our light affliction, which is but for a moment, worketh for us a far more exceeding and eternal weight of glory.

Hold on. Your glory is coming.

"For we must all appear before the judgment seat of Christ." (2 Corinthians 5:10)

IT'S HARD TO PICTURE EXACTLY WHAT the final judgment will look like. Both Romans 14:10 and 2 Corinthians 5:9 speak of the "judgment seat." What will this moment entail for us?

---

3. *Strong's,* 639.
4. Jeffrey R. Holland, "The Cost—and Blessings—of Discipleship, *Ensign,* May 2014, 7.

The phrase "judgment seat of Christ" is a translation of one Greek word: *bema*.[5] In New Testament times, the *bema* was a raised platform where a Roman magistrate or ruler sat to make decisions and pass sentences.[6] It was used in Greek and Isthmian athletic contests, where the contestants would compete for the prize under the scrutiny of judges who would ensure every rule of the contest was obeyed[7] The winner was led by the judge to the *bema*. There the laurel wreath was placed on his head as a symbol of victory.[8] Theologian Lewis Sparry Chafer wrote:

> Paul was picturing the believer as a competitor in a spiritual con-test. As the victorious Grecian athlete appeared before the Bema to receive his perishable award, so the Christian will appear before Christ's Bema to receive his imperishable award.[9]

Think about that! Rather than the final judgment being a time of stress and worry and wonder, it may be more like an awards ceremony. At that point in our existence, we've already "finished the race," or mortality, and the final judgment is more of an acknowledgement of what we have earned through our efforts.

Take heart knowing that one day you'll have the joy of appearing before the "judgment seat of Christ." In this final "*bema*," you will be rewarded. Elder Holland wrote that we get credit for trying in the gospel:

> With the gift of the Atonement of Jesus Christ and the strength of heaven to help us, we *can* improve, and the great thing about the gospel is we get credit for *trying*, even if we don't always succeed.[10]

What a blessing and promise! Look forward to your *bema* moment with the Savior.

---

5. *Strong's*, 968.
6. You'll see references to this in Matthew 27:19 and John 19:13.
7. See Clarence L. Haynes, Jr, "Will All Christians Experience the Judgment Seat of Christ?" *Crosswalk.com*, 12 Aug. 2021, www.crosswalk.com/faith/bible-study.
8. You'll see reference to this in 1 Corinthians 9:24–25.
9. Lewis Sperry Chafer and John F. Walvoord, *Major Bible Themes: 52 Vital Doctrines of the Scripture Simplified and Explained* (Grand Rapids: Zondervan Publishing House, 1974), 282.
10. Jeffrey R. Holland, "Tomorrow the Lord will do Wonders Among You," *Ensign*, May 2016, 125–26.

"And all things are of God, who hath reconciled us to himself by Jesus Christ, and hath given to us the ministry of reconciliation." (2 Corinthians 5:18)

"RECONCILIATION" IS NOT AN UNCOMMON WORD (think of *reconciling* one's bank account or *reconciling* with a spouse after a disagreement). "Reconciliation" in this passage in 2 Corinthians is *katallaxantos* in Greek, which comes from Latin roots. The *re* means "again," *con* means "with," and *sella* means "seat." *Re-con-ciliation*, therefore, literally means "to sit again with."[11]

William W. Phelps, a former member of the First Presidency and Joseph Smith's close friend, left the Church and became a traitor who caused extraordinary damage to the lives of the early Saints and to the Church itself. Later, upon realizing his own wrongs and the injuries he had caused in so many lives, he wrote a letter to Joseph Smith, seeking reconciliation. His desire was true reconciliation as he wanted to "sit again with" the Saints. He wrote:

> I . . . ask my old brethren to forgive me, and though they chasten me to death, yet I will die with them, for their God is my God. The least place with them is enough for me. . . . I ask forgiveness of all the Saints. I want your fellowship; if you cannot grant that, grant me your peace and friendship, for we are brethren, and our communion used to be sweet.

Joseph Smith responded in a letter:

> Dear Brother Phelps: . . . We have suffered much in consequence of your behavior—the cup of gall, already full enough for mortals to drink, was indeed filled to overflowing when you turned against us. . . . However, the cup has been drunk, the will of our Father has been done, and we are yet alive, for which we thank the Lord. . . . Believing your confession to be real, and your repentance genuine, I shall be happy once again to give you the right hand of fellowship, and rejoice over the returning prodigal. . . . Come on, dear brother, since the war is past, For friends at first, are friends again at last. Yours as ever, Joseph Smith, Jun.[12]

---

11. *Strong's,* 2644.
12. "Letter to William W. Phelps, 22 July 1840," p. 157, The Joseph Smith Papers, accessed September 15, 2022, https://www.josephsmithpapers.org/paper-summary/letter-to-william-w-phelps-22-july-1840/1.

We have been commanded to seek reconciliation when wrongs have occurred, and the Lord will help along the way (see Mormon 9:27; Moroni 7:26, 33). The Savior promised:

I will . . . ease the burdens which are put upon your shoulders, that even you cannot feel them upon your backs, even while you are in bondage; and this will I do that ye may know of a surety that I, the Lord God, do visit my people in their afflictions. (Mosiah 24:14)

As we seek to be reconciled to God and His children in our shared "ministry of reconciliation" (see 2 Corinthians 5:18), let us try our best to seek forgiveness from God and to be peacemakers with our fellow man. Restoring what seems impossible to restore and healing wounds that seem impossible to heal are some of the purposes of the Atonement of Christ. Reconciliation has marvelous power.

If it's time to make amends and choose to make *reconciliation*, you will feel the power of forgiveness flow into your life. To "be seated again with" God and with our friends and family is a blessing that is beyond our understanding.

What can you do today to start that reconciliation process?

"Godly sorrow worketh salvation." (2 Corinthians 7:10)

IN THE BOOK OF MORMON, THE term "remorse" is often used to describe "godly sorrow" (see Alma 5:18; 29:5; 42:18). A "morsel" of pie or a "morsel" of cake or even a "morsel" of praise from a parent or friend are wonderful things. A "morsel" refers to a small piece of something good. Its root is in the Latin *morsus* which means, "a bite." The English word "mordant" (sharp, critical, or biting) shares the same root.

The word "remorse" (as you have probably guessed), comes from the Latin *remorsum* and literally means "to bite back."[13] Remorse is the feeling of our conscience gnawing at us. The hypothesized root of "remorse" is *mer-*, meaning "rub away" or "harm" (think of words like "morbid," "nightmare," and "mortgage"; "mortgage" literally means "death pledge").[14]

Remorse is a critical part of the repentance process. We must feel godly sorrow—remorse—for our mistakes. This *biting* feeling of remorse should lead us to confess our sins to those we have injured and, in serious cases, to

---

13. "Remorse," *Online Etymology Dictionary.*
14. See Stan Carey, "Etymology bites back," *Macmillan Dictionary Blog,* 2015, www.macmillandictionaryblog.com/etymology-bites-back.

our bishop as well. The biting feelings of remorse are much like spurs used to encourage a horse.

It is important to note a crucial difference between remorse and shame.[15] Remorse leads to a desire to make amends, while shame leads to a desire to hide.[16] Shame is character-based ("I am a bad person"), whereas remorse is action-based ("I did a bad thing"). Remorse helps people to identify something regretful, prompting them to make Christlike changes, whereas shame typically makes people shrink away from change and improvement. As Elder Neal A. Maxwell taught, "Real *remorse* floods the soul. This is a 'godly sorrow,' not merely the 'sorrow of the world' . . . (2 Corinthians 7:10). False remorse instead is like 'fondling our failings.' In ritual regret, we mourn our mistakes but without mending them."[17]

No matter the level of pain we may experience from the biting feelings of remorse, the suffering of repentance can be completely swallowed up in the joy of forgiveness.

15. See Janice Lindsay-Hartz, Joseph de Rivera, and Michael F. Mascolo, "Differentiating Guilt and Shame and Their Effects on Motivation," *Self-Conscious Emotions: The Psychology of Shame, Guilt, Embarrassment, and Pride*, ed. June Price Tangney and Kurt W. Fischer (Guilford Publications, 1995).

16. See McKell A. Jorgensen, "Shame versus Guilt: Help for Discerning God's Voice from Satan's Lies," *Ensign*, Jan. 2020.

17. Neal A Maxwell, "Repentance," *Ensign*, Nov.1991, 31.

FOR FURTHER STUDY

- You might recall what you learned about the word "comfort" a few weeks ago (John 13–17). There is yet another passage with the word "comfort" this week in 2 Corinthians 1:4. Look back at how its etymology fits with this week's passage.

- You may be familiar with the term "earnest money" as it relates to purchasing a home. In 2 Corinthians 1:22–23; 5:5, Paul uses the word "earnest" to refer to the Holy Ghost. Look up this word using www.biblehub.com and www.blueletterbible.org and see how it can testify of one of the missions of the Holy Ghost.

- In 2 Corinthians 2, Paul wrote that "Satan . . . has an advantage of us." Using www.biblehub.com and www.blueletterbible.org, look up these words to add clarity to this principle.

- For the last few years, we've been asked to be "ministering brothers" and "ministering sisters" to people in our lives. Consider studying the Greek meaning of the word "minister" using www.biblehub.com and www.blueletterbible.org.

- "Separate" has an interesting etymology. Look at 2 Corinthians 6:14–18 and www.etymonline.com to see what is there to be discovered from the Greek.

What other unique or insightful words did you find in your study this week?

_____

_____

_____

_____

_____

Please share with us!
Visit www.ComeFollowMeWOW.com and
share your word discoveries and insights!

Chapter 37

2 Corinthians 8-13

Don't miss these Words of the Week

"Thorn in the Flesh" (2 Corinthians 12:7)
"Simplicity" (2 Corinthians 11:3)

"Simplicity that is in Christ." (2 Corinthians 11:3)

CONSIDER THIS STORY THAT ELDER UCHTDORF shared about simplicity:

One sister, a Relief Society instructor, was known for preparing flawless lessons. One time she decided to create a beautiful quilt that would serve as the perfect backdrop to the theme of her lesson. But life intervened—there were children to pick up from school, a neighbor who needed help moving, a husband who had a fever, and a friend who felt lonely. The day of the lesson approached, and the quilt was not completed. Finally, the night before her lesson, she did not sleep much as she worked all night on the quilt.

The next day she was exhausted and barely able to organize her thoughts, but she bravely stood and delivered her lesson.

And the quilt was stunning—the stitches were perfect, the colors vibrant, and the design intricate. And at the center of it all was a single word that triumphantly echoed the theme of her lesson: "Simplify."

Brothers and sisters, living the gospel doesn't need to be complicated.[1]

It's a tricky thing—letting go. There are even TV shows about people whose homes have become personal prisons because they can't let go of things, both physical and emotional. We like to hold onto things.

The apostle Paul reminds us that *simplicity* is found in Christ (see 2 Corinthians 11:3).

The Latin word, *simplicitatem*, refers to "frankness and openness."[2] The Greek word used in this passage is *haplotētos*. While it does mean "pure" or "straightforward" (and some translations present this word as "*plain*"), the word *haplotētos* also means "sincerity" or "generosity."[3]

Think of that! "As the serpent beguiled Eve through his subtilty, so your minds should be corrupted from the simplicity [sincerity or generosity] that is in Christ" (2 Corinthians 11:3). Christ offers His sincerity and His generosity; His *simplicity* is a wonderful gift in a world filled with deceit and selfishness.

It has been wisely said that the gospel of Jesus Christ is simply beautiful and beautifully simple. But many of us complicate simple things (and our lives) to the point of causing confusion—and exhaustion.

If you ever find yourself feeling over programmed, over scheduled, or overwhelmed, remember this beautiful truth from Paul: simplicity is found in Christ.

"There was given to me a thorn in the flesh, the messenger of Satan to buffet me." (2 Corinthians 12:7)

THORNS ARE EVERYWHERE—FROM THE LITTLE OBSTRUCTIONS on roses, to the tiny needle-like pins found on raspberry plants, to the burrs that get stuck into hikers' shoes. In the New Testament, Paul talked about a "thorn in his flesh" (see 2 Corinthians 12:5–10). While the scriptures are silent about what this thorn was, most assume he was referring to a weakness that he had, which he likened to having a "thorn" in his life.

---

1. Dieter F. Uchtdorf, "It Works Wonderfully!" *Ensign*, Nov. 2015, 22.
2. "Simplicity," *Online Etymology Dictionary*.
3. *Strong's*, 572.

The word "thorn" is the Greek word *skolops*, a word used to describe "a sharp, spiked instrument or tool."[4] We can assume that Paul didn't have a literal thorn in his flesh—he was using a metaphor to try to teach us about mortal weaknesses that we all combat. We might define these mortal thorns as limitations we have as human beings living in a fallen world and living in a telestial environment. Sometimes we lack wisdom or can't find strength and we feel that holiness is far from us. These normal and natural fallen flaws and predispositions are common—and we will experience emotions like anger, sadness, frustration, and fear many times in our lives.

Doctrinally speaking, Jesus Christ knows fully how it feels to have many of these same feelings. He fully understands the condition of having mortal thorns (see 2 Corinthians 13:4). He was completely free of sin (sin is a choice to disobey God's commandments, which He never did), but He did understand weaknesses and thorns of mortality.

Thorn in the Flesh (weakness)	Rebellion against God (sinfulness)
Natural shortcomings	Conscious disobedience against commandments
Caused by our fallen state	Championed by Satan
Overcome by the enabling power of the Atonement of Jesus Christ	Overcome through repentance and the redeeming power of the Atonement of Jesus Christ

The Book of Mormon offers hope to those wanting to overcome their thorns in the flesh:

And if men come unto me I will show unto them their weakness. I give unto men weakness that they may be humble; and my grace is sufficient for all men that humble themselves before me; for if they humble themselves before me, and have faith in me, then will I make weak things become strong unto them. (Ether 12:27)

Elder Richard G. Scott added:

---

4. This word *skolops* was also used to describe the stake on which an enemy's head was stuck after being decapitated. Satan metaphorically may have wanted Paul's head on a stake! The adversary was a constant source of irritation to the apostle Paul.

The joyful news for anyone who desires to be rid of the consequences of past poor choices is that the Lord sees weaknesses differently than He does rebellion. Whereas the Lord warns that unrepented rebellion will bring punishment, when the Lord speaks of weaknesses, it is always with mercy.[5]

If the "thorns" in your life have caused you to make unwise choices, look to Christ for strength and understanding. He truly can help you overcome your weakness (even the strongest of thorns).

FOR FURTHER STUDY

- There is a wonderful study of the word "examine" from 2 Corinthians 13:5 where Paul said, "examine yourselves, whether ye be in the faith." Consider a study of this word using www.biblehub.com and www.blueletterbible.org and consider how it can apply to your life.

- The Greek language has several words for "cheerful." In this week's study, Paul shared a principle about being a "cheerful giver" (2 Corinthians 9:7). Consider researching this type of cheerfulness using www.biblehub.com and www.blueletterbible.org and see what you can do to apply it to your life today.

- The word "witness" (see 2 Corinthians 13:1) has a fascinating root in Greek. Research it using www.etymonline.com.

- Consider the words "war" and "warfare" in 2 Corinthians 10:3–4. Research their meaning using www.biblehub.com and www.blueletterbible.org and look for relevancy for your life.

---

5. Richard G. Scott, "Personal Strength through the Atonement of Jesus Christ," *Ensign*, Nov. 2013, 83.

What other unique or insightful words did you find in your study this week?

_____

_____

_____

_____

_____

Please share with us!
Visit www.ComeFollowMeWOW.com and
share your word discoveries and insights!

Chapter 38

Galatians

Don't miss these Words of the Week

"**Seed of Abraham**" (Galatians 3:16)
"**Bondage**" and "**Free**" (Galatians 5:1)
"**Overtaken**" and "**Restore**" (Galatians 6:1)

"To Abraham and his seed were the promises made." (Galatians 3:16)

THE ORATOR MARCUS GARVEY SAID, "A people without the knowledge of their past history, origin and culture is like a tree without roots." Family history work can be exhilarating (and for those that haven't started tracing their ancestors, the process can feel a bit daunting). The good news is that you know a lot about one of your ancestors: Abraham.

A beautiful doctrine of the restored gospel teaches that faithful men and women who have made and kept covenants with God are literally of Abraham's lineage (or have been adopted into that family). In Galatians 3:16, Paul reminds us of the promises made to the seed of Abraham. The Greek word for "seed" used here is *spermati*; it means "offspring or remnant."[1] Throughout the scriptures, we are taught that we are from the seed of Abraham, meaning his offspring or remnant.[2]

---

1. *Strong's*, 4690.
2. See Galatians 3:26–29; 4:1–7; D&C 84:34; 103:17; 132:30; Abraham. 2:9–11.

We learn from the Old Testament that God spoke to Abraham, saying that if they will be His people and let Him be their God, He will covenant with them, blessing and protecting them (see Jeremiah 31:33). That is, one aspect of our being of the seed of Abraham and heirs of the Abrahamic Covenant is essentially this: "Abraham, anyone that is good to you, I will be good to them! And anyone that curses you, I will deal with them. If you will simply be my people and if you will let me be your God." As many as receive this gospel are part of Abraham's family and are part of his seed.

You've probably noticed the purple streaks of your veins in your arms or hands. If it were possible to extract your blood and put it under a "celestial microscope," there's a high probability that you would see that in you flows the literal blood of Abraham.[3] Abraham and his seed (including those adopted into his family) have all of the blessings of the gospel, of the priesthood, and of eternal life. This means that you have that same promise given to Abraham, Isaac, and Jacob: God will bless those who are good to you and He will also curse those who curse you, if you will be His child and let Him be your God.

What a promise of hope! God will prevail in your life because you are of the seed of Abraham. Take heart knowing that God will help you prevail.

"Christ hath made us free, . . . be not entangled again with the yoke of bondage." (Galatians 5:1)

IN MANY DRIVER'S EDUCATION CLASSES, WE are taught to focus on our own lane, because focusing on oncoming traffic or the views on either side of the roadway may cause us to drift towards them, putting ourselves and our passengers in danger.

The "bondage" of driving in our designated lane actually brings freedom. That is, by using our agency to choose the right, we find peace and freedom through making right choices. This principle is taught by several prophets:

- "Whosoever committeth sin is the servant of sin" (John 8:34).
- "To whom ye yield yourselves servants to obey, his servants ye are to whom ye obey" (Romans 6:16).
- "They chose evil works rather than good; therefore the spirit of the devil did enter into them, and take possession of their house . . .

---

3. Those of Gentile lineage who have believed the gospel and live its laws have been adopted into Abraham's family and will inherit the blessings of the covenant as fully and completely as though they had been born in that lineage.

and this because of their own iniquity, being led captive by the will of the devil" (Alma 40:13).

The Greek word for "free" used in Galatians 5:1 is *eleutheria*, which means "a state of freedom from slavery."[4] The Greek word for "freedom" is ēleutherōsen, which means *to set free* or *liberate*.[5] To further our understanding of this passage, the Borean Bible, using modern Greek lexicons, renders Galatians 4:9 as, "But now that you know God, or rather are known by God, how is it that you are turning back to those weak and worthless principles? Do you wish to be enslaved by them all over again?"

The principles from the acronym P.O.L.K.A. can help us avoid doing this "dance" of going from righteousness to rebellion over and over again:

P—Power to choose (see 2 Nephi 2:16). The ability to make choices.

O—Opportunity to choose (see 2 Nephi 2:11). A condition (mortality) wherein we can actually use our power to choose.

L—Laws (see 2 Nephi 2:13). Laws of God give us guidelines to follow.

K—Knowledge (see 2 Nephi 2:5). Through scriptures and prophets, we know the consequences of obeying a law and breaking it.

A—Agency (see 2 Nephi 2:27). With the Power to choose, the Opportunity to choose, Laws to guide us in our choices, and Knowledge of what is good and what is evil, Agency can be employed.

Seek today for true freedom. Look to make choices that will keep you far from the bondage that always accompanies sin. And if you've slipped into the binds of bondage through some sins or mistakes, remember that repentance is the good news of the gospel. Guilt can be swept away and freedom can be restored and we escape the bondage of sin through the Savior's Atonement.

"If a man be overtaken in a fault . . . restore such an one." (Galatians 6:1)

BROTHER JOSÉ DE SOUZA MARQUES WAS the type of leader who truly understood what it looked like when a person was *overtaken* by temptation and what it meant to *restore* them to a better place. While serving as a leader in his branch in Brazil, a young man named Fernando wrote of his experience with Brother Marques:

---

4. *Strong's,* 1659.
5. *Strong's,* 1397.

I became involved in surfing competitions on Sunday mornings and stopped going to my Church meetings. One Sunday morning Brother Marques knocked on my door and asked my nonmember mother if he could talk to me. When she told him I was sleeping, he asked permission to wake me. He said to me, "Fernando, you are late for church!" Not listening to my excuses, he took me to church.

The next Sunday the same thing happened, so on the third Sunday I decided to leave early to avoid him. As I opened the gate I found him sitting on his car, reading the scriptures. When he saw me he said, "Good! You are up early. Today we will go and find another young man!" I appealed to my agency, but he said, "We can talk about that later."

After eight Sundays I could not get rid of him, so I decided to sleep at a friend's house. I was at the beach the next morning when I saw a man dressed in a suit and tie walking towards me. When I saw that it was Brother Marques, I ran into the water. All of a sudden, I felt someone's hand on my shoulder. It was Brother Marques, in water up to his chest! He took me by the hand and said, "You are late! Let's go." When I argued that I didn't have any clothes to wear, he replied, "They are in the car."

That day as we walked out of the ocean, I was touched by Brother Marques's sincere love and worry for me. He truly understood the Savior's words: "I will seek that which was lost, and bring again that which was driven away, and will bind up that which was broken, and will strengthen that which was sick" (Ezek. 34:16).[6]

In Galatians 6:1, Paul shared a similar principle of helping those that have been *overtaken* by temptation or sin. The Greek word *prolēmphthē* was used by Paul to describe what it means to be "overtaken." It literally means "to be taken by surprise"[7] (and isn't it true that oftentimes our sins simply overtake us by surprise?). The Greek word for "restore" found in the same passage (*katartizete*) means "to completely and thoroughly repair."[8]

The English standard version of Galatians 6:1 reads beautifully:

Brothers, if anyone is caught in any transgression, you who are spiritual should restore him in a spirit of gentleness. Keep watch on yourself, lest you too be tempted.

.

---

6. Qtd. in Mervyn B. Arnold, "Strengthen Thy Brethren," *Ensign*, May 2004, 46–47.
7. *Strong's*, 4301.
8. *Strong's*, 2675.

In modern revelation, this principle was taught by the Savior in this way:

And if any man among you be strong in the Spirit, let him take with him that is weak, that he may be edified in all meekness, that he may become strong also. (D&C 84:106)[9]

If you are in a good place, seek out those that may have been overtaken by things of this world and look to strengthen and restore them. As the Savior admonished:

For I was an hungred, and ye gave me meat: I was thirsty, and ye gave me drink: I was a stranger, and ye took me in; Naked, and ye clothed me: I was sick, and ye visited me: I was in prison, and ye came unto me. (Matt. 25:35–36)

Go, and seek to restore someone you love.

---

9. In Doctrine and Covenants 20, the Savior invites us to "watch over," "take the lead," "expound," "visit," "pray," "strengthen," "warn," "teach," "exhort," and "invite all to come unto Christ" (D&C 20:42, 44, 46–47, 53, 59, 81–82).

FOR FURTHER STUDY

- There is a wonderful study of the word "liberty" in Galatians 5:13 if you would like to go on a journey of discovery.
- Genesis 5:18–21 lists several words with rich roots. Consider looking several up using www.biblehub.com and www.blueletterbible.org.

What other unique or insightful words did you find in your study this week?

_____

_____

_____

_____

_____

_____

**Please share with us!
Visit www.ComeFollowMeWOW.com and
share your word discoveries and insights!**

Chapter 39

Ephesians

Don't miss these Words of the Week

"Apostle," "Prophet," "Evangelist," "Pastors,"
and **"Teachers"** (Ephesians 4:11)

"Corrupt Communication" (Ephesians 4:29)

"Bitterness," "Wrath," "Anger," "Clamour," and
"Evil speaking" (Ephesians 4:31)

"Good will" (Ephesians 6:7)

"And he gave some, apostles; and some, prophets; and some, evangelists; and some, pastors and teachers." (Ephesians 4:11)

WHAT A BLESSING TO BELONG TO a living church (see Doctrine and Covenants 1:30). Understanding the doctrine that a living prophet and living apostles walk the earth can bring us joy as members of The Church of Jesus Christ of Latter-day Saints. While there are things about this life that are difficult to understand and at times we feel confused or downtrodden, Church leaders have always been sent to help.

Ephesians 4 provides a list of some of the ordained leaders that the Lord has provided to our Church (and other faiths) to help guide His children:

- Apostles (Greek *apostolous*): An ambassador of the gospel; a commissioner of Christ.

- Prophet (Greek *prophētas*): A foreteller or seer; an inspired speaker.
- Evangelist (Greek *euangelistas):* Bearer of good tidings. "An evangelist is a Patriarch. . . . Wherever the Church of Christ is established in the earth, there should be a Patriarch for the benefit of the posterity of the Saints, as it was with Jacob in giving his patriarchal blessing unto his sons."[1]
- Pastor (Greek *poimenas*): A shepherd; the feeder, protector, and ruler of a flock of men. For Latter-day Saints, pastors are bishops and stake presidents.[2]
- Teacher (Greek *didasko*): An instructor (and think of the endorsement the Lord gave to people called to teach in our Church; they are esteemed in the list including prophets, apostles, patriarchs, bishops, stake presidents!)

The choice is now ours: Will we follow His prophets and His apostles? Will we seek blessings from patriarchs and heed council from bishop and stake presidents? Will we prepare to be taught by inspired teachers at Church or in our homes? With our sustaining votes, we should do more than just raise our hands. We will feel a little less lonely and a lot more empowered as we follow those the Lord has called and ordained to lead us in these days.

"Let no corrupt communication proceed out of your mouth." (Ephesians 4:29)

HUMOR IS A GREAT WAY TO reduce stress, but in Ephesians 4:29, Paul addresses what he called "corrupt communication." The Greek word chosen for "corrupt" is *sapros* and the Latin counterpart, *corruptus,* share the definitions, "rotten, spoiled, useless, corrupt, worthless."[3] And if there is one type of humor or communication that truly is worthless and that Christians should try to avoid, it's sarcasm.

The Greek root for "sarcasm" is *sarkazein* and means "to strip the flesh."[4] One dictionary defines "sarcasm" as "irony designed to give pain."[5] A visual that may amplify this definition is to picture sarcasm as humor wrapped in barbed wire.

---

1. *History of the Church*, 3:381; from a discourse given by Joseph Smith on June 27, 1839, in Commerce, Illinois; reported by Willard Richards.
2. Bruce R. McConkie, *Doctrinal New Testament Commentary* (Bookcraft, 1966), 2:510.
3. *Strong's*, 4554.
4. See "sarcasm," *Online Etymology Dictionary.*
5. See Merriam-Webster Dictionary, "sarcasm."

Sarcasm has many uses in our communication: it can convey an insult, it can be used to dominate or intimidate, and it can communicate contempt and anger. Not all sarcasm is intentionally sinister, but it has an edge to it because it requires us to say the opposite of what we mean. Some use it for humor, but it often damages our relationships because it leaves our friends and family doubting our sincerity and confused by what we say.[6]

We are counseled to live with "cheerful hearts and countenances," but also to avoid "much laughter, for this is sin" (D&C 59:15). Puns, exaggeration, understatement, irony, and clever wit can help build relationships and cause happiness to be felt. Sarcasm, in contrast, can wound more than help. Sarcasm is rampant in American culture and media. It can be the most damaging form of humor through the cutting, hostile, and contemptuous feelings it creates. President Gordon B. Hinckley identified the damage that sarcasm inflicts on our relationships:

> Everywhere is heard the snide remark, the sarcastic gibe, the cutting down of associates. Sadly, these are too often the essence of our conversation. In our homes, wives weep and children finally give up under the barrage of criticism leveled by husbands and fathers. Criticism is the forerunner of divorce, the cultivator of rebellion, sometimes a catalyst that leads to failure. . . . I am asking that we look a little deeper for the good, that we still voices of insult and sarcasm, that we more generously compliment virtue and effort.[7]

All our communication should uplift and strengthen others and never tear down. In contrast to corrupt communication, Elder Richard G. Scott of the Quorum of the Twelve Apostles has taught that "a good sense of humor helps revelation" and that it "is an escape valve for the pressures of life."[8]

Good humor truly is a gift. It can act as a medicine to the soul by relieving tension and bringing comfort to potentially embarrassing situations (see Proverbs 17:22). It can change attitudes, generate love, and add joy to life. But the use of corrupt communication, including sarcasm, can be spiritually destructive without a proper understanding of the situation and audience.

As believers in Christ, we should shape our humor in the light of Christ's teachings and never use any corrupt communication, especially sarcasm, to

---

6. See Jennifer Grace Jones, "No Corrupt Communications," *Ensign*, Aug. 2013.
7. Gordon B. Hinckley, "The Continuing Pursuit of Truth," *Ensign*, Apr. 1986.
8. Richard G. Scott, "How to Obtain Revelation and Inspiration for Your Personal Life," *Ensign*, May 2012, 46.

"strip the flesh" from other people. Always strive to be careful as you communicate with others.

"Let all bitterness, and wrath, and anger, and clamour, and evil speaking, be put away." (Ephesians 4:31)

AVOIDING ANGER CAN BE SO CHALLENGING! From annoying drivers on the road to a spouse's frustrating actions to disagreements at work or on social media, ridding our lives of anger is daunting. In *Handbook for Families*, it says that anger is a choice:

> Thus, to be angry is a choice we make; it is not "caused" by anything or anyone outside ourselves. If we can teach our children, in both words and actions, that choosing not to respond in anger *is* within our control, we will teach them one of life's most valuable lessons.[9]

Anger is a secondary emotion. We don't instantly feel angry. We usually feel undervalued or misunderstood or mistreated, and our "natural man" coping mechanism is to contend with anger (see 3 Nephi 11:29). Although some may argue there is a healthy way to release anger, our goal from a gospel perspective is to both control and eliminate it.

In Ephesians 4, the apostle Paul lists several emotions that we should guard against:

- Bitterness (Greek *pikria*): Harshness, embittered (resentful) spirit.
- Wrath (Greek *thymos*): An outburst of passion.
- Anger (Greek *orgē*): Violent passion; abhorrence.
- Clamour (Greek *blasphēmia*): Abusive language; vilification (same root as "blasphemy")
- Evil speaking (Greek *kakia*): badness, depravity, malignity, or trouble.

Picture our world (or your life) free from harshness and embittered (resentful) feelings. Free of passionate outbursts of rage. Without abhorrence for other people and without any abusive language or vilification. A world (and life) free of trouble.

Here are a few questions to ask when you feel the feelings anger bubbling up inside:

9. "Dealing with Anger and Contention," *Ensign*, Sept. 1988.

- Am I assuming the best intentions of those that upset me?
- Was the offense a one-time incident or was there a pattern of behavior/rhetoric?
- Is there "more"? Have I misunderstood or misinterpreted their words or actions?
- Is there a chance I may be wrong?
- Was the individual acting in their ordained role as a leader or was their humanity on display?
- Am I willing to give grace to the individual?
- Is my response to their action founded on humility?
- Am I going through the proper channels to share my concerns?
- Am I more focused on my relationship with the Savior or on the incident?

Don't get discouraged when you are trying to school your feelings of anger. Remember perfection cannot be achieved in this life. However, with help from the Savior and His Atonement, we can continue to improve and live a life with better and holier expressions.

"Husbands, love your wives." (Ephesians 5:25)

CAN YOU REMEMBER A GROUP PROJECT that you liked? Whether it's at school, work, or church, trying to bring a group of different personalities together to accomplish anything is a difficult, often frustrating, challenge. But every so often, you get a group member whose skills match your weaknesses, and you're able to accomplish the impossible together. In that way, marriage is the greatest group project we've ever been assigned.

In the first marriage, Eve was created as Adam's "help meet." The Hebrew term for the phrase "help meet" (*ezer kenegdo*) literally means "a helper suited to, worthy of, or corresponding to him."[10] The King James translators rendered this phrase "help meet" which to them meant, "fitting" or "proper."[11] The phrase "help meet" might be easier to understand were there a comma after "help"; were such the case, the passage from Genesis would read: "I will make him an help, meet for him."[12]

---

10. As indicated in the footnote to Genesis 2:18 in the Latter-day Saint edition of the Bible (footnote note 18b)
11. See www.biblehub.cominterlinear/genesis/2-18.htm.
12. See David Rolph Seely, "What does it mean when the Lord said he would create for Adam 'An Helpmeet for Him'?" *Ensign*, Jan. 1994.

In the phrase *ezer kenegdo*, *ezer* describes an equal partner. The Old Testament describes how God is an *ezer* (or partner) to man. Historical and etymological evidence indicates that *ezer* originally meant "to rescue; to save; or to be strong." Other Biblical scholars have rendered the translation as "to save from extremity," "to deliver from death."[13] It refers to the actions of one who gives water to someone dying of thirst, thus saving his life.[14]

Historically, there have been some misunderstandings about what the phrase "help meet" means.[15] In the seventeenth century, "help" and "meet" were mistaken as one word that meant wife. Then in the eighteenth century, the spelling "helpmate" was introduced.

Elder Earl C. Tingey of the Presidency of the Seventy taught that a help meet is an equal companion and partner:

> A helpmeet is a companion suited to or equal to [the other]. [They] walk side by side . . ., not one before or behind the other. A help-meet results in an absolute equal partnership between a husband and a wife. Eve was to be equal to Adam as a husband and wife are to be equal to each other.[16]

Eve was designed to be Adam's mirror opposite, possessing the other half of the qualities, responsibilities, and attributes that he lacked. Taking these insights and etymology together, we might translate Genesis 2:18 as, "It is not good that man should be alone. I will make him an equal companion of strength with power to save."

When Adam gave names to every living creature, Eve was not included among the creations he was given dominion over. Eve was (figuratively) created from Adam's rib.[17] One biblical scholar noted that the rib symbolized

---

13. See "A Suitable Helper (in Hebrew)" *Marg Mowczko: Exploring the biblical theology of Christian egalitarianism,* 8 Mar. 2010, margmowczko.com/a-suitable-helper.

14. See Samuel L. Terrien, *Till the Heart Sings: A Biblical Theology of Manhood and Womanhood* (Fortress Press, 1985), 10.

15. The American Heritage Dictionary further explains: "In the 17th century the two words 'help' and 'meet' in this passage were mistaken for one word, applying to Eve, and thus 'help meet' came to mean 'a wife.' Then in the 18th century, in a misguided attempt to make sense of the word, the spelling 'helpmate' was introduced" (Second college edition, [Boston: Houghton Mifflin, 1982], 604).

16. Earl C. Tingey, "The Simple Truths from Heaven—The Lord's Pattern," Church Educational System fireside for young adults, 13 Jan. 2008, speeches.byu.edu.

17. See Spencer W. Kimball, "The Blessings and Responsibilities of Womanhood," *Ensign,* Mar. 1976.

their physical union and "that she is his companion and partner, ever at his side."[18]

Eve was created to help Adam rule and give helpful support, feedback, council, and suggestion so they could rule *together* as equal partners. The prophet Peter advised that husbands counsel with their wives:

> Likewise, ye husbands, dwell with them according to knowledge, giving honour unto the wife . . . that your prayers be not hindered. (1 Peter 3:7)

If we as spouses don't consult with each other, we will be helpless, and Peter taught that our prayers will be hindered.[19]

General authorities have often expressed the equality of husband and wife.[20] President Howard W. Hunter counseled that priesthood holders must accept their wives as equal partners in leading their homes and families:

> A man who holds the priesthood accepts his wife as a partner in the leadership of the home and family with full knowledge of and full participation in all decisions relating thereto.[21]

The etymology behind the word "helpmeet" reveals a beautiful root. It doesn't mean a couple is the same in everything, only that they fit together in harmony. They complement each other; they are co-equals in their relationship. Just as the B-flat key on the piano is not the same as the F key, together they make a harmonious chord. Similarly, the best group member is one who is different from us, but well-suited to us, one who completes us in every way and who brings harmony, not discord, to the relationship. As *helpmeets*, a couple can rule their home and family in harmony with each other and within the Lord's parameters.

---

18. Nahum M. Sarna, *Genesis: The Traditional Hebrew Text with new JPS Translation/Commentary by Nahum M. Sarna* (Philadelphia, New York, Jerusalem: The Jewish Publication Society, 1989), 22.

19. Remember that Adam doesn't have absolute authority: he has authority under the one he has submitted to. He's not the man WITH authority, he's the man UNDER authority.

20. Elder Boyd K. Packer counseled Fathers to remember that "Your wife is your partner in the leadership of the family and should have full knowledge of and full participation in all decisions relating to your home" (see "The Father and the Family," *Ensign*, May 1994, 21).

21. Howard W. Hunter, "Being a Righteous Husband and Father," *Ensign*, Nov. 1994, 50.

"With good will doing service." (Ephesians 6:7)

WHEN MOST PEOPLE HEAR THE TERM "good will" their minds think of stores that take in old or used items to resell to the poor and needy. Others, when they hear the term "good will" think of the beloved Christmas song echoing, "Peace on earth and *good will* toward man."

The word translated as "good will" in Ephesians 6:7 is *eunoias* in Greek.[22] This word happens to be where our English word "enthusiasm" originates. Both the term "good will" used by Paul and the word "enthusiasm" have the same meaning and share synonyms such as "excitement" or "passion" or "energy."

The word "enthusiasm" was first coined in 1603 from the Middle French word *enthousiasme*, from the Latin *enthousiasmus*, and from the Greek *enthousiasmos*. Each of these words, in French, Latin, and Greek mean something remarkable: "possessed by gods" (the prefix *en*, meaning "within," and *theos*, meaning "God").[23] In fact, the word "enthusiasm" was once used to describe people who possessed God-like abilities or God-inspired wisdom or conviction.

Ralph Waldo Emerson wrote that enthusiasm leads to success:

Enthusiasm is one of the most powerful engines of success. When you do a thing, do it with all your might. Put your whole soul into it. Stamp it with your own personality. Be active, be energetic, be enthusiastic and faithful, and you will accomplish your objective. Nothing great was ever achieved without enthusiasm.[24]

When people are truly filled with "good will" there is a natural enthusiasm about them. They seem to be lead by a power that is greater than themselves. Rather than simply just "going through the motions," those with true *enthusiasm* do things out of alignment with God's will and with God's power within them. Without enthusiasm—without "God within"—nothing eternally great can be achieved. With enthusiasm, all things are possible—and will last.

As you seek to magnify a calling or as you show "good will" to friends and neighbors, do so with true *enthusiasm*, knowing you are God's errand, and that God is "within" you.

---

22. *Strong's,* 2133.
23. "Enthusiasm," *Online Etymology Dictionary.*
24. Ralph Waldo Emerson, *The Collected Works of Ralph Waldo Emerson: Society and solitude,* ed. Alfred Riggs Ferguson, et al. (Harvard University Press, 1971), 415.

FOR FURTHER STUDY

- The etymology of the word "gather" (see Ephesians 1:10) has wonderful applications to us today. Consider looking up its origin and meaning using www.etymonline.com to find relevant meaning.

- Paul wrote about "the power of [the Lord's] might" (see Ephesians 6:10–13). The word "might" is instructive, so consider a study of its Greek meaning using www.biblehub.com and www.blueletterbible.org.

- The word "quench" is used in a few New Testament passages. This week we find it in Paul's message about the armor of Go (see Ephesians 6:10–18). Look up this word "quench" and what it means using www.biblehub.com and www.blueletterbible.org and consider how it applies to the armor of God.

What other unique or insightful words did you find in your study this week?

_____

_____

_____

_____

_____

_____

Please share with us!
Visit www.ComeFollowMeWOW.com and
share your word discoveries and insights!

Chapter 40

Philippians; Colossians

Don't miss these Words of the Week

"Passeth all understanding" (Philippians 4:7)
"Redemption" (Colossians 1:14)
"Content" (Philippians 4:11)

"Peace that passeth all understanding."
(Philippians 4:7)

FRENZIED FEELINGS OF PANIC OR ANXIETY are so common today. Maybe it doesn't happen continually, but every once in a while, something happens, or someone says something that pushes a button inside of us and throws us into a spiral of emotion. When this occurs, many of us say and do things we later regret (and we feel silly that we let the adversary get ahold of our hearts).

In Philippians 4:7, the apostle Paul writes, "And the peace of God, which passeth all understanding, shall keep your hearts and minds through Christ Jesus." The word "passeth" is the Greek word *huperecho*, which is a compound of the words *huper* and *echo*.

The word *huper* literally means "over, above, and beyond."[1] It depicts something that is way beyond measure. The peace that Christ offers is above all description, superior to anything else in this world; it is incomparable to any other feeling in mortality.

---

1. *Strong's*, 5242.

The second part of the word "passeth" is the Greek word *echo*, which means "to keep or possess."

When these words are compounded, they form the Greek word *huper-echo*, a word denoting a peace so superior that it is held high above all other types of peace.

You may have tried to find peace in other places, but there is no peace like the peace of God. The peace of God completely outshines every other attempt. There is absolutely nothing in the world that can compare with the peace of God. When this peace operates in you, it dominates your mind and your life. It stands at the gate of your heart and mind, disabling the devil's ability to disturb you.

In every situation of stress, let God's supernatural peace rise up to dominate your heart and protect your mind and emotions.

"I have learned, in whatsoever state I am, therewith to be content." (Philippians 4:11)

CORRIE AND BETSIE TEN BOOM WERE courageous, compassionate Dutch Christians who were imprisoned at Ravensbrück, a German concentration camp. To their utter annoyance, the barracks in which they were imprisoned was infested with fleas. *Fleas.* It was so badly infested that the guards would rarely check on them for fear of being bitten themselves.

One day, Corrie drew out the small Bible she had managed to smuggle into the concentration camp. She read, "Rejoice always, pray constantly, give thanks in all circumstances; for this is the will of God in Christ Jesus" (1 Thessalonians 5:14–18).

Teaching a similar principle, the apostle Paul wrote, "I have learned, in whatsoever state I am, therewith to be content" (Philippians 4:11). The Greek word employed here by Paul is *autarkēs* and the Latin equivalent, *contentus,*2 both mean "self-sufficient, contented, satisfied, independent."3

We can learn a lot from these passages: as we give thanks in all circumstances and as we learn to be content in all things, we can start to feel power in our lives. The two sisters, amid the constant bites of the little fleas, decided to thank God for every single thing about their barracks. Betsie prayed:

"Thank you for the fleas and for . . ." It was too much for Corrie. She cut in on her sister: "Betsie, there's no way even God can make

2. "Content," *Online Etymology Dictionary.*
3. *Strong's,* 842.

me grateful for a flea." "'Give thanks in all circumstances,'" Betsie corrected. "It doesn't say, 'in pleasant circumstances.' Fleas are part of this place where God has put us."

So they gave thanks for the fleas. Though Corrie thought Betsie was completely wrong at first, she later came to realize that because of the fleas the Nazi soldiers stayed away from their barracks, and because of that, their Bibles were never found and confiscated, and she remembered Betsie bowing her head and thanking God for creatures that Corrie could see no use for. [4]

May our own hearts and lips overflow with gratitude this Thanksgiving season and throughout the year. Even when faced with deeply trying and discouraging circumstances, we can identify numerous blessings that the Lord continues to pour into our lives. Some of those blessings come as a result of the difficulties we're facing. As we focus on the Lord's blessings, we will be heartened and enabled to persevere through life's discouragements. And we'll never fail to appropriately honor God by thanking Him for His ever-present blessings.

"In whom we have redemption through his blood, even the forgiveness of sins." (Colossians 1:14)

IT HAS BEEN REPORTED THAT THERE are nearly 200 names for Jesus in the New Testament.[5] Among the most significant is the title *Redeemer*.

The word "redeem" (Greek *apolytrōsin*) means "to pay off a debt or to ransom in full"[6] (if someone makes a mistake and corrects it, we say he or she has redeemed themself). The Latin *redemptionem* means "a buying back, or a releasing."[7] This is the crux of Paul's message to the saints in Colosia in Colossians 1:14: "In whom we have *redemption* through his blood, even the forgiveness of sins" (Colossians 1:14).

To *redeem* something means to buy it back or to restore it. People use the word "redeem" when they buy something back.[8] We also use the word

---

4. Corrie ten Bloom, *The Hiding Place*, ed. Elizabeth Sherrill and John L. Sherrill (Hendrickson Publishers, 2009), 179.
5. Alexander Cruden, *A Complete Concordance to the Holy Scriptures of the Old and New Testament: or a Dictionary and Alphabetical Index to the Bible* (commonly called Cruden's Concordance) first edition (MA, 1737), and successive editions (publishers vary).
6. *Strong's*, 629.
7. "Redemption," *Online Etymology Dictionary*.
8. If you had a major economic downturn and had to sell an expensive piece of jewelry for cash—but then wound up with enough money in time—you could buy back the

"redeem" when we trade in a coupon, or *redeem* it, as we are given the cash equivalent for its value. You see, through presenting your faith in and testimony of the Savior and His Atonement, redemption will come to you. Jesus paid the full price to buy us back—to *redeem* us—from the eternal condemnation of sin. He offers His redemption to us freely, but it wasn't free. It cost Him everything.

The Plan of Salvation required a redeemer:

Whom shall I send? [Who will be the Redeemer?] And one answered like unto the Son of Man: Here am I, send me. And another answered and said: Here am I, send me. And the Lord said: I will send the first. And the second was angry and kept not his first estate; and, at that day, many followed after him. (See Abraham 3:22–28)

The Lord taught Moses more about this defining moment:

That Satan, whom thou hast commanded in the name of mine Only Begotten, is the same which was from the beginning, and he came before me saying—Behold, here am I, send me, I will be thy son, and I will redeem all mankind, that one soul shall not be lost, and surely I will do it; wherefore give me thine honor.

But, behold, my Beloved Son, which was my Beloved and Chosen from the beginning, said unto me—Father, thy will be done, and the glory be thine forever. (Moses 4:1–2)

Jesus Christ is the great Redeemer of mankind. Through His Atonement, He paid the price for the sins of mankind and made possible the resurrection of all. Consider a few ways that you can show your personal gratitude for the gift that your Redeemer offers you.

FOR FURTHER STUDY

- There is a theme of joy and rejoicing in this week's study. Consider a study of these two words and their origins using www.biblehub.com, www.blueletterbible.org, and www.etymonline.com.
- The words "grounded" and "rooted" are used by Paul in Colossians 1:23; 2:7. Each has a fascinating history, so consider a study of each of them using www.etymonline.com.

---

jewelry. That buy-back process is known to some as "redeeming."

What other unique or insightful words did you find in your study this week?

_____

_____

_____

_____

_____

_____

Please share with us!
Visit www.ComeFollowMeWOW.com and
share your word discoveries and insights!

Chapter 41

1 and 2 Thessalonians

Don't miss these Words of the Week

"**Defraud**" (1 Thessalonians 4:6)
"**Caught Up**" (1 Thessalonians 4:17)
"**Edify**" 1 Thessalonians 5:11)
"**Quench**" (1 Thessalonians 5:19)

"That no man go beyond and defraud his brother." (1 Thessalonians 4:6)

From failed business dealings, to outright lies being told about us, to being sucked into a scam promising big financial returns, elements of *fraud* plague our society. These entrapments can wreck families, injure reputations, and put financial constraints on people for years.

It appears that only on rare occasions throughout history have societies been free from contention, envyings, strifes, tumults, whoredoms, lyings, murders, and "any manner of lasciviousness" (see 4 Nephi 1:15–16). And when people have unshackled themselves from these societal ills, it's usually because they chose to love God more deeply. It seems that loving God is a precursor to loving our fellow man.

The English word "defraud" used by Paul is *hyperbainein* in Greek.[1] It means "to transgress against" or "to overreach." The Latin word *fraudem* means "cheater or deceiver."[2]

In Doctrine and Covenants 50:2–3, the Lord taught about deception:

> Behold, verily I say unto you, that there are many spirits which are false spirits, which have gone forth in the earth, deceiving the world. And also Satan hath sought to deceive you, that he might overthrow you.

Yes, and sadly, the Lord saw people in our day who would try to defraud others.

Since you are reading this book, it's unlikely that you are actively seeking to defraud those around you, but it may be wise to take a quick inventory. Are there any actions you are engaged in that might be dangerous to other people emotionally, financially, or spiritually? Is there any sign of overreach in your relationships? Is there anything small you are doing that is actually cheating? Is there any element of your communications with others that might be a bit deceptive?

A life that is transparent and free from the stains of any form of fraud is a life founded in happiness. And as we truly avoid fraud of any kind, we, like the Nephites, "could not be a happier people among all the people who had been created by the hand of God" (4 Nephi 1:16) as we show our love to our fellow man by acting without deceit, overreaching, or cheating.

"Then we which are alive and remain shall be caught up together with them in the clouds." (1 Thessalonians 4:17)

PICTURE YOURSELF SITTING QUIETLY AT HOME one day, enjoying some music and drinking a favorite drink. As you gaze out the window, much to your surprise, you see several neighbors floating up toward the skies. Amazement and wonder (and a mix of confusion) fill your mind as you cannot comprehend what is happening.

Insert the doctrine of the Saints being "caught up" to the clouds (1 Thessalonians 4:17).

The term "rapture" is used by many Christian-based faiths for this event. They, along with Latter-day Saints, teach that when Christ comes, all

---

1. *Strong's*, 5233.
2. "Fraud," *Online Etymology Dictionary*.

living believers will be "caught up" to meet Him in the clouds and experience a translation of their bodies from mortal to immortal (without experiencing physical death).

The word "rapture" is said to come from a Latin translation of the Greek word *harpazo* (see 1 Thessalonians 4:17). *Harpazo* is translated in English as "caught up." It means literally "to seize or snatch."[3]

Jesus taught that angels shall gather God's elect in the last days:

> Immediately after the tribulation of those days shall the sun be darkened . . . And then shall appear the sign of the Son of man in heaven . . . And he shall send his angels with a great sound of a trumpet, and they shall gather together his elect. (Matt. 24:29–31)

Modern revelation adds:

> But before the arm of the Lord shall fall, an angel shall sound his trump, and the saints that have slept shall come forth to meet me in the cloud. (D&C 45:45)

Publications by The Church of Jesus Christ of Latter-day Saints do not use the word "rapture" when referring to the events of the Second Coming of Christ.[4] Rather, our leaders have focused their messages on being prepared materially, physically, and spiritually for the Second Coming.

If the Second Coming were to happen today, would you feel ready to be "caught up" to meet Him in the clouds? If not, seek to make a few adjustments so you could more confidently greet Him in a future day.

"Edify one another." (1 Thessalonians 5:11)

PAUL SEEMS TO HAVE A CATCHPHRASE in the New Testament: "edify one another." In Greek, the word "edify" is translated as *parakaleite*, which means "to encourage and invoke."[5] The Latin word for "edify" means "to build a house," "to erect a building," or "to build up from the ground" (the word "edify" and the word "edifice" come from the same root).[6] "Edify" appears in the King James Bible nearly 20 times (only in the New Testament) and it's translated into phrases such as "building up" in several modern translations.

---

3. *Strong's*, 726.
4. Possibly because the root word of "rapture" is tied to *rape*.
5. *Strong's*, 3870.
6. "Edify," *Online Etymology Dictionary*.

Building a solid edifice requires a well-thought-out plan and an exact execution of that plan. Similarly, to edify others, divine plans must be in place, and those plans are foundational to the long-term and lasting establishment of the edification of one another.

By way of analogy, the arch was a very popular structure in medieval architecture. The greatest advantage of an arch in building was its strength and stability as each stone in the arch leaned on the one beside it. This system of mutual support enabled the construction of much larger structures than might otherwise have been possible.

In application, just like an arch, we all need one another to build up and strengthen one another. We can have a system of mutual support from our fellow church members *and* our fellow Christians. As soon as we stop relying on each other, we lose strength.

Edification might be best summarized by Paul's words to the Saints in Ephesus:

> Let no corrupt communication proceed out of your mouth, but that which is good to the use of edifying, that it may minister grace unto the hearers. (Ephesians 4:29)

Let us "minister grace" unto others with words that build up, rather than words that tear down, and "let us consider one another to provoke unto love and to good works" (Hebrews 10:24). We live in a time that champions individual success over the wellbeing of the whole, but as believers in Christ we can be champions of edification. This principle may be more important today than at any time in the Church's history!

"Quench not the Spirit." (1 Thessalonians 5:19)

FOR THOSE THAT HAVE PUT OUT a campfire or blown out a candle, there is something satisfying about watching the flame die and the smoke cut out. It's hard to not extinguish a flame and not stare in amazement as the life of the fire is taken away.

In several New Testament passages, Paul used the phrase "Quench not the Spirit" in his letters to believers. Other versions of the Bible render this phrase as:

- Do not stifle the Holy Spirit (New Living Translation)
- Do not extinguish the Spirit (Borean Bible)
- Don't turn away God's Spirit (Contemporary English Version)
- Do not restrain the Holy Spirit (Good News Translation)

- Do not put out the Spirit's fire (International Standard Version)

"Quench" is a fascinating word. The Greek word used here is *sbennyte* and it means "to extinguish, suppress, or thwart."[7] It also means "to cool or extinguish by means of water" (hence the terms "to drench in water" from the late 15th century).

A beloved hymn of the Latter-day Saints, "The Spirit of God," speaks of the fire of God's Spirit.[8] Can God's Spirit really be *quenched,* or *extinguished*? According to Paul, possibly so! As Elder David A. Bednar taught:

> The standard is clear. If something we think, see, hear, or do distances us from the Holy Ghost, then we should stop thinking, seeing, hearing, or doing that thing. If that which is intended to entertain, for example, alienates us from the Holy Spirit, then certainly that type of entertainment is not for us. Because the Spirit cannot abide that which is vulgar, crude, or immodest, then clearly such things are not for us. Because we estrange the Spirit of the Lord when we engage in activities we know we should shun, then such things definitely are not for us.[9]

Remember, "If there is anything virtuous, lovely, or of good report or praiseworthy, we seek after these things."[10] In other words, "quench not the Spirit"!

---

7. *Strong's*, 4570.
8. See "The Spirit of God," *Hymns*, no. 2.
9. David A. Bednar, "That They May Always Have His Spirit to Be with Us," *Ensign*, May 2006, 30.
10. Articles of Faith 1:13.

FOR FURTHER STUDY

- There is a wonderful application with the meaning of the word "weary" in 2 Thessalonians 3:13. Consider a study of this word's etymology using www.etymonline.com.

- In 2 Thessalonians 1:9, Paul speaks of being "punished with everlasting destruction." Latter-day revelation sheds light on this phrase. Consider studying D&C 19:1–5 and comparing it to this passage.

- 2 Thessalonians 2:3 uses the phrase "falling away" in reference to the Apostasy. Consider looking at this phrase in Greek using www.biblehub.com and www.blueletterbible.org to see what applications there are to the restoration of the gospel.

- Did you know that the word "busybody" is scriptural? Look at 2 Thessalonians 3:11. Study that word using www.biblehub.com and www.blueletterbible.org and see what modern-day relevance that term has.

What other unique or insightful words did you find in your study this week?

Please share with us!
Visit www.ComeFollowMeWOW.com and
share your word discoveries and insights!

Chapter 42

1 and 2 Timothy; Titus; Philemon

Don't miss these Words of the Week

"Bishop" (Timothy's calling)
"Modest" (1 Timothy 2:9)
"Example" (1 Timothy 4:12)
"Canker" (2 Timothy 2:17)
"Endure" (2 Timothy 4:3)
"Full Proof" (2 Timothy 4:5)

**"Women adorn themselves in
modest apparel." (1 Timothy 2:9)**

SOME MIGHT THINK THAT *MODESTY* IS a topic for girls and women, but nothing could be further from the truth! The word "modesty" in both Greek and Latin means "well arranged, ordered or measured, and of good behavior."[1] In other words, when people are modest, they *arrange* and *measure* their lives in an *orderly* way; their words are chosen carefully, as are their clothes and their thoughts. That is something that we all can aspire to!

Being modest connotes balance, proportion, restraint, and moderation ("moderation" shares the same root as "modest"). Similar to its cousin characteristic charity, modesty "vaunteth not itself, . . . doth not behave itself unseemly" (see 1 Corinthians 13:4–5). Being modest and measured means

---

1. "κόσμιος", *Blue Letter Bible*, www.blueletterbible.org/lexicon/g2887/kjv/tr/0-1/, accessed on 15 July 2021.

that one does not seek personal attention, does not flaunt, but shows respect for others—showing sensitivity and tact. "Modesty" means "measured." Its opposites would include words like "excess," "extreme," "lack of restraint," and so forth.

The Greek word for "modesty" (*kosmiō*) used by Paul in 1 Timothy translates essentially as "being respectable."[2] How beautiful is that definition! Modesty originally knew no gender boundary. The Church's website reflects the genderless application of modesty by stating:

> Modesty is an attitude of propriety and decency in dress, grooming, language, and behavior. If we are modest, we do not draw undue attention to ourselves. Instead, we seek to "glorify God in [our] body, and in [our] spirit" (1 Corinthians 6:20; see also 1 Corinthians 6:19).
>
> . . . In dress, grooming, and manners, we should always be neat and clean, never sloppy or inappropriately casual. . . . We should express ourselves through clean, positive, uplifting language and in actions that bring happiness to those around us.[3]

Thus, modesty includes measured dress, speech, conduct, and thoughts. Think on that word today as you go about your daily tasks. What can you do to make your life more measured and orderly?

"If a man desire the office of a bishop, he desireth a good work." (1 Timothy 3:1)

THINK OF HOW MANY DIFFERENT BISHOPS have presided over your wards over your lifetime. It's amazing to think of their various personalities and professions and approaches to their ministries.

Timothy (Greek *Timótheos*, meaning "honouring God" or "honoured by God") was the first bishop in the New Testament church.[4] Paul wrote to him, "If a man desire the office of a bishop, he desireth a good work" (1 Timothy 3:1). The Latin word for "bishop" is *episcopus* and resonates with the Greek *episkopos* which means "watcher" or "overseer"[5] (from *epi-* "over" and *skopos* "one that watches.") Indeed, bishops are guardians and protectors

---

2. *Strong's*, 2887.
3. Gospel Topics, "Modesty," topics.churchofjesuschrist.org.
4. Eusebius, "3.4," *Historia Ecclesiastica [The History of the Church]* translated by Harmondsworth (Williamson, G.A.: Penguin, 1965), 109.
5. *Strong's*, 1984.

who oversee their wards through their priesthood keys. The bishop's duties are complex as he acts as the president of the ward's Aaronic Priesthood, is the presiding high priest in the ward (see D&C 107:15–17) who determines the worthiness of all members of his ward and directs the performance of sacred ordinances (see D&C 107:68–76) and also oversees records, finances, and the use of the meetinghouse.[6]

Elder Quintin L. Cook taught of bishops:

Some words and the sacred callings they describe are imbued with almost a spiritual, transcendent significance. The calling of *bishop* is definitely in the top tier of such words. To serve the Lord in this capacity is remarkable in so many ways. The calling, sustaining, and setting apart of a bishop is a never-to-be-forgotten experience.[7]

To better understand what Timothy, the first bishop—and your current bishop—may endure during their calling as *overseer*, consider these tenderly written words by a former bishop:

I pulled into my driveway at 12:30 this morning.

I sat in the car in front of our dark house for a few minutes. Everyone inside was asleep. The whole neighborhood was still. And yet my mind was racing. So many questions. So many emotions. Sadness. Hope. Inadequacy.

Welcome to the life of a Mormon bishop. . . .

They come to us for various reasons. Because of guilt. Because they have lost hope. Because they have been betrayed. Because they don't know where else to go. Because they feel worthless. Because the person they are isn't the person they want to be. Because they have questions. Because they have doubts. Because they believe in a forgiving God yet feel disconnected from Him. . . .

I did not ask for this opportunity. I never considered I might someday have an office in a church. I have no professional training for this position. I am not a scriptural scholar. . . . All I did was answer a phone call. Show up for a meeting. And nod when asked if I would serve. . . .

---

6. *General Handbook: Serving in the Church of Jesus Christ of Latter-day Saints*, 6.1.5, churchofjesuschrist.org.

7. Quintin L. Cook, "Bishops—Shepherds over the Lord's Flocks," *Liahona*, May 2021.

I'm not sure any of them have learned from me. But, I have learned so much in the hours I've sat in that office listening to them.[8]

I recommend reading the rest of this article; it is illuminating. We can learn a lot about the callings of bishops as we study the books of 1 & 2 Timothy. As you read these books, consider what you can do to sustain your bishop in his calling. Our blessed bishops are keyholders. They hold doors open for us with those keys and that mantel.

"Be thou an example of the believers." (1 Timothy 4:12)

CAN THE INFLUENCE OF ONE RIGHTEOUS man or woman make a difference in the world? The answer is a resounding yes! Paul admonished the faithful to "be thou an example of the believers" (1 Timothy 4:12).

Our English word for "example" is taken from the Latin *exemplum* meaning, "a sample, precedent, or one that serves as a warning."[9] The Greek word for "example" is *typos*; it refers to "a die" or "a stamp" or even "a scar."[10] Think of that: our examples literally become imprinted on others! Each conversation we have—each interaction—leaves an imprint on the people we are around. Each word, each vacation, each text, and every email leaves its impression. What kind of impression are we leaving?

When we think about what it means to be "an example of the believers," we might imagine that we should be walking the pavement like a missionary, handing out pass-along cards to every person we see. But think about the examples in your life who have left an impression on you. Most likely, their example was more in the way that they made you feel than whether or not they were directly preaching the gospel.

You can be an example in your everyday actions, from the way that you listen to others to the way you say hello. Think about what you want to leave with people. How do you want to make them feel? More importantly, how would Christ want you to make them feel?

Today, Heavenly Father performs most of His miracles through His children. If you will allow Him to, He will help you be in the places where

---

8. "'I did not ask for this opportunity:' Confessions of a Mormon bishop," *Deseret News*, 25 Mar. 2013.
9. "Example," *Online Etymology Dictionary*.
10. *Strong's*, 5179.

He needs you to help the people who need you and stand as an example of Him and what He has done for you.

"And their word will eat as doth a canker."
(2 Timothy 2:17)

Ever had an annoying canker sore? Yuk! They are painful, distracting, and, for some people, debilitating.

A church, like a body, can suffer maladies. "Canker" is a word used to describe sores or abscesses on the body, usually around the mouth. The Oxford English Dictionary defines "canker" as "a destructive or corrosive agent; a chronic, non-healing sore or ulcer, especially one that extends into surrounding tissue." Today, we use the root words for "canker" in two ways. We have "canker sores" (which are mostly painful, yet endurable) and we also have another word for "canker" from Latin: it's the word "cancer."[11]

It may be that the Biblical translators saw both canker sores *and* cancer and used the word to warn us about both uncomfortable spiritual ulcerations and possible spiritual debilitation and destruction.

As Paul saw the conditions in Timothy's area, he noted that people were engaged in "profane and vain babblings", and he taught Timothy that their messages would spread like cancer (see 2 Timothy 2:16–17). This is still true in our day. Elder Maxwell said regarding a doctrinally unsound book that was circulating, "It never ceases to amaze me how gullible the Latter-day Saints can be. Our lack of doctrinal sophistication makes us an easy prey for such fads;"[12] his solution for avoiding deceptions regarding doctrine is to learn the true doctrines more fully through daily scripture study.

The canker of which Paul speaks is transmitted verbally and usually comes without physical contact. It goes from the mouth of one person to the ear of another. He counseled, "But shun profane and vain babblings: for they will increase unto more ungodliness" (see 2 Timothy 2:16).

One of the duties of a bishop (remember, Timothy was a bishop), his councilors, and the Sunday School presidency is to see to it that false teachers and false doctrines do not take root in a ward. In the Book of Mormon, Alma commanded the priests he ordained to teach that they only teach gospel truths:

---

11. "Canker," *Online Etymology Dictionary.*
12. Ryan Morgenegg, "Five Ways to Detect and Avoid Doctrinal Deception," *Church News*, 17 Sept. 2013.

And he commanded them that they should teach nothing save it were the things which he had taught, and which had been spoken by the mouth of the holy prophets. (Mosiah 18:19)

Further, the Savior's twelve Nephite disciples followed this same principle as they taught only what Jesus had taught:

They . . . ministered those same words which Jesus had spoken—nothing varying from the words which Jesus had spoken. (3 Nephi 19:8)

Following this precedent, President Harold B. Lee encouraged us to teach doctrines to prevent misunderstanding:

You're to teach the old doctrines, not so plain that they can just understand, *but you must teach the doctrines of the Church so plainly that no one can misunderstand.*[13]

As teachers of the gospel at home or in formal Church meetings, we should ensure that we keep the doctrine pure, that we avoid speculation, misquoting, sensationalism, and private interpretation of doctrine.[14] Why? Those ideas will spread like *cancer.* Be sure to always check (and double check) your sources before you teach or before you speak. Having the full story—and the true doctrine—is crucial, and it can prevent spiritual canker.

As we are prayerful, prepared, and focused on simple and direct doctrine, teaching the scriptures and the words of the prophets and apostles, there is safety. This practice makes for a ward or family free of cankerous infections which can spread quickly.

"For the time will come when they will not endure sound doctrine." (2 Timothy 4:3)

WE USUALLY ASSOCIATE THE WORD "ENDURE" with the phrase "endure to the end" (see D&C 14:7). Paul used the word endure to teach a different principle: *enduring sound doctrine* (see 2 Timothy 4:3).

The Greek word for "endure" is *anexontai* and means "bear with, have patience with, suffer, admit, persist."[15] The Latin term here, *endurer,*

---

13. Harold B. Lee, "Loyalty," in *Charge to Religious Educators,* 2nd ed. (1982), 64.

14. See *Teaching, No Greater Call* (The Church of Jesus Christ of Latter-day Saints, 2013), chapter 11.

15. *Strong's,* 430.

means "to undergo or suffer" (especially without breaking).[16] Using these etymological roots with 2 Timothy 4:3, we learn that in the latter-days, some people would not be able to bear, be patient with, admit, or persist (stay with and not reject) doctrines of the gospel.

Knowing that many would not be able to endure sound doctrine, the Lord encourages all of us to "seek learning, even by study and also by faith" (see Doctrine and Covenants 88:118). From time to time, Church leaders provide information to help answer some of our questions, but it's unlikely they will be able to answer every single question. And that's where our journey comes in—and our test. Can we endure (bear, be patient with, admit, or persist) with sound doctrines of the gospel?

Don't feel embarrassed or unworthy when you have questions or concerns. Almost everyone has questions or concerns at one time or another. When we feel confused or conflicted, we can seek answers using Paul's wise counsel to Timothy to continue in the things that he had "been assured of" (2 Timothy 3:14).

Elder Jeffrey R. Holland gave good advice to those of us who may be feeling a lack of confidence in enduring sound doctrine:

> In moments of fear or doubt or troubling times, hold the ground you have already won, even if that ground is limited. . . . When those moments come and issues surface, the resolution of which is not immediately forthcoming, *hold fast to what you already know and stand strong until additional knowledge comes.* . . . The size of your faith or the degree of your knowledge is not the issue—it is the integrity you demonstrate toward the faith you do have and the truth you already know.[17]

If you are struggling with questions or doubts, know that you are okay. Your feelings and questions are valid—and even foreseen by Paul and other prophets! Take heart, knowing that answers will come as you humbly seek to endure sound doctrines of the gospel.

---

16. "Endure," *Online Etymology Dictionary.*
17. Jeffrey R. Holland, "'Lord, I Believe,'" *Ensign,* May 2013, 93–94.

"Make full proof of thy ministry." (2 Timothy 4:5)

EACH OF US HAS A PERSONAL ministry and calling on the earth. From raising children to being a good spouse or great neighbor, we have several roles to play in addition to formal church callings.

In a letter to Timothy, Paul counseled him to "make full proof of thy ministry" (see 2 Timothy 4:5). Much debate has been made over the term "full proof" and its connection to the phrase "fool proof."[18] The Greek word employed here is *plērophorēson* and means "to carry out fully."[19] In modern terms, we might use the phrase, "magnify your calling." In other words, we are to be "all in."

There is no room for mediocrity. Interestingly, the word "mediocre" is from Latin *mediocris*, meaning "of middling height or state"[20] or, originally, "halfway up a mountain" (from *medius*, "middle," and the word *ocris*, "jagged mountain.")[21]

How many of us are satisfied with mediocrity in our faith? That is, with settling for "halfway up the mountain" levels of faithfulness and devotion? God has so much more for us!

Sir Edmund Hillary was the first to summit Mount Everest. When asked what he thought the key to his success was, he stated:

I have very modest abilities. Academically I was very modest. Mediocre perhaps, and I think perhaps physically I did not have a great athletic sense . . .. But, I think maybe the only thing in which I was less than modest was in motivation. I really wanted very strongly to do many of these things and once I started I didn't give up all that easily.[22]

No one begins to climb any mountain with their hearts set on their car or on their base camp—their hearts are set on the summit. No matter what your calling or ministry is, seek to provide "full proof" of your efforts. Because of our Savior, all of the effort we put into our assignments and roles will be worth it! Why settle for mediocrity when we can climb far higher?

---

18. See, for example, grammarist.com/usage/foolproof/.
19. *Strong's*, 4135.
20. We read an application of the meaning behind the word "mediocre" in Lahonti and Amalickiah's story in Alma 47:10-13.
21. "Full proof," *Online Etymology Dictionary*.
22. Edmund Hillary as quoted on "Sir Edmund Hillary on Perseverance," *Academy of Achievement*, achievement.org/video/edmund-hillary-1/.

FOR FURTHER STUDY

- The Greek word for "adorn" (see 1 Timothy 2:9–10) has a wonderful history. Consider doing some research on what it meant originally using www.biblehub.com and www.blueletterbible.org.

- There is a wonderful history behind the terms "perilous times" from 2 Timothy 3:1; consider looking at its Greek roots using www.etymonline.com, www.biblehub.com, and www.blueletterbible.org.

- In 1 Timothy, Paul's messages about women can feel infuriating and misogynistic without an understanding of the Greek meanings of some words and phrases he used. Consider a deep dive to those verses using www.biblehub.com and www.blueletterbible.org to discover applications.

- Paul spoke of evils that "creep in our houses and lead us captive" (see 2 Timothy 3:6). Consider studying the root of the word "creep" using www.etymonline.com and look for its relevance.

- "Profitable"? Used to describe scripture? Yes! Take a look at that word in Greek using www.biblehub.com and www.blueletterbible.org as you study 2 Timothy 3:14–17.

What other unique or insightful words did you find in your study this week?

_____

_____

_____

_____

_____

_____

Please share with us!
Visit www.ComeFollowMeWOW.com and
share your word discoveries and insights!

Chapter 43

Hebrews 1-6

Don't miss these Words of the Week

"**Catholic**" (Hebrews 1:1)
"**Iniquity**" (Hebrews 1:9)
"**Mercy**" (Hebrews 4:16)

"God, who at sundry times and in divers manners spake in time past unto the fathers by the prophets." (Hebrews 1:1)

THE BEAUTIFUL CATHOLIC FAITH LINKS ITS beginning with the charge given by Jesus when He commissioned His apostles with the words:

> Go ye therefore, and teach all nations, baptizing them in the name of the Father, and of the Son, and of the Holy Spirit: Teaching them to observe all things whatsoever I have commanded you: and, lo, I am with you alway, even unto the end of the world. (Matthew 28:19–20)[1]

Notice first the threefold "all"—*all* nations, *all* things, *alway*. Those of the Catholic faith understand this word to mean, "universal"—all.[2]

---

1. In 2 Timothy 4:21, Linus is listed. According to Catholic tradition, Pope Linus was the second bishop of Rome. Clement I, a contemporary and in the same papal line, is mentioned in Philippians 4:3.
2. Frank Sheed, *Theology and Sanity* (San Francisco, CA: Ignatius Press, 1993), 284.

The word "catholic" comes from the Greek *katholikos*, the combination of two words: *kata* which means "concerning," and *holos* which means "whole."[3] The first recorded use of the word is found very early in Christian literature. We find in the first instance the writings of St. Ignatius of Antioch.[4] During its genesis, the word "catholic" hardly seemed to apply. But as the Church grew and spread, Jews, Gentiles, Romans, freemen, and slaves began to embrace the faith.

In March 2019, President Russell M. Nelson visited the Vatican and met Pope Francis. After the meeting, President Nelson remarked, "The differences in doctrine are real—and they're important—but they're not nearly as important as the things we have in common."[5] He went on to speak of our many commonalities, including:

> Our [common] concern for human suffering, our desire for and the importance of religious liberty for all of society, and the importance of building bridges of friendship instead of building walls of segregation.[6]

On this same subject, Professor Luis Ladaria once wrote in an essay:

> Catholics and Mormons often find themselves working together on a range of problems regarding the common good of the entire human race. It can be hoped therefore that through further studies, dialogue and good will, there can be progress in reciprocal understanding and mutual respect.[7]

This meeting between President Nelson and Pope Francis was indeed historic, healing—and unifying. The Roman Catholic Church has incorrectly been accused of being the "great and abominable church" that Nephi saw in vision (see 1 Nephi 13–14, Revelation 17).[8] Of this fallacy, Elder Stephen E. Robinson of the Seventy stated:

3. "Catholic," *Online Etymology Dictionary*.
4. Letter to the Smyrnaeans 8, J.R. Willis translation.
5. The remarks echoed what Archbishop George Niederauer said at the 2010 ground-breaking ceremony for the Rome, Italy temple: "We cannot pretend there are not differences, but we can recognize that what is in common is much stronger than what is different."
6. See Sarah Jane Weaver, "President Nelson Meets with Pope Francis at the Vatican," *Church News*, 9 Mar. 2019.
7. Fr. Luis Ladaria, S.J., "The Question of the Validity of Baptism Conferred in The Church of Jesus Christ of Latter-day Saints," *L'Osservatore Romano*, 1 Aug. 2001, 4, www.vatican.va, as accessed 9 May 2021.
8. In the 1958 edition of *Mormon Doctrine*, on page 129, Elder Bruce R. McConkie, in defining the "Church of the Devil," cites the Roman Catholic Church specifically as

This is . . . untenable, primarily because Roman Catholicism as we know it did not yet exist when the crimes described by Nephi were being committed. . . .The notion of shifty-eyed medieval monks rewriting the scriptures is unfair and bigoted. We owe those monks a debt of gratitude that anything was saved at all.[9]

As we look at an application to the word Catholic, its root reminds us of wholeness and unity. And the Lord has revealed the way to find unity. His way is for us to share the gospel and offer priesthood ordinances for the salvation of all of Heavenly Father's children. True and *universal* unity can only occur when believers unite with each other and build on common beliefs during this time of the "restitution of all things" (see Acts 3:21). That is the goal for which all Catholics and Latter-day Saints should pray universally.

"Thou hast loved righteousness, and hated iniquity." (Hebrews 1:9)

THE SCRIPTURES ARE FULL OF PASSAGES addressing sin, transgression, and iniquity. In Hebrews, Paul reminds us that the Lord is a champion of righteousness (remember from our earlier study that the root of "righteous'" is simply "right"—the Lord loves the right). In the same verse, Paul teaches that the Lord hates iniquity (see Hebrews 1:9). Used here, the English word for "iniquity" is taken from the Greek word *anomian* and means "lawlessness"; it's from *anomos* which means "illegal or violation of law."[10]

---

being "most abominable above all other churches." The statement was later removed in the 2nd edition published in 1966. The publication now reads on pages 137–138, "The titles *church of the devil* and *great and abominable church* are used to identify all churches or organizations of whatever name or nature—whether political, philosophical, educational, economic, social, fraternal, civic, or religious—which are designed to take men on a course that leads away from God and his laws and thus from salvation in the kingdom of God."

9. Stephen A. Robinson, "Warring against the Saints of God," *Ensign*, Jan. 1988. In recent years, there have been awards and commendations shared and given between The Church of Jesus Christ of Latter-day Saints and the Roman Catholic church. President Russell M. Nelson, then-president of the Quorum of the Twelve, was honored on Nov. 4, 2016, by the Catholic Community Services of Utah. In turn, The Church of Jesus Christ of Latter-day Saints honored Cardinal Timothy Dolan with the Visionary Leadership Award. Catholic Archbishop Joseph Kurtz said of the Latter-day Saint-Catholic relationship, "We stand together on issues that are good for America." (see *Newsroom*, The Church of Jesus Christ of Latter-day Saints, 6 May 2016).

10. *Strong's*, 458.

While *iniquity* is akin to illegality, the Hebrew definition of this word is even more fascinating. Iniquity means to "bend, to curve, to twist, to distort."[11] Notice that iniquity is more of a precursor to sin than actually committing the sin. That is, when people bend and twist God's law, they are on a slippery slope that typically ends with sin and transgression.[12]

Rather than bending and curving and twisting God's laws to conform to what we want, we should instead bend and curve and twist our lives to conform to God's law. President Dieter F. Uchtdorf has said that through obedience we can learn what we're truly made of:

> Maybe obedience is not so much the process of bending, twisting, and pounding our souls into something we are not. Instead, it is the process by which we discover what we truly are made of. . . . We come to see obedience not as a punishment but as a liberating path to our divine destiny. . . . Eventually, the priceless, eternal spirit of the heavenly being within us is revealed, and a radiance of goodness becomes our nature.[13]

This week, consider how you might better practice obedience to God's laws in your life.

"Let us therefore come boldly unto the throne of grace, that we may obtain mercy." (Hebrews 4:16)

MOST NATIVE ENGLISH SPEAKERS HEAR THE root of "thanks" (*mercis*)[14] resonate when they hear the word "mercy" spoken. Mercy is treatment greater than what is deserved—and it is made possible through the Atonement of our Savior Jesus Christ.

Mercy encompasses a spirit of tenderness and forgiveness (see Bible Dictionary, "Mercy"). The scriptures are replete with passages of His mercy:

- "His *mercy* endureth forever" (1 Chr. 16:34)

---

11. *Strong's*, 5753.
12. The Old Testament King David, who learned much about sin, transgression, and iniquity wrote in Psalm 32:5, "I acknowledged my sin unto thee, and mine iniquity have I not hid. . . . I will confess my transgressions unto the Lord." Did you notice that he used all three words, "sin," "transgression," and "iniquity" in the same passage? What are we to learn from that and what light does it shed on Hebrews 1:9?
13. Dieter F. Uchtdorf, "He Will Place You on His Shoulders and Carry You Home," *Ensign*, May 2016, 103–4.
14. "Mercy," *Online Etymology Dictionary*.

- "Blessed are the *merciful*: for they shall obtain *mercy*" (Matt. 5:7, 3 Ne. 12:7)
- "According to his *mercy* he saved us (Titus 3:5)
- "The tender *mercies* of the Lord are over all (1 Ne. 1:20)
- "*Mercy* hath no claim on the unrepentant (Mosiah 2:38–39)
- "Little children are alive in Christ because of his *mercy*" (Moro. 8:19–20, D&C 29:46)
- "They who have kept the covenant shall obtain *mercy*" (D&C 54:6)
- "I, the Lord, show *mercy* unto all the meek" (D&C 97:2)

Because Heavenly Father knows our weaknesses and tendencies toward sin as a fallen people, He shows *mercy* to help us return to dwell in His presence.

Historically, the "mercy seat" (Exodus 25:19; 37:6) was a cover for the ark of the covenant. It was made from pure gold. Once a year, on the Day of Atonement, a designated high priest would sprinkle the blood of a sacrificed animal onto the mercy seat as an atonement for the sins of the people of Israel. This act symbolized the redemptive nature of the Atonement of Jesus Christ.

If you were to search for the word "earn" in the scriptures or Bible Dictionary, you would not find any references; the same is true for the word "deserve." In contrast, the scriptures are replete with passages that include the words "merit" and "mercy," teaching God's children that there is nothing they can do to "earn" or "deserve" our celestial inheritance (see Doctrine and Covenants 45:3–5).

"Mercy" shares the same root with the word "market." Other words in mercy's word family are "merchant," "mercenary," and "merchandise." Each of these words are akin to the Latin word "*merces*," which means "price paid for goods" or "wages."[15] There is an overall sense of a purchase or transaction having been paid when the word "mercy" is used. Indeed, we, as begotten and redeemed children of God, are "bought with a price" (see 1 Corinthians 6:20). Once we realize this, we may wish to shout a heartfelt "thank you" when we consider what His redemption purchased—and what His forgiveness and mercy mean!

Considering the Lord's command to "be ye . . . merciful, as your Father also is merciful" (Luke 6:36), we should be merciful in our relationships with others. As we remove pride, arrogance, and unforgiveness from our nature, His examples of mercy and forgiveness, afforded by the *payment* He

---

15. Ibid.

made, may help others feel of God's mercy, and give a proper *thanks* to their Savior, Jesus Christ.

FOR FURTHER STUDY

- Hebrews 1:10 speaks of "foundation." In recent years, modern apostles and prophets have spoken often of the need to secure our foundations. Consider looking up this word's history and original meaning using www.etymonline.com, www.biblehub.com, and www.blueletterbible.org to strengthen your faith in Christ.

- There is a rich etymological meaning behind the word "harden" used in Hebrews 3:7–19; 4:1–11. Consider researching this word and its use in the context of Hebrews 3 using www.etymonline.com, www.biblehub.com, and www.blueletterbible.org.

- The word "captain" is worth an exploration. See how it's used in Hebrews 2:9–10 and how it helps us learn of Christ using www.biblehub.com, and www.blueletterbible.org.

What other unique or insightful words did you find in your study this week?

_____

_____

_____

_____

**Please share with us!
Visit www.ComeFollowMeWOW.com and
share your word discoveries and insights!**

Chapter 44

Hebrews 7-13

Don't miss these Words of the Week

"**Melchizedek**" (Hebrews 7:1)
"**Pitch**" (Hebrews 8:2)
"**Covenant**" (Hebrews 8:6)
"**Faith**" (Hebrews 11:1)
"**Framed**" (Hebrews 11:3)
"**Adversity**" (Hebrews 13:3)

"Melchisedec, king of Salem, priest of the most high God." (Hebrews 7:1)

THE SCRIPTURES ARE FULL OF GREAT men and women of God who demonstrated their faith and exemplified righteousness. And none might have been as great as Melchizedek.

He was a high priest living in the days of Abraham and was an example of righteousness—and the namesake of the higher priesthood. Though living in a time of wickedness, Melchizedek "exercised mighty faith, and received the office of the high priesthood according to the holy order of God" (Alma 13:18). The Book of Mormon prophet Alma said of him, "None were greater" (Alma 13:19). The Doctrine and Covenants states that Melchizedek was "such a great high priest" that the higher priesthood was named after his name:

Before his day it was called the Holy Priesthood, after the Order of the Son of God. But out of respect or reverence to the name of the Supreme

Being, to avoid the too frequent repetition of his name, they, the church, in the ancient days, called that priesthood after Melchizedek, or the Melchizedek Priesthood. (D&C 107:2–4)

So what of the name *Melchizedek*? From the Hebrew *Melchiah*, the root points to the phrase "Jehovah is king."[1] The Hebrew suffix *Zadok* means "righteous." Thus, *Melchizedek* means, "King of righteousness" (see also Hebrews 7:2).

The ultimate King of Righteousness is Jesus Christ. Thus, the translated word *Melchizedek* also represents the Savior. Therefore, when we speak of the Melchizedek priesthood and those men who bear it, we are pointing our minds to the source of that divine power: the King of Righteousness, Jesus Christ. Those that hold this priesthood—and the women of faith that access this same power through their covenants—are to represent the Savior Himself and use His power to bless the lives of those they serve and minister to.

The priesthood of Melchizedek is truly the power and authority of the King of Righteousness, even Jesus Christ. Regardless of gender, that gift is accessed by all. Consider ways that you can feel the power of the priesthood in your life today.

"The true tabernacle which the Lord pitched." (Hebrews 8:2)

"HEY! BATTER BATTER! HEY!" NO—NOT THAT kind of "pitch"! The word "pitched" had several different meanings during the time of the Bible.

Hebrews 8:2 deals with the verb "to pitch" (as in "pitching a tent").[2] However, the noun "pitch" was a substance used to waterproof the ark of Noah (see Genesis 6:14). And the English word "pitch" used in Genesis 6:14 comes from the Hebrew word *kopher*, meaning "the price of a life; ransom."[3] Interestingly, the Latin root for "pitch" is *kaphar*, meaning, "to cover, make an atonement, make reconciliation."[4]

There are several ways in which Noah's ark and the use of pitch can point our minds to Jesus Christ:

---

1. See "Melchizedek," *Online Etymology Dictionary*.
2. *Strong's*, 4078.
3. See "pitch," *Online Etymology Dictionary*.
4. *Kopher* is found 17 times in the Old Testament. *Kopher* is translated as "pitch" in the book of Genesis, but translated as "ransom" other times. 73 times in the Old Testament it is translated as "atone" or "make atonement."

There was only one way to enter the ark—and only one way to enter the tabernacle that the Lord pitched: through the one and only door. Jesus calls Himself the one and only way (John 14:6).

Noah trusted the ark—and the people were told to trust the Lord in the tabernacle—as we can trust in Christ.

Both the ark and the tabernacle frames were made of wood, just as the cross was.

The pitch protected the people that followed Noah, and the tabernacle pitched by the Lord points our minds to Jesus's atoning blood and how it covers our sins when we repent.

Just as God prepared a place for Noah and his family when the ark settled, Jesus said He will prepare a place for us (John 14:3).

Hence, both the ark and the tabernacle become obvious types of Christ. They give us a picture of what Jesus did for us. He made atonement and paid the ransom, completely covering our sins. When we make covenants with Him, we step into a metaphorical ark or tabernacle, and we are saved from the spiritual death that would otherwise come. Jesus atoned, or "covered" our sins, just like the pitch covered the ark—and pitched tabernacle—and protected the people against God's judgment. The pitch was a covering for the Ark, and the life blood of our Savior is a covering for the soul.

The next time you see a picture of a temple or enter a temple and participate in ordinances, picture the Lord pitching that building, erecting it for you to cover and protect you. Picture as well the pitch that Noah might have used to seal his ark—and the seal by which you are connected to Christ through your covenants.

"He is the mediator of a better covenant." (Hebrews 8:6)

Baptismal covenants. Sacrament covenants. Temple covenants. Sealing covenants. The oath and covenant of the priesthood. *Covenants* are central to the gospel of Jesus Christ. The Bible Dictionary teaches that we receive the gospel through our covenants:

The gospel is so arranged that principles and ordinances are received by covenant, placing the recipient under strong obligation and responsibility to honor the commitment.[5]

---

5. Bible Dictionary, "Covenant."

The word "covenant" is found 555 times in the standard works, almost as often as the word "faith" is mentioned (627 occurrences) or the word "repent" (628 occurrences). In fact, the word "covenant" is linked directly with the word "gospel": the Lord called the fullness of the gospel "the covenant" (D&C 39:11) and the "everlasting covenant" (D&C 66:2).

The Greek word used here is *diathēkēs* (which means "a contract").[6] Interestingly, the Latin root for "covenant" is *convenire,* from *com* "together" and *venire* "to come," so another way to define "covenant" would be "to come with."[7] When we covenant with the Lord, we agree to go with Him and He agrees to come with us.

The Hebrew word is *kārat berît,* literally meaning "to cut a covenant" (the verb *kārat* means "cut off" and the noun *berît* means "covenant"). Ancient covenants often became binding by killing and cutting an animal. These rituals are seen in English idioms such as "let's cut a deal" and "to strike a bargain."

Several examples of how a covenant was literally "cut" are found in the Old Testament wherein an animal was killed and then cut into pieces (see Genesis 15:7–21; Jeremiah 34:8–22). The ancient practices of cutting animals in relation to making or restoring covenants graphically illustrated the curse for violating covenants; divine warnings of a sword to come down upon and cut a covenant-breaking people are found in several passages (see Leviticus 26:25; Deut. 32:41; Jer. 46:10; Alma 9:13; 36:1, 30; 37:13; 38:1).[8]

The ultimate *covenant* is found in the Atonement of Jesus Christ, who was rent, cut, torn, and broken for us. This was powerfully shown when "the veil of the temple was rent in twain from the top to the bottom" (Matt. 27:51). In finishing His Atonement, our covenants, which are cut with God,

---

6. *Strong's,* 1242.

7. "Covenant," *Online Etymology Dictionary.*

8. In a pivotal moment in Nephite history, Captain Moroni "went forth among the people, waving the rent [cut] part of his garment in the air, that all might see the writing" (Alma 46:20). The faithful followers, upon seeing this Title of Liberty then "came running together with their armor girded about their loins, rending [cutting] their garments in token, or as a covenant, that they would not forsake the Lord their God" (Alma 46:21). Notice that Captain Moroni waved the "rent part" of his garments. Why the emphasis on the rent part of his garment? For those with covenant eyes, it was a reminder of the Lord's history of using a cut or cutting when making covenants with believers. Those under Captain Moroni's leadership, seeing the rent part of his garment used to create the Title of Liberty, must have had their minds connect the dots between the rent or cut garment and the process of cutting as related to making covenants. The focus in this moment is not upon a flag-waving patriot, but on the importance of making and keeping covenants.

are valid because Christ was cut, enabling us to return to His presence and the presence of God the Father. Brigham Young University professor Jamie Ann Steck wrote that we should remember the symbolism of cutting covenants as we make our own covenants:

> As people today cut sacred and binding covenants with the Lord and with others, let them remember to not only symbolically cut covenants but to literally break themselves off from the world and tear the inhibiting sin from their lives. Let them remember he who was symbolically cut so that they might honorably keep their covenants and return to live with God the Father.[9]

Today, choose to remember your covenants. Remember Christ's being cut for you and how you can express your gratitude for His sacrifice. He truly is the "mediator of a better covenant" (Hebrews 8:6).

"Now faith is the substance of things hoped for, the evidence of things not seen." (Hebrews 11:1)

WHAT DOES FAITH MEAN TO YOU? Elder Dallin H Oaks taught, "Faith means trust—trust in God's will, trust in His way of doing things, and trust in His timetable."[10] The Latin word for "faith," *fides*, defines it as "trust, confidence, and reliance."[11] However, in most New Testament instances, the word "faith" is the Greek word *pistis* which is defined as a "mutual trust and loyalty between two parties."[12]

Pistis (faith) in essence, means *trust*.

Faith in Jesus Christ requires complete and total trust and reliance on Him and in His promises to us. Elder Holland taught, "The size of your faith or the degree of your knowledge is not the issue—it is the integrity you demonstrate toward the faith you do have and the truth you already know."[13] Our faith in the Savior is best shown by our demonstration of *trust* in His promises that He has revealed.

9. Jamie Ann Steck, "Cutting a Covenant: Making Covenants and Oaths in the Old Testament and the Book of Mormon," *Studia Antiqua*, 4.1.2, Apr. 2005, scholarsarchive.byu.edu/studiaantiqua/vol4/iss1/2.

10. Dallin H. Oaks, "Timing," Brigham Young University devotional, 29 Jan. 2002, speeches.byu.edu.

11. "Faith," *Online Etymology Dictionary*.

12. *Strong's*, 4102.

13. Jeffrey R. Holland, "'Lord I Believe,'" *Ensign*, May 2013, 94.

Just as married couples demonstrate their trust and faithfulness to each other through keeping their marriage covenants, so too do we demonstrate our faithfulness to the Lord by not violating our covenants by being "unfaithful" to Him. As we seek to be faithful to God, we show our faith (or *trust*) in Him.

When a topic arises that causes us to doubt, let us strive to look unto Christ in every thought and completely trust what has already been revealed (See D&C 6:36). To those of us whose faith or trust is lacking, President Dieter F. Uchtdorf taught:

> Some struggle with unanswered questions about things that have been done or said in the past . . . Sometimes questions arise because we simply don't have all the information and we just need a bit more patience. When the entire truth is eventually known, things that didn't make sense to us before will be resolved to our satisfaction . . . Therefore, please, first doubt your doubts before you doubt your faith.[14]

When a trial comes our way, we can choose to study and pray for greater trust in the light that has already been revealed and then humbly seek further light about how to proceed. When we reach the edge of current understanding and become concerned about a Church doctrine or principle, we can find peace as we choose to trust in the Lord's ability to make connections we haven't thought of before based on what He has already revealed.

This level of "trust-faith" can help us when discouragement settles in. When we choose to walk in humility before the Lord, recognizing and trusting Him as the source of knowledge, He will reveal more light as the timing becomes right.[15]

Faith is *trust*, focusing our minds on what we know to be true through the power of the Holy Ghost. As the scriptures say: "Faith is not to have a

---

14. Dieter F. Uchtdorf, "Come Join with Us," *Ensign*, Nov. 2013.

15. Ammon, in speaking about King Lamoni's wife in Alma 19:11, said: "Blessed art thou because of thy exceeding faith; I say unto thee, woman, there has not been such great faith among all the people of the Nephites." This is quite a compliment! If we include Nephi and Jacob and father Lehi and Enos and Alma into the list of Nephites who demonstrated faithfulness, to think that this non-Christian woman's faith is to the same degree of each of these great Nephite prophets is indeed a compliment to end all compliments. How could she have faith that exceeded all others? She showed through her actions that faith is choosing to act on what one knows and what the Lord has revealed. She held onto what she knew (which is very little at this point in her life). Because she truly treasured the revelations she had received and because she was willing to act on the revelation she had received, she indeed had "exceedingly great" faith.

perfect knowledge of things; therefore if ye have faith ye hope for things which are not seen, which are true" (Alma 32:21).

"Through faith we understand that the worlds were framed by the word of God." (Hebrews 11:3)

WHEN WE HEAR THE PHRASE, "He was *framed!*" most of the time we think of it as a bad thing. We think that someone has been set up or made to look like they did something that they didn't do. But the scriptures talk about a different type of frame. In his letter to the Hebrews, Paul wrote, "The worlds were framed by the word of God" (Hebrews 11:3).

The word "framed" in Greek is *katērtisthai* and means, "to complete thoroughly" or "repair" or "adjust."[16] "Framed" is from Old English and once meant, "To profit, be helpful, benefit."[17] Doctrinally speaking, Heavenly Father has a type of "frame" around our lives. Through His omniscience, there is a boundary around each of our lives (see Luke 1:37; Matthew 19:26; D&C 82:10).

The "frames" He has placed in our lives will profit, help, and benefit us. They, like the root for "frame," will help us "complete thoroughly" our lives and our personal missions as we make necessary repairs and adjustments.

Troubles, trials, sickness, and accidents can happen, but they will be used for our benefit and blessing, and each boundary to them has been set by Him, the Framer and Creator of the universe. As the Lord declared in the Doctrine and Covenants:

> Hold on thy way, and the priesthood shall remain with thee; for their bounds are set, they cannot pass. Thy days are known, and thy years shall not be numbered less; therefore, fear not what man can do, for God shall be with you forever and ever. (D&C 122:9)

By way of application, our loving Heavenly Father often sends the right person to say the right thing to us in our lives in an effort to keep us on the right path. Those messages may be found in the form of friends, family, priesthood leaders, or scripture passages. Each resource can help us to accomplish our missions on earth.

Our sacred scriptures expose a grand truth: "He knoweth our frame" (Psalm 103:14) and one day, we will know why things happened to us:

---

16. *Strong's*, 2675.
17. "Frame," *Online Etymology Dictionary.*

Yea, verily I say unto you, in that day when the Lord shall come, he shall reveal all things— (D&C 101:32)

The *frames* in our lives will indeed help us more than we may ever know.

"Them which suffer adversity." (Hebrews 13:3)

IN OUR PREMORTAL EXISTENCE, WE SHOUTED for joy over the idea of coming to earth (see Job 38:7), even though we knew that part of mortality would entail adversity. While adversity is experienced differently by everyone, one truth is constant: adversity is universal and everyone experiences suffering at one point or another.

The Greek work for the apostle Paul's word for "adversity" in Hebrews 13:3 is *kakouchoumenōn.18* It means "to treat evilly, hurt, torment." "Adversity," based on its Latin root, means "to be turned, converted, transformed, to be changed."[19] Adversities may appear in the form of illness, accidents, death, or other trials. Each of these maladies have the power to *change* or *transform* us into becoming more like our Heavenly Parents.

President Brigham Young assured:

Every vicissitude we pass through is necessary for experience and example, and for preparation to enjoy that reward which is for the faithful.[20]

Elder Neil L. Anderson further taught:

Like the intense fire that transforms iron into steel, as we remain faithful during the fiery trial of our faith, we are spiritually transformed and strengthened.[21]

Yes, joy can be found only in the life and mission of Jesus Christ and His marvelous Atonement, but that does not mean that we will be spared from adversity. Sometimes, as we struggle to understand why adversity was sent our way, we may ask "Why?" or begin to doubt God's care or closeness.

If left unchecked, those feelings can lead us to lose our faith, but if we are anchored to Christ and understand that adversities will transform and change us for the better, those challenges will truly transform us into new

---

18. *Strong's,* 2558.
19. "Adversity," *Online Etymology Dictionary.*
20. *Teachings of Presidents of the Church: Brigham Young* [1997], 262.
21. Neil L. Anderson, "Trial of Your Faith," *Ensign,* Nov. 2012, 42.

beings. Joseph Smith once remarked, "I think I could never have felt as I do now if I had not suffered the wrongs I have suffered. It has awakened my soul to the love of God."[22]

Because of Christ's incredible suffering, He is better equipped than anyone to help us through our challenges. Adversities can become easier to endure as we seek Christ and view our challenges within the context of Heavenly Father's plan for us: our adversities help transform us to become more like Him.

FOR FURTHER STUDY

- There are two words that greet you in Hebrews 10:32–38 that have great etymology: "reproaches" and "afflictions." Consider digging into their historical meanings using www.etymonline.com.

- The word "martyr" has an interesting history and meaning. Consider a study of that word using www.biblehub.com and www.blueletterbible.org.

- Paul uses the word "ordinance" in Hebrews 9:1–28; 10:1–22. This word has modern-day relevance, so consider a study of it using www.biblehub.com and www.blueletterbible.org.

- The phrase "illuminated by truth" found in Hebrews 10:32–36 makes for a deep study. See www.biblehub.com and www.blueletterbible.org to get started.

- "Chasten" is found in Hebrews 12:5–11 and has a wonderfully rich history and meaning. See www.biblehub.com and www.blueletterbible.org to get started.

---

22. *History of the Church*, 3:290.

What other unique or insightful words did you find in your study this week?

_____

_____

_____

_____

_____

_____

Please share with us!
Visit www.ComeFollowMeWOW.com and
share your word discoveries and insights!

Chapter 45

James

Don't miss these Words of the Week

"Wisdom" (James 1:5)
"Religion" (James 1:27)
"Criticism" (James 4:11)

"If any of you lack wisdom, let him ask of God." (James 1:5)

"O BE WISE; WHAT CAN I say more?" (Jacob 6:12). This famous one liner from Nephi's brother captures so much truth in just one sentence! Indeed, wisdom is a treasured gift given to many.

A unique lesson about one of the meanings of *wisdom* is found in Exodus 28. The Lord instructs Moses to fashion garments for those who participate in worship within the tabernacle. Verse 3 reads:

> And thou shalt speak unto all that are wise hearted, whom I have filled with the spirit of wisdom, that they may make Aaron's garments . . . that he may minister unto me in the priest's office.

Interestingly, the virtue of *wisdom*, as taught in this particular passage, is linked to the ability to follow a sewing pattern—the Lord was seeking out wise people based on their ability to follow a pattern. Indeed, wise people are simply willing to follow the Lord's pattern with exactness.

The Hebrew word for "wisdom" is *chakam,* which means "expert or skillful."[1] Related, the Greek word often used for "wisdom" is *sophias,* which means "insight, skill, [and] intelligence."[2] We see the derivations of these two roots in the beautiful passage from James 1:5, "If any of you lack *wisdom,* let him ask of God."

The receipt of wisdom is inseparably connected with a person's willingness to follow God's pattern for receiving wisdom. Elder Dale G. Renlund taught that principle this way when he wrote:

> I have learned that the command to "ask of God" is not merely to satisfy our curiosity. God wants us to seek more than facts; He wants us to be prepared to act. His desire is to give us not only the understanding or knowledge, but the opportunity to "practice" becoming like Him.[3]

Wisdom is a capacity of the mind that allows us to understand life from God's perspective. Throughout the book of Proverbs, Solomon encourages us to "get wisdom" (see Proverbs 4:5). He teaches that those who get wisdom love life (see Proverbs 19:8), that it's better to get wisdom than gold (see Proverbs 16:16), and that those who get wisdom find life and receive favor from the Lord (see Proverbs 8:32–35).

Obtaining wisdom comes from a deep study of the word of God (see Psalm 19:7). We shouldn't rely merely on our own understanding, but lean on the truths found in the scriptures and in the words of prophets and then align our will to what has been revealed. This is where divine wisdom lies.

Since the fear of the Lord is the beginning of wisdom (Proverbs 9:10), the surest way to become wise is to have reverence and love for God. As we come to know more about Him, the foundation for wisdom becomes firmer in our lives, and we grow in our ability to discern things according to His revealed truth. If wisdom is to be attained, it will be done so through a study of the Author of scripture, who is the source of all *wisdom.*

---

1. See "Wisdom," *Online Etymology Dictionary.*
2. *Strong's,* 4678.
3. Dale G. Renlund, Facebook, 5 Feb. 2017, www.facebook.com/DaleGRenlund/posts/pfbid0nDaSleFk7NV8PQXb7YzPBTKWx6fWA6xrlfm7pYYxRG53VvFnhbUnFJq-jAvoaJAnql.

"Pure religion ... is this, To visit the fatherless and widows." (James 1:27)

EDWARD L. HART WROTE THE TEXT of the much-loved hymn, "Our Savior's Love":[4]

> The Spirit, voice of goodness, whispers to our hearts
> A better choice than evil's anguished cries.
> Loud may the sound of hope ring till all doubt departs,
> And we are bound to him by loving ties.

The last line's reference to "loving ties" points our mind to a word and its unique origin: religion. While the Greek word for "religion" is *thrēskos*, which speaks to ceremonial worship,[5] the English word "religion" comes from the Latin word *religare,* meaning to "tie," or more literally, to "re-tie."[6] The English word "ligature" (what a doctor uses to sew us up if we have a wound) shares the same root, as well as the word "ligament" (a connective tissue that attaches bone to bone and usually serves to hold structures together and keep them stable).

Based on its origin and its shared root with "ligament," *religion* is designed to hold people and society together. Ligaments hold our body structure together and keep us stable (just ask anyone who has ever torn an ACL or other ligament). Ligaments by themselves will not move us; they must be connected to bone, which is connected to tendons and muscle—all of which work together and help our bodies to move. Like ligaments, *religion* provides the structure and stability needed for each of us to experience essential ordinances and covenants that enable us to move forward and return to our Heavenly Father.

As we seek to live our religion, we want to conduct ourselves in Christlike ways and treat others kindly, tying ourselves to our God in Heaven and also to those in need. As the Apostle James wrote:

> If any man among you seem to be religious, and bridleth not his tongue, but deceiveth his own heart, this man's religion is vain. Pure religion and undefiled before God and the Father is this, To visit the fatherless and widows in their affliction, and to keep himself unspotted from the world. (James 1:26–27)

---

4. *Hymns,* no. 113.
5. *Strong's,* 2357.
6. "Religion," *Online Etymology Dictionary.*

Practicing religion is practicing connecting ourselves to God and to others around us.

Governor Morris, a signer of the Articles of Confederation as a New York delegate to the Continental Congress, must have been familiar with the origin and definition of the word "religion." He insisted:

> There must be religion. When that ligament is torn, society is disjointed and its members perish ... [T]he most important of all lessons is the denunciation of ruin to every state that rejects the precepts of religion.[7]

Will Durant, an American author, historian, and philosopher, wrote, "There is no significant example in history ... of [any] society successfully maintaining moral life without the aid of religion."[8] Indeed, religion and its natural binding process has helped to weave the fabric of nations since the dawn of time. Of that principle, Elder Jeffrey R. Holland penned:

> True religion brings understanding of and loyalty to our Father in Heaven and His uncompromised love for every one of His spirit children—past, present, and future. True religion engenders in us faith in the Lord Jesus Christ and hope in His Resurrection. It encourages love, forbearance, and forgiveness in our interactions with one another, as He so magnanimously demonstrated them in His. True religion, the tie that binds us to God and each other . . .[9]

Today, many people describe themselves as being "spiritual but not religious." While one can be religious without being spiritual, it doesn't really go the other way, based on the word's origin and definition. Spirituality hangs on religious discipline just as muscles hang on bone. Faithful believers see religion as something that vitally connects them with heaven. These "loving ties" are the essence of *religion*.

---

7. Collections of the New York Historical Society for the Year 1821 (New York: E. Bliss and E. White, 1821), pp. 32, 34, from "An Inaugural Discourse Delivered Before the New York Historical Society by the Honorable Gouverneur Morris, (President,) 4 Sept. 1816."

8. Will and Ariel Durant, *The Lessons of History* (Simon and Schuster, 1968), 51.

9. Jeffrey R. Holland, "Religion: Bound by Loving Ties", BYU Campus Education Week devotional, 16 Aug. 2016, speeches.byu.edu.

"Speak not evil one of another." (James 4:11)

IT'S HARD TO BE VULNERABLE IN today's world, especially online. It can feel like there's someone lurking in every corner, just waiting for the right moment to pop out and judge you for your choices. This digital age has more communication than ever before, making it tough to go a single day without hearing or reading words of criticism.

Based on James's admonition in James 4:11, it looks like the same struggle was alive and well in his day, and he felt strongly about the blessing of positive communication. He may have experienced this firsthand, hearing verbal assaults heaped upon Jesus, his half-brother, and perhaps even on his mother as a result of her being pregnant before she was married.

The Greek word *kakologeō* translates to English as "speak evil." It means "to revile, abuse, or to curse."[10] A cousin word might be "criticize." The word "criticize" is derived from the Green *krinein*, which means the "middle voice." One fascinating word that is derived from *krinein* is *krisis*, meaning "crisis," which in Greek means "the turning point in a disease."[11]

We, as agents endowed with power to act and choose, can employ our agency to critique and evaluate. Sports writers, book reviewers, music enthusiasts, investment consultants, and product testers inform the public by way of criticism and critique. This type of criticism is welcomed and usually very constructive.

Fault finding, in contrast, is destructive—and that's what James was tackling here. Pointing out other people's faults, especially ones that are petty or inconsequential, by "speaking evil" can lead to discord and feelings of hatred and disdain. When the character or reputation of a person is attacked, it is destructive.[12]

President Gordon B. Hinckley advised that, while correction and repentance are important, we should seek to focus on the good:

> I am not asking that all criticism be silenced. Growth comes of correction. Strength comes of repentance. Wise is the man who can acknowledge mistakes pointed out by others and change his course.

---

10. *Strong's*, 2551.
11. See "Crisis," *Online Etymology Dictionary*.
12. The scriptures commands us to avoid "evil speakings," to "let all bitterness, and wrath, and anger, and clamour, and evil speaking, be put away from [us]" and to avoid "backbiting," "evil speaking," and "find[ing] fault one with another" (see Doctrine and Covenants 20:53–54; 42:27; 88:124; 136:23).

What I am suggesting is that each of us turn from the negativism that so permeates our society and look for the remarkable good among those with whom we associate, that we speak of one another's virtues more than we speak of one another's faults.[13]

Just as justice must be constrained by the principle of mercy (see Alma 42:33–42), so must the use of truth be disciplined by the principle of love. As Paul instructed the Ephesians, we "grow up into" Christ by "speaking the truth in love" (see Ephesians 4:15).[14]

Looking again at "evil speaking" and the meaning of the word "criticize," it's important to note that when constructive feedback and analysis turns into contemptuous criticism, that is the turning point of the conversation, as implied in the root word *crisis* of "criticize" which means the turning point in a disease. The prophet Isaiah advised us to use our words carefully when he denounced those who "make a man an offender for a word, and lay a snare for him that reproveth in the gate" (Isaiah 29:21; see also 2 Nephi 27:32). And in our own relationships, be them between husband and wife, parent and child, or teacher and student, we should exercise great caution so as to not let meaningful correction drift into the hurtful area of all-out criticism.

---

13. Gordon B. Hinckley, "The Continuing Pursuit of Truth," *Ensign*, Apr. 1986, 3–4.
14. See Dallin H. Oaks, "Criticism," *Ensign*, Feb. 1987.

FOR FURTHER STUDY

- Earlier this year, you studied the word "meek." James has another message about meekness in James 1:21. Consider reviewing the meaning of the word "meek" using www.biblehub.com and www.blueletterbible.org to help amplify James's words.

- The word "patience," as used in James 1:2–4; 5:7–11, has a wonderful root meaning. Go on a journey of exploration to look up its meaning using www.etymonline.com, www.biblehub.com, and www.blueletterbible.org.

- There are several words that James uses in James 3:1–18 that have interesting meanings and definitions. As you read that passage, look up a few of these words using www.biblehub.com and www.blueletterbible.org to supplement your study.

What other unique or insightful words did you find in your study this week?

_____

_____

_____

_____

_____

Please share with us!
Visit www.ComeFollowMeWOW.com and
share your word discoveries and insights!

Chapter 46

1 and 2 Peter

Don't miss these Words of the Week

"Priesthood" (1 Peter 2:5)
"Peculiar" (1 Peter 2:9)
"Right" and **"Left"** (1 Peter 3:22)
"Manifold" (1 Peter 4:10)
"Humility" (1 Peter 5:5)

"Ye also, as lively stones, are built up a spiritual house, an holy priesthood." (1 Peter 2:5)

THERE ARE TIMES WHEN WE NEED a mediator—someone to help us to communicate with someone else. This can be as small as speaking with a receptionist to make an appointment to see the dentist, or as big as seeing a couples therapist to solve relationship issues.

The suffix "hood" shows a current condition or state. For example, "motherhood" is a condition or state of being a mother, "fatherhood" is a condition or state of being a father, "childhood" is a condition or state of being a child, and "neighborhood" is the condition or state of being neighbors in a proximity. Likewise, the word "priesthood" simply means "the quality or state of being a priest."[1]

---

1. See "priesthood," *Online Etymology Dictionary.*

What is a *priest*? According to the Bible Dictionary, "Priests are mediators between us and God." Therefore, priesthood connotes "the condition or state of being mediators between man and God."

The account of the restoration of the Melchizedek Priesthood gives us an example of how the priesthood helps with mediation between man and God. After being incarcerated for preaching the gospel in Coleville, Addison Everett wrote that Joseph Smith and Oliver Cowdery traveled all night through the wood and at the break of day Peter, James, and John came to them and ordained them to apostleship:

> Mr. Reid [Joseph's lawyer] said that there was a mob in front of the house and hosting [hoisting] the window. Joseph and Oliver went to the woods in a few rods, it being night, and they traveled until Oliver was exhausted and Joseph almost carried him through mud and water. They traveled all night and just at the break of day Oliver gave out entirely and exclaimed "O Lord, How long Brother Joseph have we got to endure this thing?" Brother Joseph said that at that very time Peter, James and John came to them and ordained them to the apostleship. They had 16 or 17 miles to travel to get back to Mr. Hale's, his father-in-law, and Oliver did not complain any more of fatigue.[2]

The Doctrine and Covenants adds more detail to this story, describing how they heard the voice of Michael detecting the devil, and they heard the voices of Peter, James, and John declaring that they possessed the priesthood keys:

> And again, what do we hear? . . . The voice of Michael on the banks of the Susquehanna, detecting the devil when he appeared as an angel of light! The voice of Peter, James, and John in the wilderness between Harmony, Susquehanna county, and Colesville, Broome county, on the Susquehanna river, declaring themselves as possessing the keys of the kingdom, and of the dispensation of the fulness of times! (D&C 128:20)

---

2. Letter of Addison Everett to Oliver B. Huntington, St. George, Utah, 17 Feb. 1881, recorded in "Oliver Boardman Huntington, Journal #14, [under back-date of] 31 Jan. 1881," Harold B. Lee Library, Brigham Young University. See also O. B. Huntington Diary #15, 18 Feb. 1883, 44–47.

Alvin R. Dyer added that Joseph and Oliver were unable to detect the presence of Lucifer, who appeared as an angel to deceive them, but Michael warned them of his presence:

> Apparently, not having yet received the Higher Priesthood, they were not able to detect the presence of Lucifer, who, according to the words of the Prophet Joseph Smith, appeared on the Susquehanna River as an angel of light to deceive them and no doubt to attempt to interfere with the conferring of the Holy Priesthood upon them. We are informed by the Prophet of the appearance there of Michael, the archangel, who came to detect the deception of Lucifer and banish him from the scene.[3]

Michael, acting in his role as a bearer of the holy priesthood, was a mediator between man (Joseph and Oliver) and God. His assistance on the banks of the Susquehanna shows the primary function of those who hold the priesthood: to be protectors of God's children and intervene to help them grow closer to God.

This role is on display each Sunday when priesthood holders administer the sacrament (a tangible time wherein they act as mediators between the congregation and God); this role is also seen as priesthood holders visit homes in a ministering capacity to provide service.

Jesus Christ is the ultimate mediator between God and man. His Atonement made possible a way for people to repent of their sins and become reconciled to God—and priesthood holders help teach that principle as they worthily carry out their priesthood duties.

"But ye are a chosen generation, a royal priesthood, an holy nation, a peculiar people." (1 Peter 2:9)

TODAY THE WORD "PECULIAR" CONNOTES THE odd, unusual, strange, and possibly weird of our world. The earliest uses of the word, however, related to animals with the idea that they were movable and had value.[4] Hence, *peculiar* once meant things owned that could be traded or bartered (think of the word "pecuniary," meaning "money").

---

3. Alvin R. Dyer, *Meaning of Truth* (Salt Lake City: Deseret Book Company, 1961), 153–54.
4. See "peculiar," *Online Etymology Dictionary*.

Throughout time, "peculiar" has been used to identify something exclusively owned by someone. In the footnote found in 1 Peter 2:9, "peculiar" comes from a Greek word meaning "purchased or preserved"; there we also learn that it is related to a Hebrew word meaning "special possession or property."

In the Greek translation of the New Testament, it substitutes the word "peculiar" for the phrase "people for God's own possession."[5] In the Old Testament, peculiar is used in the sense of a special treasure. The Lord, through Moses, taught that "if ye will obey my voice indeed, and keep my covenant, then ye shall be a peculiar treasure unto me above all people" (Exodus 19:5).

We are a peculiar people because of the Atonement of Jesus Christ, for we "are not [our] own . . . [but] are bought with a price" (1 Corinthians 6:19–20). The Savior symbolically purchased us and we, therefore, are His *private property*, as taught by the Apostle Paul: "Our Savior Jesus Christ; Who gave himself for us, that he might redeem us from all iniquity, and purify unto himself a peculiar people, zealous of good works" (Titus 2:13–14). Indeed, the price that was paid was "not redeemed with corruptible things, as silver and gold . . . but with the precious blood of Christ, as of a lamb without blemish and without spot" (1 Peter 1:18–19).

In our strivings to become more like Him, we may indeed endure the looks, jeers, and sneers of the world, or feel lonely and isolated from our peers, friends, or family, but ultimately, we will feel peace and protection from God because we are His *peculiar* people.

"On the right hand of God." (1 Peter 3:22)

THERE IS AN 11% CHANCE THAT you are left-handed. And chances are much higher that you know someone that is a lefty.

Historically, the left hand was once called the "sinister hand."[6] Consider the negative connotations of the word "left" in our language: the phrase "over the left (shoulder)" once meant "not at all," people who are poor at dancing are said to have "two left feet," and the phrase "out in left field" means that someone is out of touch with reality. Conversely, the English

5. "1 Peter 2:9," subheading "Greek," *Bible Hub*, www.biblehub.com1_peter/2-9. htm#lexicon.
6. See "The Left Hand of (Supposed) Darkness: On 'sinister,' dexterity,' 'gauche,' and 'adroit'," *Merriam-Webster Dictionary*, www.merriam-webster.com/words-at-play/sinister-left-dexter-right-history.

word "right" is used to mean "correct," "true," or "ethically sound;" phrases like "a right answer" or "the right thing to do" demonstrate this bias.

The Latin word "sinister" literally means "left" and is the opposite of *dexter,* meaning "skillful" or "clever."[7] In olden times, those with a dominant left hand were accused of demonic possession, leading to accusations of witchcraft. We don't really know why "left" is associated with evil, but Merriam Webster's Dictionary has a theory:

> The association of the directional left with evil is likely attributed to the dominance of right-handed people within a population, and consequently the awkwardness of motions made from the left side of the body. . . . The historical association of sinister with evil or backwardness is balanced linguistically by the fact that dexter, the Latin word meaning "on the right side," comes with a largely positive connotation that survives throughout its linguistic descendants. To be dexterous, for example, is to be good with the hands (like a surgeon) or a clever thinker, while one who is ambidextrous uses one's left and right hand equally well.[8]

In the Bible, to be at the "right side" or "right hand" is to be in a place of honor.[9] The scriptures are replete with references to the *left* and to the *right.* Jesus gave a parable using goats on the left and sheep on the right (Matthew 25:33); Jesus also told Peter that if he wanted to catch fish to throw his net from the right side of the boat (John 21:6). At the Second Coming, being on the right hand of God is most favorable (see Mark 16:19; Luke 22:69; Matthew 22:44; 1 Peter 3:22).[10]

Whether we're right-handed or left, as children of God, we can live in the joy of knowing that God's *right hand* of protection, promise, and provision rests over us as we seek to keep our covenants and we choose the right. As the song goes:

---

7. See "sinister," *Online Etymology Dictionary.*
8. "The Left Hand of (Supposed) Darkness," Merriam-Webster, www.merriam-webster. com/words-at-play/sinister-left-dexter-right-history.
9. Leland Ryken, James Wilhoit, Tremper Longman III, et al., ed, "Right, Right Hand," *Dictionary of Biblical Imagery* (InterVarsity Press, 1998), 727–28.
10. What is the scriptural difference between left and right? Ecclesiastes 10:2 reads, "A wise man's heart is at his right hand; but a fool's heart at his left." Psalm 16:11 adds, "Thou wilt shew me the path of life: in thy presence is fullness of joy; at thy right hand there are pleasures for evermore" and Isaiah penned, "Fear thou not; for I am with thee: be not dismayed; for I am thy God: I will strengthen thee; yea, I will help thee; yea, I will uphold thee with the right hand of my righteousness" (Isaiah 41:10).

Choose the right when a choice is placed before you.
In the right the Holy Spirit guides;
And its light is forever shining o'er you,
when in the right your heart confides.
Choose the right!
Choose the right!
Let wisdom mark the way before.
In its light, choose the right!
And God will bless you evermore.[11]

God will bless us as we make choices that will bring us closer to His right hand.

"Good stewards of the manifold grace of God." (1 Peter 4:10)

"MANIFOLD," A WORD WE RARELY HEAR today, is penned twice in the New Testament. Paul, in his letter to the Saints in Ephesus, spoke of "the *manifold* wisdom of God" (Ephesians 3:10), and Peter wrote about "the *manifold* grace of God" (1 Peter 4:10). The original meaning of the adjective "manifold" (*poikilēs* in Greek[12]) meant "various, of different colors, diverse." It may have been a loan-translation of the Latin word *multiplex* (a root for the word "multiply"). [13]

One place that we do hear "manifold," surprisingly, is with modern vehicles. A manifold is a pipe that runs from the carburetor to the cylinders in the engine; pipes that ensure the air coming into the engine is evenly distributed to all the cylinders. A manifold's primary purpose is to divide and distribute air.

A surprising connection can be made between the Lord's "manifold mercies," "manifold wisdom," and "manifold grace," and the modern-day engine's manifold. The beauty of God's grace is that His mercy, His works, and His grace are distributed evenly to all of His children. He does so in various ways "of different colors." He does not "play favorites." He loves all of His children. As Nephi wrote:

---

11. "Choose the Right," *Hymn*, no. 239.
12. *Strong's*, 4164.
13. "Multiply," *Online Etymology Dictionary*.

He inviteth them all to come unto him and partake of his goodness; and he denieth none that come unto him, black and white,
bond and free, male and female; and he remembereth the heathen;
and all are alike unto God, both Jew and Gentile. (2 Nephi 26:33)

He is "no respecter of persons" (see Acts 10:34–35).

In our daily discipleship, we should strive to be modern-day manifolds
of God's love and blessings, helping to distribute His mercies to those around
us. As President Thomas S. Monson reminded: "Love is the very essence of
the gospel, and Jesus Christ is our Exemplar. His life was a legacy of love."[14]
It's our responsibility to love God and love our neighbor, and the word "manifold" teaches us that we can do so "in many different colors" and in many
different ways that fit the natural gifts God has given to each of us.

"Be clothed with humility." (1 Peter 5:5)

THE GREEK WORD TRANSLATED AS "HUMILITY" is *tapeinophrosynēn*, which
means "lowliness of mind" or literally refers to height and suggests making
oneself low or close to the ground.[15] Even today, we use height when referring
to a person's status: higher class, upper class, lower class, etc. C.S Lewis wrote
about this principle of height and humility when he said: "It is the comparison that makes you proud: the pleasure of being above the rest."[16]

One of the Latin roots of the word "humble" is *humus* and means
"ground" or "dirt" or "the earth."[17]

There is a unique paradox with the principle of humility: on one hand,
scriptures confirm that "the worth of souls is great in the sight of God"
(D&C 18:10), yet, on the other hand, Mormon reminded us that we are
even "less than the dust of the earth" (Helaman 12:7). King Benjamin
added: "Can ye say aught of yourselves? I answer you, Nay. Ye cannot say
that ye are even as much as the dust of the earth" (Mosiah 2:25).

In a clarifying message, Joseph Fielding Smith said, "[T]he dust of the
earth is obedient. . . . Everything in the universe obeys the law given unto
it, so far as I know, except man. . . . But man rebels."[18]

---

14. Thomas S. Monson, "Love—the Essence of the Gospel," *Ensign*, May 2014, 91.
15. *Strong's*, 5012.
16. C. S. Lewis, *Mere Christianity* (HarperCollins, 1952); note also that Dieter F. Uchtdorf
taught, "We don't discover humility by thinking less *of* ourselves; we discover humility
by thinking less *about* ourselves" ("Pride and the Priesthood," *Ensign*, Nov. 2010, 58).
17. "Humility," *Online Etymology Dictionary*.
18. Joseph Fielding Smith, in Conference Report, Apr. 1929, 55.

To this message, Brigham Young added:

The whole earth and all things pertaining to it, except man, abide the law of their creation. . . . We tame the animals and make them do our drudgery and administer to our wants in many ways, yet man alone is not tamed-he is not subject to his Great Creator. How often have we witnessed a faithful animal conveying his master home so drunk that he could not see his way or sit up; yet his faithful animal will plod through mud, shun stumps, trees, and bad places, and land him safely at home.[19]

Humility, by its definition and through our scriptural application, may be summarized by us as "trying to become as obedient as dirt is to the Lord!" Humility and obedience to God go hand in hand.[20] Neal A. Maxwell emphasized this:

The submission of one's will is really the only uniquely personal thing we have to place on God's altar. The many other things we "give" . . . are actually the things He has already given or loaned to us. However, when you and I finally submit ourselves, by letting our individual wills be swallowed up in God's will, then we are really giving something to Him! It is the only possession which is truly ours to give![21]

Contrary to what we might often think, greatness does not come only because of strength and power; true greatness requires humility. To be truly grounded is to be truly humble. Humility is not about thinking little of yourself, but seeing yourself accurately in the service of others. Jesus Christ (the creator of all dirt and all dust) is our greatest example of humility as He said, "I can of mine own self do nothing. . . . I seek not mine own will, but the will of the Father which hath sent me" (John 5:30).

Think about the wonderful phrase from Paul: "Be clothed in humility" as you go throughout your day today.

---

19. Brigham Young, *Journal of Discourses,* volume 9, 246–47.
20. Note that seeking low self-worth is not humility. By excessively pointing out our own flaws and weaknesses or by dismissing compliments, we deny a truth that divinity is found within us. Don't confuse self-degradation with humility.
21. Neal A. Maxwell, "Swallowed Up in the Will of the Father," *Ensign,* Nov. 1995, 24.

FOR FURTHER STUDY

- There are several articles written about the phrase found in 1 Peter 1:1 about "girding up our loins" that have great relevance to our day. Go on a study of that unique phrase. See the Maranatha Baptist Seminary's article "Gird Up Your Loins" (www.mbu.edu/seminary/gird-up-your-loins/) to get started.

- Peter presents several words worth exploring: heaviness, temptations, grief, fiery trial, and sufferings (see 1 Peter 1:6; 2:19; 4:12–13). Consider researching a few of them using www.biblehub.com and www.blueletterbible.org.

- The phrase "divine nature" has a rich meaning in Greek. Consider studying that phrase found in 2 Peter 1:1–11 using www.biblehub.com and www.blueletterbible.org.

- "Cornerstone" is a unique word with a fun history. Consider a study of this word found in 1 Peter 2:5–10 using www.biblehub.com and www.blueletterbible.org.

- What does it mean to be an "eyewitness?" Read 2 Peter 1:16–21, including the footnotes, to find the answer to this question.

What other unique or insightful words did you find in your study this week?

_____

_____

_____

_____

_____

_____

Please share with us!
Visit www.ComeFollowMeWOW.com and
share your word discoveries and insights!

Chapter 47

1–3 John; Jude

Don't miss these Words of the Week

"**Sin**" and "**Sins**" (1 John 1:7–9)
"**Advocate**" (1 John 2:1)
"**Confidence**" (1 John 2:28)

"If we say that we have no sin, we deceive ourselves, and the truth is not in us. If we confess our sins, he is faithful and just to forgive us our sins." (1 John 1:8–9)

A FASCINATING PASSAGE ABOUT SINFULNESS (AND fallenness) is found in 1 John 1:8–9: "If we say that we have no *sin*, we deceive ourselves, and the truth is not in us. If we confess our *sins*, he is faithful and just to forgive us our *sins* and to cleanse us from all unrighteousness" (emphasis added). You may have noticed that "sin" appears to be a general word and that "sins" seems to be a more specific word that is probably the result of the first.

We were born into a fallen world of sin—and saying there is no sin is silly.[1] It reminds us of what Nephi taught on this topic:

> And others will he pacify, and lull them away into carnal security, that they will say: All is well in Zion; yea, Zion prospereth, all is well—and thus the devil cheateth their souls, and leadeth them

---

1. Many prophets have addressed our sinful nature (see Mosiah 3:19; Romans 6:6). Because of Adam's fall (1 Corinthians 15:22), we are prone to sin.

away carefully down to hell. . . . Therefore, wo be unto him that is at ease in Zion! Wo be unto him that crieth: All is well! (2 Nephi 28:21, 24–25)

While it does seem that John appears to have used the same word for "sin" in both verse 8 and verse 9 (*hamartian*, the Greek word for sin[2]), a principle might be drawn from how that one word became two different words in the translation process. Indeed, what John and Nephi may have been trying to teach is this: sin is part of this world and sins will inevitably become part of our lives.[3] That is, *sin* is at the root - and *sins* are the fruits. And the Atonement of Jesus Christ can help us overcome both!

"We have an advocate with the Father." (1 John 2:1)

MANY PEOPLE PICTURE A COURTROOM SCENE when they try to imagine the final judgment. This may be linked back to the many mentionings of Jesus Christ as our *advocate*. Consider the many meanings of the word "advocate" (*paraklēton* in Greek): intercessor, consoler, comforter, helper, consoler.[4]

Jesus Christ is indeed our Advocate with the Father. The word "advocate" has Latin roots meaning "one who pleads for another."[5] John S. Tanner said, "In 1 John 2:1, the Greek *parakletos*, which connotes one who is at our side, is translated as 'our helper.' The same Greek term is used for the Holy Ghost in His role as comforter. The idea here is that Christ is by our side, as our helper and our defender; He speaks on our behalf."[6]

Elder D. Todd Christofferson emphasized the significance of Christ pleading our case:

> It is of great significance to me, that I may at any moment and in any circumstance approach through prayer the throne of grace, that my Heavenly Father will hear my petition, that my Advocate, him who did no sin, whose blood was shed, will plead my cause.[7]

---

2. *Strong's*, 266.
3. The only one who was born into a fallen and sinful world—and successfully avoided sin—was Jesus Christ. He was "without sin" (Hebrews 4:15).
4. *Strong's*, 3875.
5. See Russell M. Nelson, "Jesus Christ—Our Master and More," Brigham Young University fireside, 2 Feb. 1992), 4; speeches.byu.edu.
6. John S. Tanner, "Christ, Our Advocate and High Priest," *Religious Educator* 8, no. 2 (2007): 26–34.
7. D. Todd Christofferson, "I Know in Whom I Have Trusted," *Ensign*, May 1993, 83.

Advocate denotes not merely a lawyer but literally one who speaks for us. Read of His tender advocacy:

Listen to [Jesus Christ] who is the advocate with the Father, who is pleading your cause before him—saying:

Father, behold the sufferings and death of him who did no sin, in whom thou wast well pleased; behold the blood of thy Son which was shed, the blood of him whom thou gavest that thyself might be glorified;

Wherefore, Father, spare these my brethren that believe on my name, that they may come unto me and have everlasting life. (See Doctrine and Covenants 45:3–5)

Christ, through His perfect Atonement, extends to us the promise of everlasting life if we will have faith in Him. This week, consider what you can do to better accept this gift.

"When he shall appear, we may have confidence." (1 John 2:28)

FROM SUCCESS AT WORK TO A feeling of accomplishment at school, *confidence* is a feeling that is absolutely wonderful. The Latin root word *com* means "with" and *fid* means "faith" or "trust."[8] Bringing these two words together, the word "confidence" is formed—"confidence" literally means "with faith."

From descriptions of *fidelity* to a person that is a *confidant* for information that is to be kept *confidential*, the Latin root words of *com* and *fid* depict scenarios or people who proceed "with faith."[9] The Lord has sought several truths about confidence and proceeding "with faith":

- "It is better to trust in the Lord than to put confidence in man" (Psalms 118:8)
- "The Lord shall be thy confidence" (Proverbs 3:26)
- "Hold the beginning of our confidence steadfast" (Hebrews 3:14)
- "Cast not away therefore your confidence" (Hebrews 10:35)

Understanding the etymology of the word "confidence" may not increase our confidence in ourselves, but it establishes a confidence in the

---

8. "Confidence," *Online Etymology Dictionary.*
9. The word "infidel" is confidence's etymological opposite.

Lord and His ability to help us do more and become more than we possibly could on our own. Elder Dieter F. Uchtdorf taught that Heavenly Father sees our true potential:

> [I]f we look at ourselves only through our mortal eyes, we may not see ourselves as good enough. But our Heavenly Father sees us as who we truly are and who we can become. He sees us as His sons and daughters, as beings of eternal light with everlasting potential and with a divine destiny.[10]

Take *confidence* knowing that Heavenly Father loves you. He sees you. Take *confidence* knowing that Jesus Christ suffered in Gethsemane and on the cross for you (both our Heavenly Father and His Son knew you would sin and need a Redeemer). Take *confidence* knowing that They want you to come home. As you act "with faith" you will find your divine confidence.

FOR FURTHER STUDY

- The JST uses the word "testimony" in 1 John 1:1. Do you know what that word meant historically? If not, consider a study of exploration using www.biblehub.com and www.blueletterbible.org.

- There is a synonym for atonement in 1 John 2:2. Look at it and study its origin using www.etymonline.com.

- 1 John 2 is the only use of the word "antichrist" in the scriptures. Consider studying its origin and meaning using www.etymonline.com, www.biblehub.com, and www.blueletterbible.org.

- 1 John 2:20 uses the word "unchion." Consider seeing what that word means and how it points to Christ using www.biblehub.com and www.blueletterbible.org.

- 1 John 4 uses the word "love" several times. And in many cases, it's a different type of love in Greek. Take a journey to look up each type of love taught by John using www.biblehub.com and www.blueletterbible.org.

What other unique or insightful words did you find in your study this week?

10. Dieter F. Uchtdorf, "It Works Wonderfully!" *Ensign*, Nov. 2015, 23.

_____

_____

_____

_____

_____

_____

Please share with us!
Visit www.ComeFollowMeWOW.com and
share your word discoveries and insights!

Chapter 48

Revelation 1-11

"To him be glory." (Revelation 1:6)

TODAY, WHEN YOU WOKE UP, OUR Heavenly Father suited up to go to battle in your defense (see the Lord's teaching in Moses 1:39 and the meaning of the word "glory").

The Greek word for "glory" is *doxa* and the Latin word is *gloria*, both of which connote "fame, renown, great praise or honor."[1] What a great message comes from the meaning of the word "glory"!

We do not have to worry or become discouraged when bad things happen in our lives. Sometimes we are tempted to doubt God, but His work and *glory*—His weapons and His defenses—are for us! Sometimes God will place a protective shield around us where nothing will be able to get through to attack. Sometimes He will fight the actual battle for you and through you. Other times He will tell you to hold your position and do absolutely nothing, and then He will go to work on your behalf (see Exodus 14:13).

---

1. "Glory," *Online Etymology Dictionary.*

If you're in the heat of a battle right now, or if you worry that your enemies are gaining ground in your life, please know you're not alone, not ever. God is the One who fights on our behalf, constantly shielding, protecting, strengthening, even when we're unaware. We never have to struggle to fend for ourselves.

Consider these vital verses:

- "For the Lord your God is he that goeth with you, to fight for you against your enemies, to save you" (Deuteronomy 20:4).
- "Have not I commanded thee? Be strong and of good courage; be not afraid, neither be thou displayed: for the Lord they God is with thee whithersoever thou goest" (Joshua 1:9).
- "If God be for us, who can be against us?" (Romans 8:31).
- "The glory of God is intelligence, or, in other words, light and truth. Light and truth forsake that evil one" (D&C 93:36–37).

Fittingly, our Lord's glory—His power and defense—comes from His light and His truth. Lucifer, in stark contrast, has no light and limited truth and therefore has less power than our God. This is why we have been commanded to "put no confidence in the flesh" (Philippians 3:3). Our confidence should be placed exclusively in God, who will fight our battles and bring us safely home (see Jude 1:24–25). "Some trust in chariots, and some in horses: but we will remember the name of the Lord our God" (Psalm 20:7).

Elder Holland reminded us of God's glory and His power to fight for and defend those that trust Him when he said:

[Y]ou have help from both sides of the veil, and you must never forget that. When disappointment and discouragement strike—and they will—you remember and never forget that if our eyes could be opened we would see horses and chariots of fire as far as the eye can see riding at reckless speed to come to our protection.[2]

Even if we can't see or feel them, God and His angels are always there to help us fight our battles through this life.

2. Jeffrey R. Holland, "For Times of Trouble," Brigham Young University devotional, 18 Mar. 1980, speeches.byu.edu.

"These things saith the Amen, the faithful and true witness." (Revelation 3:14)

WE SAY *AMEN* AT THE END of prayers, testimonies, talks, and several priesthood ordinances. It connotes "may it be so" or "so it is." The Greek word, *amēn*, was borrowed from Hebrew and means, "properly, firm, surely."[3] It also means "certainty" and "truth." The pronouncement of Amen indicates acceptance and agreement (see Deuteronomy 27:14–26) or truthfulness (see 1 Kings 1:36). When people hear public prayers or messages, they are encouraged to say an audible amen to indicate agreement and acceptance.

In English, the word "amen" has two primary pronunciations: "ah-men" and "ey-men." Despite misconceptions, *amen* has nothing to do with the words "man" or "men"; in January 2021, Missouri Representative Emanuel Cleaver closed his opening prayer on the first day of the 117th Congress by saying "amen, and a-woman" to try to be gender-neutral.[4]

Jesus Christ is called "the Amen, the faithful and true witness" (Revelation 3:14). Christians, Jews, and Muslims all use a version of the word; in Judaism, congregants say amen in response to the words of the rabbi, or as part of their prayers; in Islam, amen is used as an appropriate way to end any sort of prayer.

For most, saying amen is a form of spiritual applause. The combined amens from listeners, be them in a ward, during an ordination, or at a family prayer, will foster unity and closeness and increased spirituality as we place our verbal approval and consent on the truth that was spoken.

"The children of Israel." (Revelation 7:4)

THE NAME *ISRAEL* WAS GIVEN TO Jacob at Penuel (Gen. 32:28) and again at Bethel (Gen. 35:10). After the division of the kingdom, the northern tribes retained the name *Israel*, while the southern kingdom was called Judah. The word "Israel" appears more than a thousand times in the scriptures. It can apply to Jacob's (Israel's) family (see Genesis 35:23–26; 46:7) or geographically as a place on planet Earth, but its doctrinal use applies to people who are willing to let God prevail in their lives.

---

3. *Strong's*, 281.
4. Emily Brooks, "'Amen and a-woman': House opening prayer goes gender-inclusive," *Washington Examiner*, 3 Jan. 2021, www.washingtonexaminer.com.

According to the Bible Dictionary, "In another sense Israel means the true believer in Christ . . . regardless of their lineage or geographical location."[5]

Adding to this definition, President Russell M. Nelson, after studying and praying and feasting on every scripture he could find about the doctrine of the gathering of Israel for 36 years shared:

> [I]magine my delight when I was led recently to a new insight. With the help of two Hebrew scholars, I learned that one of the Hebraic meanings of the word *Israel* is "let God prevail." Thus the very name of *Israel* refers to a person who is *willing* to let God prevail in his or her life. That concept stirs my soul!
>
> The word *willing* is crucial to this interpretation of *Israel*. We all have our agency. We can choose to be of Israel, or not. We can choose to let God prevail in our lives, or not. We can choose to let God be the most powerful influence in our lives, or not. . . .
>
> Are *you* willing to let God prevail in your life? Are *you* willing to let God be the most important influence in your life? Will you allow His words, His commandments, and His covenants to influence what you do each day? Will you allow His voice to take priority over any other? Are you *willing* to let whatever He needs you to do take precedence over every other ambition? Are you *willing* to have your will swallowed up in His?[6]

President Nelson invites us to ponder these questions for ourselves. Consider taking his invitation this week.

"He should offer it with the prayers of all saints upon the golden altar." (Revelation 8:3)

CHARLES HUTCHINSON GABRIEL WAS A WRITER of gospel songs. He is said to have written and/or composed between 7,000 and 8,000 songs. Even though he never had any formal training in music, he began to travel and taught singing in schools in various locations when he was only seventeen years old.[7]

---

5. See Bible Dictionary, "Israel."
6. Russell M. Nelson, "Let God Prevail," *Ensign*, Nov. 2020, 92, 94; emphasis in original.
7. See Kenneth W. Osbeck, *101 More Hymn Stories* (Grand Rapids, MI: Kregel Publications, 1985), 120.

Charles faced many struggles, including his father's death when Charles was a teenager and a failed marriage later on in his life. One of his greatest works, inspired by some of His triumphs over his challenges, is the sacred *Hymn* no. 193, "I Stand All Amazed."

In speaking of Christ's grace, he penned, "I stand all amazed at the love Jesus offers me, Confused at the grace that so fully he proffers me." In Charles's day (the early 1900s), "confused" meant "a state of perplexity and bewilderment, a state of awe." He was absolutely amazed and mystified by the grace of God.

In the book of Revelation (and 400 times in scripture), the word "offer" is used. The Greek word used here is *dōsei* and means "to put or place."[8] Interestingly, in "I Stand All Amazed," the word choice for how the Lord's grace is presented is unique. Charles used the word "proffer" rather than "offer." The English word "proffer" is from a Latin word meaning "to bring forward" (*pro* "forward" + *ferre* "to bring").[9]

Today, we more commonly use the word "offer" when we give a gift because the root of "offer" is the Latin word *offrir,* which simply means "to present." In other words, when we *offer* something, it's simply a presentation of something to another. In contrast, when we *proffer* something, we literally bring the item forward, offering it directly and intimately to the recipient. For example, if I were to *offer* a person a drink of water, I would fill a glass of water and simply offer it to that person, but if I were to *proffer* a person a drink of water, I would fill the glass and then bring it over to the person and offer them a drink. *Proffer* is a proactive offering.

Each week during sacrament meeting, the sacrament is *proffered,* brought literally within arm's reach, much like the offering mentioned in Revelation 8, which was offered upon the golden altar before the throne (see Revelation 8:3). This is a sweet symbol of how the grace of God is given, or proffered. He doesn't simply (passively) *offer* His love and forgiveness, He (actively) *proffers* it to us, begging us to partake of His mercy and love.

When you go to church this next week, think about the words "offer" and "proffer" as priesthood holders bring the sacrament to you. And during the week, think about the Savior's offer (and proffer) of His Atonement.

---

8. *Strong's,* 1325.
9. "Proffer," *Online Etymology Dictionary.*

"Where also our Lord was crucified"
(Revelation 11:8)

AT THIS POINT IN YOUR STUDY of the New Testament, you've read the word "crucify" or "crucified" over 20 times. The Greek word is *estaurōthē* and means "to impale on a cross."[10]

But there's another word that shares its root with "crucify." It's a word that may be used errantly and without the reverence it deserves: excruciating.

We may say, "That was excruciating!" to describe a painful experience, whether physical or emotional.[11] However, the root of "excruciating" means "to crucify."

The Latin root of "excruciating" is *crux*, referring literally to a cross, which points our minds toward the cross and crucifixion of Jesus Christ.[12] In 1986, the Journal of the American Medical Association published:

> Although the Romans did not invent crucifixion, they perfected it as a form of torture and capital punishment that was designed to produce a slow death with maximum pain and suffering. It was one of the most disgraceful and cruel methods of execution . . .[13]

Jesus was staked to a cross with nails approximately nine inches long (John 20:25; cf. Psalm 22:16) that were driven through His wrists and feet. His legs were most likely bent and rotated, making His slow death excruciatingly painful.

Philippians 2:8 reads, "And being found in fashion [appearance] as a man, he humbled himself, and became obedient unto [to the point of] death, even the death of the cross." The extreme and *excruciating* pain that Jesus endured showed His supreme level of love for us (see John 3:16).

Our use of the word "excruciating" may need to be carefully considered. Understanding the origin of the word "excruciating" can provide us with a deep appreciation for what Jesus Christ was willing to endure to make eternal life available to each of us—as well as give us pause to consider our use of this word more carefully in the future.

---

10. *Strong's*, 4717.
11. The word "excruciating" was used since at least the mid-16th century to mean "very painful."
12. "Crucify," *Online Etymology Dictionary*.
13. W. D. Edwards, W. J. Gabel, F. E. Hosmer, "On the physical death of Jesus Christ," *JAMA*, 21 Mar. 1986, 255(11):1455-63.

FOR FURTHER STUDY

- Numerology is rich in meaning and application. Consider looking up the meanings of numbers as you study the book of Revelation this week. See the Encyclopedia Britannica article "number symbolism" (https://www.britannica.com/topic/number-symbolism) to get started.

- Revelation 1:1 uses the word "signified," which has a root possibly tied to the temple. Consider researching its meaning in Greek using www.biblehub.com and www.blueletterbible.org.

- John wrote that the "countenance was as the sun shineth in his strength" (Revelation 1:14–16). Consider looking up the meaning of the word "countenance" using www.biblehub.com and www.blueletterbible.org and see what application its meaning has.

- It's hard to pass up looking up the meaning of "alpha" and "omega" in Revelation 1:8. See www.biblehub.com and www.blueletterbible.org to get started.

- Each church listed in Revelation 2–3 has significant meaning and history. Look up the meaning of each of the seven churches that John wrote to in Revelation 2–3. See the www.gotquestions.org article "What do the seven churches in Revelation stand for?" (https://www.gotquestions.org/seven-churches-Revelation.html) to get started.

- Revelation 6 is full of colors. Consider a research project looking up the meaning and symbolism of colors in scripture. See the www.gotquestions.org article "Is there any significance to colors in the Bible?" (https://www.gotquestions.org/colors-Bible.html) to get started.

- The restoration is mentioned by John in Revelation 7. Understanding the definition of the word "restoration" builds testimony, so consider a study of its meaning using www.biblehub.com and www.blueletterbible.org.

What other unique or insightful words did you find in your study this week?

_____

_____

_____

_____

_____

_____

Please share with us!
Visit www.ComeFollowMeWOW.com and
share your word discoveries and insights!

Chapter 49

Christmas

THE NAME *JESUS*, ANNOUNCED TO JOSEPH and Mary through the angels (see Matthew 1:21; Luke 1:31) means "Yahweh saves" or "Yahweh is salvation." The transliterated word from Hebrew and Aramaic is *Yeshua*, a combination of *Ya* (short for *Yahweh* or *Jehovah* in passages like Exodus 3:14).[1] When combined with the verb *yasha*—which means "rescue," "deliver," or "save"—the name-title *Jesus* is powerful: "Jesus" means "Jehovah will save" (see Philippians 2:9–10).[2]

Many people have the name Jesus today and it was quite common in first-century Galilee.[3] Archaeologists have unearthed the tombs of dozens of *Yeshuas* (the Hebrew name for Jesus) from the period around the Messiah's death.[4] The name also appears 30 times in the Old Testament in reference to four separate people—including a descendent of Aaron who helped to distribute offerings of grain (see 2 Chronicles 31:15) and a man who accompanied former captives of Nebuchadnezzar back to Jerusalem (see Ezra 2:2).

The Savior received His name by revelation. To Joseph of Nazareth, the angel of the Lord appeared in a dream, saying:

---

1. Durham, G. Homer, "Jesus the Christ: The Words and Their Meaning," *Ensign*, May 1984, 14–16.
2. "Jesus," *Online Etymology Dictionary.*
3. Susan Ward Easton, "Names of Christ in the Book of Mormon," *Ensign*, Jul. 1978, 60–61.
4. Werner Foerster, "[Jesus]," *Theological Dictionary of the New Testament.* 10 vols. Edited by Gerhard Kittel and Gerhard Friedrich. Translated by Geoffrey W. Bromiley (Grand Rapids, MI: Eerdmans, 1964–76), 3:284–93.

Joseph, thou son of David, fear not to take unto thee Mary thy wife: for that which is conceived in her is of the Holy Ghost. And she shall bring forth a son, and thou shalt call his name JESUS: for he shall save his people from their sins. (Matthew 1:20–21)

Luke similarly recorded, "And, behold, thou shalt conceive in thy womb, and bring forth a son, and shalt call his name JESUS" (Luke 1:31). The formal naming of the child when eight days old is recorded by Luke: "His name was called JESUS, which was so named for the angel before he was conceived in the womb" (Luke 2:21).

Many have wondered about Jesus's last name. It was not "Christ," as last names were not commonly used until the 16th century. Instead, Galileans distinguished themselves from others by using their given name and then adding either "son of" and their father's name, or their place of birth. Therefore, Jesus's contemporaries most likely would have called him *"Yeshua Bar Yehosef"* or *"Yeshua Nasraya"*; that is, "Jesus, son of Joseph" or "Jesus of Nazareth."

What other unique or insightful words did you find in your study this week?

_____

_____

_____

_____

_____

Please share with us!
Visit www.ComeFollowMeWOW.com and
share your word discoveries and insights!

Chapter 50

Revelation 12-22

Don't miss these Words of the Week

"**Angel**" (Revelation 14:6)
"**Babylon**" (Revelation 18:21)
"**Marriage**" (Revelation 19:7)
"**Hell**" (Revelation 20:12)
"**Garnished**" (Revelation 21:11)

"I saw another angel fly." (Revelation 14:6)

UNDERSTANDING THE DOCTRINE OF ANGELS CAN bring comfort and peace to our souls. Knowing that our beloved departed are ministering to us is one of the greatest truths found in the word of God.

Revelation 14:6 speaks of an "angel fly[ing] in the midst of heaven, having the everlasting gospel to preach unto them that dwell on the earth." The Greek word *angelon* was leaned on by John here for the English word "angel" and it simply means "a messenger,"[1] while the Latin word *angelus* specifies "one that announces."[2]

President Gordon B. Hinckley revealed that the angel described in this scripture was Moroni: "That angel has come. His name is Moroni. His is

---

1. *Strong's*, 32.
2. "Angel," *Online Etymology Dictionary.*

a voice speaking out from the dust, bringing another witness of the living reality of the Lord Jesus Christ."[3]

Moroni has played a major role in our faith and in the American nation. It has been reported that Moroni may have visited the Prophet Joseph Smith at least 22 times,[4] kept the golden plates safe from robbers and apostates,[5] died as a martyr,[6] helped Christopher Columbus in his voyage[7], inspired the founding fathers to sign the Declaration of Independence,[8] dedicated the land for the building of the Manti temple,[9] and helped design the temple garment.[10]

The Lord has promised that angels would be around us: "I will go before your face. I will be on your right hand and on your left, and my Spirit shall be in your hearts, and mine angels round about you, to bear you up" (D&C 84:88). Surely angelic attendants surround us today. Just as it was in the days of Elisha, so it will be for us: "Fear not: for they that be with us are more than they that be with them" (2 Kings 6:16). As Elder Jeffrey R. Holland testified:

> I testify of angels, both the heavenly and the mortal kind. In doing so I am testifying that God never leaves us alone, never leaves us unaided in the challenges that we face. "[N]or will he, so long as time shall last, or the earth shall stand, or there shall be one man [or woman or child] upon the face thereof to be saved" (Moroni 7:36). On occasions, global or personal, we may feel we are distanced from God, shut out from heaven, lost, alone in dark and dreary places. Often enough that distress can be of our own making, but even then the Father of us all is watching and assisting. And always there are those angels who come and go all around us, seen and unseen, known and unknown, mortal and immortal.[11]

---

3. Gordon B. Hinckley, "Stay the Course—Keep the Faith," *Ensign*, Nov. 1995, 70.
4. H. Doni Peterson, "Moroni—Joseph Smith's Tutor," *Ensign*, Jan. 1992, 66.
5. Jack M. Lyon, Linda Ririe Gundry, Jay A. Parry (eds.), *Best-Loved Stories of the LDS People* (Salt Lake City: Deseret Book, 1997), 39; See also Millennial Star No. 49, llred5.htm, accessed Jun. 9, 2017.
6. Charles D. Evans, "The Fate of Moroni," Archives Division (Salt Lake City: Church Historical Division, 1897).
7. Ibid.
8. Orson Pratt, "Celebration of the Fourth of July," *Journal of Discourses*, 4 Jul. 1854, 367–71.
9. Orson F. Whitney, *Life of Heber C. Kimball* (Salt Lake City: Kimball Family, 1888), 447.
10. "Early Pioneer History of James Allred: related by Eliza M. A. Munson," Diary kept by James T. S. Allred (typescript copy, BYU Harold B. Lee Library).
11. Jeffrey R. Holland, "The Ministry of Angels," *Ensign*, Nov. 2008, 31.

Today, look for angels. They may be nearer than you realize.

"Blessed is he that watcheth and keepeth his garments, lest he walk naked." (Revelation 16:15)

When members of The Church of Jesus Christ of Latter-day Saints are endowed, we receive temple garments that clothe our bodies with sacred blessings. Fittingly, one root of the word "endow" is "to clothe" or "to put on as a garment" or "to sink into a garment; to cover."[12] The Greek word for "garment" in Revelation 16:15 is *himatia* and refers to a flowing garment.[13]

Temple *garments* provide a constant reminder of temple covenants. When worn properly, the garment provides protection against temptation. As endowed members of the Church "sink into their garment," they put on a tangible reminder of our Savior Jesus Christ.

Wearing priesthood garments is an outward expression of an inward covenant to be an endowed disciple of Jesus Christ. As endowed members of the Church properly wear the garment, they are reminded each moment of each day they have put on Christ, a principle taught by Paul in his letters to the Hebrews. He wrote:

Having therefore, brethren, boldness to enter into the holiest by the blood of Jesus, by a new and living way, which he hath consecrated for us, through the veil, that is to say, his flesh. (Hebrews 10:19–20)

In the temple, as we make covenants and ultimately pass through the veil and enter the Celestial Room, we symbolically, as Paul taught, pass through Christ (symbolized by the veil) to return to God's presence. President Joseph F. Smith emphatically taught, "[The garment] should be held by them most sacred of all things in the world, next to your own virtue, next to your own purity of life."[14]

Hugh Nibley taught a fascinating insight about the garment made for Adam and Eve.[15] His research suggests that Adam's garment was passed down to Enoch and then to Noah, whose son, Ham, stole it (see Genesis 9:22; note that the Hebrew word used here means "skin covering," not nakedness). Ham's descendants (Cush and Nimrod) claimed to possess the priesthood by virtue of possessing the garment and its insignia. Pharaoh (a descendant of Ham through Nimrod) then became in possession of the

12. See "endow," *Online Etymology Dictionary.*
13. *Strong's,* 2440.
14. Joseph F. Smith, *Improvement Era,* Aug. 1906, 813.
15. *Collected Works of Hugh Nibley,* Vol.5, Part.2, Ch.1, 169–71.

garment and offered Abraham the privilege of wearing his royal insignia in hopes that Abraham would allow Pharaoh to wear his garment (see Abraham 1:26–27). The garment was then passed from Abraham to Isaac and then to Esau, who later traded the garment (and his birthright) for a mess of pottage, giving it to Jacob.[16] Jacob had twelve sons, including Joseph, to whom Jacob gave a coat of many colors (see Genesis 37:3). However, it may have been more than just a coat of many colors. Hugh Nibley taught:

> If you look in your Bible, every time it mentions *many colors,* a garment of *certain marks* is the term that's used. It was the garment of the priesthood. No wonder they were jealous of him, they being the elder brothers and he the younger in the patriarchal line coming down from Abraham.[17]

In terms of application, we have been counseled to wear our garments always and consider them sacred. The First Presidency stated regarding garments, "The fundamental principle ought to be to wear the garment and not to find occasions to remove it." They went on to counsel:

> Members should not remove either all or part of the garment to work in the yard or to lounge around the home in swimwear or immodest clothing. Nor should they remove it to participate in recreational activities that can reasonably be done with the garment worn properly beneath regular clothing.[18]

Just as the Lord *covered* Adam and Eve with coats of skins, so too each of us can be *covered* through the atonement of the Savior—a token of which are the garments we receive as part of the endowment ceremony. This covering provides spiritual protection and a confidence that we will one day stand again in our Heavenly Father's presence, because of the Atonement of His son, Jesus Christ.

This week, consider these truths about the history, blessings, and protections of having temple garments available to endowed members in our day.

---

16. This garment may have been the very garment of skins that John the Baptist wore, called "the garment of Elias" and which was brought to him by Gabriel (*Collected Works of Hugh Nibley,* 5:2:1, 169–71).

17. Hugh Nibley, *Teachings of the Book of Mormon,* vol. 3, 51–52.

18. First Presidency letter, 10 Oct. 1988; as appears in Carlos E. Asay, "The Temple Garment," *Ensign,* Aug. 1997.

"Thus with violence shall that great city Babylon be thrown down, and shall be found no more at all." (Revelation 18:21)

BABYLON WAS, IN THE TIME OF ancient Israel, a city which had become corrupt. In fact, it's become one of the most common metaphors for wickedness in scripture. The focal point of ancient Babylon was a temple built to a false god, Bel (or Baal). The Greek rendition of the word "Babylon" (*Akkadian Bab-ilani*) means, "the gate of the gods" (from *bab* "gate" + *ilani*, plural of *ilu* "god").

Babylon was constructed in the third millennium near the Tigris and Euphrates rivers under Nebuchadnezzar II who built 56 miles of walls over 300 feet high.[19] The city appeared to be impenetrable—at least until in 539 BC when the Persian king Cyrus diverted the Euphrates north of the city until it became so shallow that the Persians could enter Babylon along the river bed under its mighty walls.[20] In one day, the great impregnable city Babylon fell.

In our latter days, Babylon will also fall quickly—apparently "overnight" or within one hour's time: "And they cast dust on their heads, and cried, weeping and wailing, saying, Alas, alas, that great city, wherein were made rich all that had ships in the sea by reason of her costliness! *for in one hour is she made desolate*" (Revelation 18:19, emphasis added). It's no wonder that John, throughout Revelation 18, invites his readers to flee Babylon.[21] If we are tangled up in modern-day Babylon, our end will come surprisingly sudden.

While it's clear that those who do not flee from Babylon will be destroyed with the wicked in the destruction leading to the second coming of Christ,[22] Babylon has much more to do with our heart than our zip code. As we strive to repent and become less contaminated with worldliness, the internal Babylon within us begins to be destroyed, leaving us more pure and more worthy to be called His children.

---

19. See Joshua J. Mark, "Wall," *World History Encyclopedia,* 2 Sept. 2009, www.worldhistory.org/wall/.
20. "1.2.1. Babylon's Historic Fall," *Bible Study Tools,* www.biblestudytools.com/commentaries/revelation/related-topics/babylons-historic-fall.html, accessed Nov. 2021.
21. This same message is echoed in Doctrine and Covenants 133:1–19.
22. See D&C 64:24.

"The marriage of the Lamb is come, and his wife hath made herself ready." (Revelation 19:7)

HEAVENLY FATHER ESTABLISHED THE DIVINE PATTERN of marriage with Adam and Eve in the Garden of Eden. The Greek word for "marriage," *gamos*, means a "wedding-ceremony."[23] Today, the First Presidency and Quorum of the Twelve Apostles have confirmed this pattern by stating, "Marriage between a man and a woman is ordained of God."[24]

The word "ordain" has its root from the Latin *ordinare*, which means "to put in order or appoint."[25] Fittingly, "ordain" has the same root as the English words "order" and "ordinance." Marriage is indeed ordained (decreed and defined and ordered) by God.

So what is "the marriage of the Lamb" and who is "his wife"? One biblical scholar has noted: "It almost seems as if the relationship of Husband and Bride between Jehovah and His people, so frequently insisted upon, not only in the Bible, but in Rabbinic writings, had always been standing out in the background. Thus [a] bridal pair on the marriage-day symbolized the union of God with Israel."[26]

At the time of Christ, there were three parts to getting married:

First was the betrothal period, when a contract was signed and a dowry was paid; this is the stage that Mary and Joseph were in when she conceived Christ (see Matthew 1:18; Luke 2:5).

Second was a parade about a year after the initial betrothal, when the bridegroom and his male friends would go to the bride's home at midnight and she and her maidens would join them and travel back to the bridegroom's home; this tradition is the basis of the parable of the ten virgins (see Matthew 25:1–13).

Third, and finally, was the wedding supper, which was a huge celebration that could go on for days (see John 2:1–2).[27]

In this scripture, "the marriage of the Lamb" refers to the third step—the wedding supper. For anyone who has helped plan a wedding, you can imagine the relief and excitement of finally reaching the wedding itself after months, even years, of preparation. It's significant that this scripture refers

---

23. *Strong's*, 1062.
24. "The Family: A Proclamation to the World," *Ensign*, Nov. 2010, 129.
25. "Ordain," *Online Etymology Dictionary*.
26. Alfred Edersheim, *The Life and Times of Jesus the Messiah* (New York: Longmans, Green, and Co., 1899), 353.
27. Sidney B. Sperry, "Hebrew Manners and Customs," *Ensign*, May 1972, 33.

to that last step as, like a wedding, this is the moment we're all waiting for: Christ's Second Coming.[28]

And who is Christ's wife in this metaphor, who has "made herself ready"? Consider Ephesians 5:25–27:

> Husbands, love your wives, even as Christ also loved the church, and gave himself for it;
>
> That he might sanctify and cleanse it with the washing of water by the word,
>
> That he might present it to himself a glorious church, not having spot, or wrinkle, or any such thing; but that it should be holy and without blemish.

In this metaphor, Christ's wife is the Church,[29] and the Church is composed of people—us—who have chosen to follow Him and believe in His name. How vital it is then that we make ourselves ready to meet Him!

"Death and hell delivered up the dead which were in them." (Revelation 20:13)

When we first chose to come to earth, we were given bodies. Along with this gift came the promise that, although we would all eventually die, we would all be resurrected and our spirits and bodies would reunite once again—never to be separated. This is a promise that we have *all* received, no matter the quality of life we choose to live.[30] Resurrection is a gift that is given to all through Christ's Atonement, but what about the judgment seat? What about . . . hell?

We may think about the concept of "hell" in the way that many Christian faiths do, with all the fire and brimstone, but did you know that there are multiple meanings for the word "hell"? In fact, *hell* can refer to at least three things: a temporary location for the dead who died without the gospel or who weren't valiant in their faith, an eternal location for the rebellious and wicked, or a state of mind as a consequence for sin.

"Hell" is an English translation of the Hebrew word *Sheol.* It signifies a place for departed spirits and corresponds to the Greek word *Hades. Hades*

---

28. "What is the marriage supper of the Lamb?" *Got Questions,* www.gotquestions.org/marriage-supper-Lamb.html, accessed 16 Nov. 2021.
29. "What does it mean that the church is the bride of Christ?" *Got Questions,* www.gotquestions.org/bride-of-Christ.html, accessed 16 Nov. 2021.
30. Gospel Topics, "Resurrection," topics.churchofjesuschrist.org.

is the word used in Revelation 20:13 and refers to a temporary location for the dead.[31] Paul taught therein that "death and hell delivered up the dead which were in them: and they were judged every man according to their works." All who have died will be resurrected and stand before the Lord to make an accounting of their lives, but our spirit bodies will be in different places depending on our faith, hence "death and hell."

Modern revelation generally calls this idea of "hell" *spirit prison*.[32] Alma taught that those that are in spirit prison are tormented with an unsettled state of mind (based on the misuse of agency) and they anticipate the wrath of God to fall upon them (see Alma 40:13–14).[33]

Another Greek word for "Hell" (*Gehenna*) is used in a few New Testament passages; *Gehenna* was a location outside the city walls where they burned garbage and sent lepers and outcasts. The word *Gehenna* was used to describe a permanent place of unquenchable fire where the unrepentant suffer. There is a place of endless torment, also called "hell" or "Outer Darkness,"[34] for those who cannot be cleansed by the Atonement because they committed the unforgivable and unpardonable sin of denying the truth and power of the Lord after knowing His power and gaining a testimony through the Holy Ghost (1 Ne. 15:35; D&C 76:30–49). Only this *hell* continues to operate after the Resurrection and Judgment.

Every human being who has ever lived once came here with the promise that we would try our best to prove ourselves on earth so we could one day return to live with our Heavenly Father—and we are proving ourselves every day. Consider what you can do this week to stand not in a place of indecision and torment, but instead in a place of spiritual power and valiant faith.

---

31. *Strong's*, 86.
32. Both *Hades* and *Sheol* are used to describe the temporary place or state of departed souls.
33. *Sheol* and h*ades* (both are words that mean hell and both refer to the temporary hell of *spirit prison*) are used as a place to teach deceased persons the gospel so they can have an opportunity to repent and accept ordinances of salvation (see Doctrine and Covenants 138).
34. "Eternal punishment is God's punishment. Endless punishment is God's punishment" (D&C 19:11–12).

"And the foundations of the wall of the city were garnished with all manner of precious stones." (Revelation 21:19)

As you've probably noticed through your study of the scriptures, and with the aid of this book, words often change in their meanings and sometimes even their basic definitions over time. "Garnish" is just such a word.

Today, the word "garnish" is probably most commonly associated with the sprig of parsley on the plate of food in a restaurant. Modern dictionaries state that "to garnish" is to "fit out with anything that adorns or beautifies." The Greek word used for "garnish" in Revelation 21:19 is *kekosmēmenoi* and it means "to put into order; decorate, deck, or adorn."[35]

The earliest root of the word "garnish" meant "to cover."[36] In the book *The Roots of English*, we learn that words with common roots with the word "garnish" include "garage," "garrison," and "garment." A *garage* protects vehicles, and a *garrison* protects military service members, while a *garment* equips and protects people. In English, "garnish" had the sense of fortifying, defending, and guarding oneself.[37]

Here in Revelation 21, the city is garnished with stones. When we read the word "garnish" in the Doctrine and Covenants, garnish has a much deeper meaning than simple decoration:

> Let virtue garnish thy thoughts unceasingly; then shall thy confidence wax strong in the presence of God. (D&C 121:45)

We could read this passage as an invitation to "let virtue be a defense, a warning to help guard our thoughts unceasingly."[38]

President James E. Faust stated, "[C]onscience is the only referee that can blow the whistle when we get out of control. If not bridled, our thoughts

---

35. *Strong's*, 2885.
36. "Garnish," *Online Etymology Dictionary*.
37. See Joseph A. Cannon, "The Gospel in Words: 'Garnish,'" *Deseret News*, 22 Jan. 2009.
38. One of the most tragic stories in the Bible began when a great man's thoughts were left "ungarnished." The thoughts left unguarded, unprotected, and unreinforced by *virtue* and which led to his downfall were those of King David. The scriptures say that at the time when kings went out to battle, David stayed behind (see 2 Samuel 11:1). That evening, he got up out of his bed and saw a beautiful woman named Bathsheba bathing; sadly, he did not look away. His unrighteous thoughts eventually led to adultery and a downward spiral of dishonesty and murder and his fall from exaltation (see 2 Samuel 11:2–14).

can run wild."[39] As we let virtue garnish our thoughts, and as we "Look unto me [the Lord] in every thought; doubt not, fear not" (D&C 6:36) our thoughts will be clean and pure. Remember, if a bad thought comes to mind that hasn't been invited, it's only a sin if we let it stay.[40]

Use your new understanding of the word "garnish" to take better control of your thoughts. Let them run through the check-and-balance of virtue. Evaluate what you are doing when your mind is most challenged with bad thoughts. Get rid of anything that might cause bad thoughts. Surround yourself (*garnish* yourself) with things that lift your spirit.

FOR FURTHER STUDY

- There is a fascinating definition of the Greek word for "sorcery" in Revelation 18:23. Look it up using www.biblehub.com and www.blueletterbible.org and you'll see a very modern-day application to sorcery in our day.

- John wrote to "flee" out of Babylon in Revelation 18:4. Consider a study and application of that word using www.biblehub.com and www.blueletterbible.org.

- Many people have wondered about the "mark of the beast" mentioned in Revelation 13:18. Look up the meaning of the word "mark" in the Greek using www.biblehub.com and www.blueletterbible.org and you'll discover a fascinating insight.

- What is the "book of life" mentioned in Revelation 20:12–15? Many latter-day prophets have spoken about its meaning. Go on a journey of discovery to learn what the book of life is. Read the Gospel Principles chapter "The Final Judgement" (www.churchofjesuschrist.org/study/manual/gospel-principles/chapter-46-the-final-judgment?lang=eng) to get started.

- Some of our Christian friends feel that Revelation 22:18–19 neutralizes the Book of Mormon. A study of the word "add" using www.biblehub.com and www.blueletterbible.org is helpful in understanding that passage.

---

39. James E. Faust, "The Power of Self-Mastery," *Ensign*, May 2000, 44.
40. See Boyd K. Packer, "Inspiring Music—Worthy Thoughts," *Ensign*, Nov. 1973.

What other unique or insightful words did you find in your study this week?

_____

_____

_____

_____

_____

_____

Please share with us!
Visit www.ComeFollowMeWOW.com and
share your word discoveries and insights!

— Word Index —

About the Author

Brother Richards grew up attending the Mountain View Baptist Church in San Diego before missionaries baptized him and his mom. Later, his own mission began in Honduras—and his son, Dawson, served in the same mission as well.

After meeting his wife at EFY, he moved to Utah to teach seminary, and play water polo and volleyball for Utah State University. He has served in several bishoprics and twice on high councils. He currently serves in the stake presidency.

Professionally, he teaches institute and seminary in the Utah North Area. He has spoken at several inter-faith events and is a member of the Veritas society and is a contributing author for the Patheos project. For 5 years, he and his team wrote the Online Seminary Curriculum. He presents at BYU and BYU-Idaho Education Week and is the author of *Preparing for the Second Coming* and was a contributing author for the 2020 publication "Hear Him." He has authored several articles for the *Ensign*, *New Era*, and *LDS Living magazine* and has produced six bestselling CDs at Deseret Book.

Most of all, he loves teaching and being with valiant Latter-day Saints.

Scan to visit

www.comefollowmewow.com